Season Review
1999-2000

MATCH CLUB GUIDE

MANAGING EDITOR: Chris Hunt
ART DIRECTOR: Darryl Tooth
ASSISTANT EDITOR: Ian Foster
SUB-EDITOR: James Bandy

NEWCASTLE UNITED BOOK COMPILED BY: Nick Gibbs
CONTRIBUTORS: Richard Adams, Hugh Sleight, Phil Smith,
Bev Ward, Kev Hughes, Martin Barry, David Houghton
& the correspondents of **MATCHFACTS**.
SPECIAL THANKS TO: Rick Dorling, Ian Leach,
Tony Warner & Stuart Dalrymple at Newcastle United.

First published in Great Britain in 2000 by Hayden Publishing Limited
Copyright Emap Active Ltd 2000
Produced under licence from Newcastle United Football Company Limited
All rights reserved. No part of this publication may be reproduced, stored
in a retrieval system or transmitted in any form or by any means,
electronic, mechanical, photocopying, recording of otherwise, without the
prior permission of the publisher.
Colour Origination: Gildenburgh Ltd.
Printed and bound in Italy by LEGO, Vicenza
ISBN 0 9533683 8 6
MATCH MAGAZINE, Bretton Court, Bretton,
Peterborough PE3 8DZ, England

contents

Guide to symbols and ratings

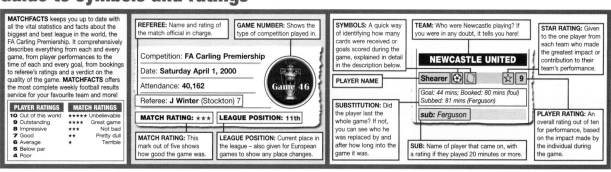

MATCHFACTS keeps you up to date with all the vital statistics and facts about the biggest and best league in the world, the FA Carling Premiership. It comprehensively describes everything from each and every game, from player performances to the time of each and every goal, from bookings to referee's ratings and a verdict on the quality of the game. **MATCHFACTS** offers the most complete weekly football results service for your favourite team and more!

PLAYER RATINGS		MATCH RATINGS	
10	Out of this world	★★★★★	Unbelievable
9	Outstanding	★★★★	Great game
8	Impressive	★★★	Not bad
7	Good	★★	Pretty dull
6	Average	★	Terrible
5	Below par		
4	Poor		

REFEREE: Name and rating of the match official in charge.

GAME NUMBER: Shows the type of competition played in.

Competition: **FA Carling Premiership**

Date: **Saturday April 1, 2000**

Attendance: **40,162**

Referee: **J Winter** (Stockton) 7

MATCH RATING: ★★★   **LEAGUE POSITION:** 11th

MATCH RATING: This mark out of five shows how good the game was.

LEAGUE POSITION: Current place in the league – also given for European games to show any place changes.

SYMBOLS: A quick way of identifying how many cards were received or goals scored during the game, explained in detail in the description below.

TEAM: Who were Newcastle playing? If you were in any doubt, it tells you here!

STAR RATING: Given to the one player from each team who made the greatest impact or contribution to their team's performance.

NEWCASTLE UNITED

PLAYER NAME

Shearer ⚽ ☆ 9

Goal: 44 mins; Booked: 80 mins (foul)
Subbed: 81 mins (Ferguson)

sub: Ferguson

SUBSTITUTION: Did the player last the whole game? If not, you can see who he was replaced by and after how long into the game it was.

SUB: Name of player that came on, with a rating if they played 20 minutes or more.

PLAYER RATING: An overall rating out of ten for performance, based on the impact made by the individual during the game.

THAT WAS THE YEAR THAT WAS...
1999-2000

> "I said, 'Look, the club is in trouble, we have to row this boat together and it's all hands to the pump — that's the only way we'll stop it sinking'."

TO SAY THAT THE 1999-2000 SEASON STARTED BADLY for Newcastle United would be a serious understatement. On August 30, 1999, the club found itself joint-bottom of the Premiership with just one point from their first six games, having just lost 5-1 to Manchester United. To compound this alarming state of affairs, the team had also lost three points at home to bitter rivals Sunderland, with local hero Alan Shearer starting the game on the bench. Not since the dark days of the 1991-1992 season, when under manager Ossie Ardiles Newcastle were staring into the gaping jaws of the old Third Division, had times been so desperate on Tyneside. On that occasion, things had been turned around by one of Newcastle's favourite sons, Kevin Keegan. Seven years on, and with the club in freefall at the start of the 1999-2000 season, the United supporters — arguably the most deserving fans in the land — needed a miracle of similar proportions.

Enter Bobby Robson. The Durham-born coach had left Newcastle over 50 years ago to play at Fulham, and after managing PSV Eindhoven, Sporting Lisbon, Porto, Barcelona and England, he came back to his home town to take charge of the club he has always worshipped. But while Robson was recognised as one of the most passionate and successful managers in world football, he still had his work cut out to save Newcastle from their kamikaze form, as he admitted at the end of last season.

"I had to do several things. The team spirit, morale and confidence had gone a little bit, there were bad results and some players had lost their way somewhat," said Robson. "Some players didn't even think they had a career left, and it looked like the club was sinking a little bit. I just said, 'Look, the club is in trouble, we have to row this boat together and it's all hands to the pump — that's the only way we'll stop it from sinking'. So the coaching staff made sure the players were fit, we made training meaningful and interesting and we put square pegs in square holes. I promised I'd give everyone a chance — have a look at everyone at the club and pick the best players for the best team. Everyone was important."

UNDER RUUD GULLIT, NEWCASTLE HAD UNDOUBTEDLY become stagnant, but nobody seemed to be blaming him. After all, this was the man who had taken The Magpies to two consecutive FA Cup Finals and become something of a folk hero on Tyneside. But the terrible start to the season, combined with the decision to leave out his captain for one of the most passionate local derbies in the Premiership, proved too much for both the board and the fans to take. Dropping Alan Shearer was widely regarded as a final gamble that didn't pay off and Gullit tendered his resignation.

The Dutchman's relaxed approach was light years away from Bobby Robson's enthusiastic demeanour, and the experienced manager set to work straight away. "I introduced some discipline within the club which I think had got very lax.

We got training started on time and it was specific to certain areas that we were failing in. We had a lot of genuine injuries, but I wasn't happy because one or two of the squad weren't even looking to get fit and I wasn't going to have that. We put in extra treatment so the players weren't allowed to think, 'Well, I'll pop in for my treatment at two o'clock and go home for three o'clock'. We stopped all that."

The new manager was amazed to learn that a Tyneside hero, Robert Lee, had been banished from the first-team squad, so one of the first things he did was to take Lee off the transfer list. "It did surprise me that Robert Lee hadn't been given a shirt number, but until you come to a club and find out what the situation is internally, you don't know that. But I came in, saw Rob train and I realised he was far from being finished as a player. It was the same with Alessandro Pistone and one or two of the others."

THIS UNDERSTANDING APPROACH TO TEAM SELECTION reaped instant benefits. Robson's first match in charge was a tough away fixture at unbeaten Chelsea, where Newcastle played their best football of the new season and were unlucky to lose by a single goal to Gianluca Vialli's Blues. But Robson was pleased with his new team. "We went to Chelsea in my first match and lost 1-0 to a suspect penalty, but we had our own spot-kick appeal turned down, so we were very unlucky. I remember saying to the players afterwards, 'If you always give me that kind of performance in terms of effort and attitude, we'll get out of trouble'."

And so it proved. In the very next game, Robson's first at St James' Park, the Toon Army were sent into dreamland. Their early chants of 'Walking In A Robson Wonderland' were tinged with understatement as The Magpies romped to a scintillating 8-0 win, with Shearer scoring a sensational five goals, equalling the Premiership record that was set by Manchester United's Andy Cole against Ipswich in 1995. "The 8-0 win against Sheffield Wednesday was a romantic scoreline," recalled Robson. "The crowd was behind us, there was a new manager and it was like the start of a new season, a new beginning almost." The win was a crucial turning point for Newcastle and there were better times ahead.

The key player in the club's revival was Alan Shearer. It was public knowledge that the England captain didn't have a good relationship with Ruud Gullit and it had started to show in his performances. Before Robson arrived, Shearer had only scored once, against Southampton from the penalty spot, so the new manager faced the challenge of getting him back to his best. "I spent some time with Alan personally, we talked about his game because it had got a bit static, maybe he had lost a bit of his movement and he didn't have a good relationship with the manager, which is not ideal at any club. I had to get him on my side, because Alan's a terrific player, he's a great leader and a good personality. I knew that if

I could turn him around there would be a terrific spin-off, so I did concentrate on him a little bit – we had to get Alan Shearer back to being the player the whole country loved. He was playing with his back to goal and the service to him had dried up. Although he wasn't playing very well, the rest of the team weren't helping him to score goals, and if you haven't got that service to the strikers you'll find it difficult to win any game of football at the top level."

To the delight of Newcastle and England fans, Robson's approach transformed Shearer's game, and the striker moved from one goal in seven games to an incredible ten goals in ten appearances. In this kind of irresistable form it was no surprise that Shearer finished the 1999-2000 season as the second highest scorer in the Premiership.

Another major influence on the team was Kieron Dyer, the club's exciting summer signing from Ipswich. The England midfielder was dogged by injury last season, but he still made a distinctive impression on his new manager. "Ruud Gullit did well to bring Kieron Dyer to the club. He's still young but he'll get better with experience – he's already improved since I've been at the club. We consider him to be a very high profile player. He's a gem, real quality." Coming from Robson, who managed a young Brazilian player called Ronaldo, that is

praise indeed, and if Dyer had been able to stay injury-free, the club's turnaround could have been even more impressive last season. He still played a significant part, though, with the highlight being his unforgettable goal in the 2-0 win at Everton. Picking up the ball on the halfway line, Dyer needed only three touches to chip David Weir, beat Abel Xavier and calmly lob the advancing goalkeeper from outside the area. The versatile midfielder was a joy to watch in a Newcastle shirt. He seemed to have no problem in adjusting to the demands of the Premiership in his first season and played a major part in getting Newcastle back on track.

AFTER THE DEFEAT AGAINST CHELSEA IN ROBSON'S first game in charge, Newcastle won six and lost only three of their next 14 league fixtures before the end of 1999. This pulled them clear of the relegation zone and into 15th place in the Premiership – a position the supporters could only dream about at the end of August. Bobby Robson wanted his team to play exciting, attacking football, but he knew they wouldn't be able to win every match, so the tactics varied between games. "We just kept going, we played differently away to the way we did at home. I thought we were good enough to win at home, to pick up three points, but I didn't

"The crowd was behind us, there was a new manager and it was like the start of a new season, a new beginning almost."

> ## "We were despondent because we knew we were the best side on the day and we should have gone through to the final."

think we were good enough, at that stage, to win away from home. For instance, we closed up shop a bit going to Arsenal, we played a bit more defensively." That might have led to a less than exciting winter encounter at Highbury last season, but it helped Newcastle to secure their first away point of the campaign, and as they continued to climb up the Premiership table, confidence soared around the club with the Robson revolution now in full swing.

The Magpies swept past Southampton 5-0 in January to avenge their defeat back in August, when a poor Newcastle side were beaten 4-2 by The Saints. But the highlight of the league season came a month later, on February 12, 2000, when Bobby Robson's side played host to treble-winners Manchester United. On that day, a sensational strike from Duncan Ferguson, plus two more from an inspired Alan Shearer, led the team to a dream 3-0 win. In Robson's eyes, the result was a magnificent achievement that spoke volumes about the club's progress.

"That was a great test for us and to beat Manchester United at home was a unique result. It showed us how near we were to them. The players just rose to the occasion. It was an open game against Manchester United because we were at home. We didn't play any heavy defensive system, we just went for it. Shearer, by that time, was playing very well with Ferguson and they were a difficult combination to handle. The team around them also played well, we gave a really good fighting performance and had a lot of quality on the pitch."

For all the euphoria that surrounded the memorable win, Newcastle's experienced manager saw it as just another piece of the jigsaw. "We had some good victories at home, not just the Manchester United game. We'd become a pretty good outfit, very difficult to beat at home. We had built a bit of a fortress at St James' Park. We only lost two games there – against Leicester and Chelsea in the Premiership – from September onwards, and that includes all our cup ties." Robson was rewarded for the incredible transformation he had achieved at Newcastle by being named the Carling Manager Of The Month for February. He accepted the award with typical modesty, but reinforced the message that there was still a long way to go. Showing his ruthless side to management, Robson put 13 players on the transfer list in an attempt to trim down the United squad to a manageable size. As promised, he had looked at everyone and decided who was surplus to requirements. It was the incentive that some players needed to improve their efforts, while others knew their time at the club was coming to an end.

AS IS ALMOST CUSTOMARY ON TYNESIDE, THE FA CUP played a huge part in Newcastle's season, and for the third season in a row, the Toon Army marched south to the Twin Towers of Wembley. Their FA Cup campaign started with a third round draw at Tottenham – the only Premiership tie of the round, and Robson's tactical nous again led the team to victory. Clinical defensive play away from home earned a 1-1 draw at White Hart Lane, before the confidence and power of Newcastle at home blew George Graham's side away 6-1, their biggest ever defeat in the competition. "Beating Spurs 6-1 at home was one of the highlights of the entire season," said Robson. "We got a draw at their place, then won 6-1 at St. James' and we were on our way."

Victories against Sheffield United, Blackburn and Tranmere followed, taking The Magpies to a semi-final against Chelsea, just one step away from another Wembley final. The way the team rose to the occasion and ran the game with sound

Unbelievable scenes at St James' Park as Shearer scores five goals in the 8-0 thrashing of Sheffield Wednesday.

tactical direction, commitment and passion was a credit to the manager and the players. Up against a star-studded Chelsea side in the pressure cooker atmosphere of Wembley, Robson's charges gave one of their best performances of the season yet still left as losers, which was a cruel blow for both the team and the supporters to suffer.

"It was hugely disappointing. It took us 48 hours to get over it because we played so well and didn't deserve to lose. You get over it if you've played badly. You get back home and you think, 'Well, we weren't good enough, we gave it a good try, but that was just par for the course'. What happened that day wasn't par for the course, we should have won 3-1. You can never say we would have gone on to win the cup, but you can say that having not won in the final for two years – and having played well at Wembley where we should have beaten a very good side – we would have stood a very good chance of winning it. We were despondent because Chelsea knew we were the best side on the day and we should have gone through to the final. Things just went against us in that particular game, like the quick free-kick that Chelsea took when the ball was rolling. Dermot Gallagher didn't see it, he should have blown – he blows for things like that all the time. He should have told the player to re-settle the ball."

The fact that the team was so devastated by failing to make the FA Cup Final was an indication of just how far Newcastle had come under Robson. The disappointment was more than the usual emotions felt by supporters and players after a defeat. It was made worse because they knew their team deserved to be in the final, and reaching that standard made them one of the best sides in the country. The Magpies started to build the confidence that was needed to challenge the leading clubs in the Premiership and beyond.

THE STRONGEST TEST OF NEWCASTLE'S RESILIENCE AND belief came in the UEFA Cup. The Magpies qualified for the competition thanks to the success of Manchester United, who beat them in the FA Cup Final the season before – if the treble-winners hadn't qualified for the Champions League in 1999, their FA Cup victory would have sent them into the UEFA Cup. Newcastle gladly took their place and made an instant impact. They brushed aside the opposition in the first two rounds, and while The Magpies may not have been up against Europe's finest, a 4-2 aggregate victory over CSKA Sofia and a 5-2 aggregate victory over FC Zurich were both impressive wins for The Black And Whites, who were now in their best form of the season.

Their opponents in the third round of the competition, Italian giants AS Roma, provided the stiffest examination of the season. But Newcastle put on a proud display against the Serie A leaders. Although they lost the tie, conceding only one goal during 180 minutes of football against the team leading the world's most talented league was immense, as Robson was keen to point out. "We played against Roma twice in the UEFA Cup and they weren't better than we were. I said, 'Look at this, one of the best teams in Europe, top of Serie A at the moment, and they only beat us 1-0 with a penalty over two legs'. Everyone was saying what a great side they were, with Delvecchio, Cafu, Candela, Totti – all those guys – but they were no better than us. I said, 'That's how good we are!'. We were very disappointed to lose the tie, we felt sick. We were only beaten by a penalty, so that was a significant game for improving our confidence."

Despite going out of the UEFA Cup, the players now realised they could take on any team in the Premiership and beat them. As the season progressed, Newcastle continued to rack up the points. "After we recovered from the poor start, we became very strong and difficult to beat at St. James'," said Robson. "I said to the players, 'The one thing that'll get us out of trouble is if we can pick up three points regularly at home – that'll be sufficient, even if we're not in the best of form away from home'. We needed to pick up points away, obviously, and we did that. We won at Aston Villa, Leicester and Everton, we got a point at Arsenal and Watford, and we should have drawn with Liverpool at Anfield, but they got a very late winner. So we played with a lot of satisfaction and a much better belief. Morale went up and there was a very good team spirit – when you've got that, you always know it's going to take a good side to beat you."

ON THE LAST DAY OF THE PREMIERSHIP SEASON, THE Magpies signed off at St James' Park with a 4-2 win over second-placed Arsenal, playing the type of football the fans had yearned for since the exciting Kevin Keegan years. The Gunners were under-strength because of their forthcoming UEFA Cup Final, but The Magpies produced a ruthless display of finishing in front of their own fans and the thrilling encounter lifted the side going into the 2000-2001 season.

Under Bobby Robson, Newcastle gained points at a faster rate than Aston Villa – who ended the season in sixth place in the Premiership, so if it hadn't been for their poor start, the team would have been pushing for a European place at the end of the season. While Alan Shearer was being written off as a has-been, the Newcastle and England captain banged in 23 Premiership goals and announced that he would retire from the international scene to concentrate on his club football, which was fantastic news for Magpies fans. Even though Shearer had a variety of strike partners, Newcastle still scored 42 goals in 19 games at St James' Park last season – only Manchester United scored more on their home turf. Everyone connected with the club can take heart from these encouraging signs as The Magpies continue to progress in the 2000-2001 campaign.

Make no mistake, this season's going to be big for Newcastle United and Bobby Robson has even higher hopes after restoring the faith of the Toon Army. "My objectives are to re-establish ourselves, to improve and be better than we were last year. We finished 11th last season and we have to do better than that. We have one of the most beautiful stadiums in Europe now – it's like a cathedral, and we just have to put out a team to match it because the supporters deserve it. My aim is to give the North East a glamour team." Magpies fans have every right to put their faith in Robson, because in this new age of foreign managers, he offers them something extra special – he understands Newcastle United, the surrounding area and the passionate support.

Last season was an unforgettable one for the club he loves, with the team experiencing everything from relegation fears to competing against the best sides in Europe, and this campaign promises even more excitement. The most improved team in the Premiership are now going all out to qualify for Europe, to finally win the FA Cup and give the best fans in the world the success they deserve.

"I know the public, I know what it means to them. I've been away for a long time but my family have always been here, so I've always come back to see them," said Robson in the close-season break. "My Dad took me to watch Newcastle so they were my favourite team and I've always listened out for their result. I've often wondered why I never signed for them when I was 17. I would have loved to play for Newcastle United, I would have loved that." ○ *Richard Adams*

"We have to do better than 11th position. We have one of the most beautiful stadiums in Europe now and we have to give the fans a team they deserve."

GAME-BY-GAME FORM GUIDE 1999-2000

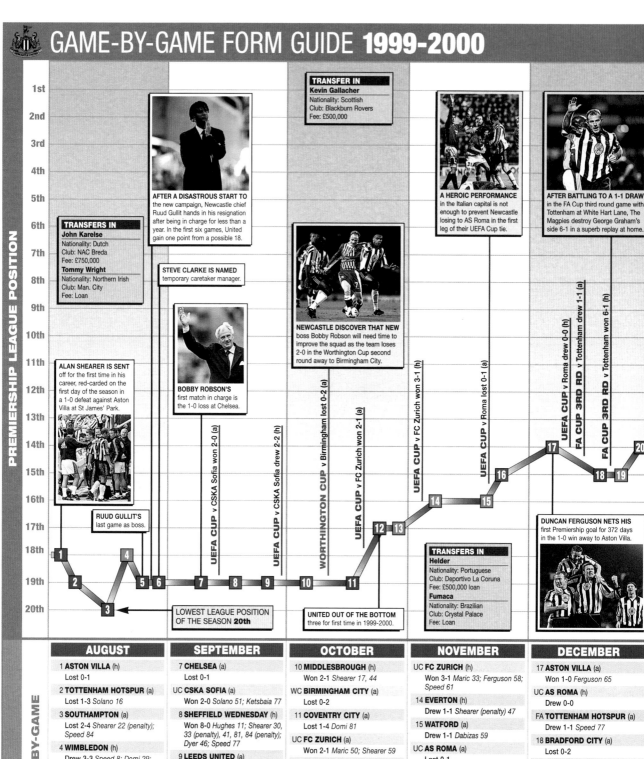

PREMIERSHIP LEAGUE POSITION (1st through 20th)

TRANSFER IN
Kevin Gallacher
Nationality: Scottish
Club: Blackburn Rovers
Fee: £500,000

TRANSFERS IN
John Karelse
Nationality: Dutch
Club: NAC Breda
Fee: £750,000
Tommy Wright
Nationality: Northern Irish
Club: Man. City
Fee: Loan

AFTER A DISASTROUS START TO the new campaign, Newcastle chief Ruud Gullit hands in his resignation after being in charge for less than a year. In the first six games, United gain one point from a possible 18.

STEVE CLARKE IS NAMED temporary caretaker manager.

A HEROIC PERFORMANCE in the Italian capital is not enough to prevent Newcastle losing to AS Roma in the first leg of their UEFA Cup tie.

AFTER BATTLING TO A 1-1 DRAW in the FA Cup third round game with Tottenham at White Hart Lane, The Magpies destroy George Graham's side 6-1 in a superb replay at home.

BOBBY ROBSON'S first match in charge is the 1-0 loss at Chelsea.

NEWCASTLE DISCOVER THAT NEW boss Bobby Robson will need time to improve the squad as the team loses 2-0 in the Worthington Cup second round away to Birmingham City.

ALAN SHEARER IS SENT off for the first time in his career, red-carded on the first day of the season in a 1-0 defeat against Aston Villa at St James' Park.

RUUD GULLIT'S last game as boss.

UEFA CUP v CSKA Sofia won 2-0 (a)
UEFA CUP v CSKA Sofia drew 2-2 (h)
WORTHINGTON CUP v Birmingham lost 0-2 (a)
UEFA CUP v FC Zurich won 2-1 (a)
UEFA CUP v FC Zurich won 3-1 (h)
UEFA CUP v Roma lost 0-1 (a)
UEFA CUP v Roma drew 0-0 (h)
FA CUP 3RD RD v Tottenham drew 1-1 (a)
FA CUP 3RD RD v Tottenham won 6-1 (h)

DUNCAN FERGUSON NETS HIS first Premiership goal for 372 days in the 1-0 win away to Aston Villa.

TRANSFERS IN
Helder
Nationality: Portuguese
Club: Deportivo La Coruna
Fee: £500,000 loan
Fumaca
Nationality: Brazilian
Club: Crystal Palace
Fee: Loan

LOWEST LEAGUE POSITION OF THE SEASON 20th

UNITED OUT OF THE BOTTOM three for first time in 1999-2000.

GAME-BY-GAME

AUGUST
1 **ASTON VILLA** (h)
Lost 0-1
2 **TOTTENHAM HOTSPUR** (a)
Lost 1-3 *Solano 16*
3 **SOUTHAMPTON** (a)
Lost 2-4 *Shearer 22 (penalty); Speed 84*
4 **WIMBLEDON** (h)
Drew 3-3 *Speed 8; Domi 29; Solano 47 (penalty)*
5 **SUNDERLAND** (h)
Lost 1-2 *Dyer 27*
6 **MANCHESTER UNITED** (a)
Lost 1-5 *Berg 31 (own goal)*

SEPTEMBER
7 **CHELSEA** (a)
Lost 0-1
UC **CSKA SOFIA** (a)
Won 2-0 *Solano 51; Ketsbaia 77*
8 **SHEFFIELD WEDNESDAY** (h)
Won 8-0 *Hughes 11; Shearer 30, 33 (penalty), 41, 81, 84 (penalty); Dyer 46; Speed 77*
9 **LEEDS UNITED** (a)
Lost 2-3 *Shearer 42, 53*
UC **CSKA SOFIA** (h)
Drew 2-2 *Shearer 36; Robinson 87*

OCTOBER
10 **MIDDLESBROUGH** (h)
Won 2-1 *Shearer 17, 44*
WC **BIRMINGHAM CITY** (a)
Lost 0-2
11 **COVENTRY CITY** (a)
Lost 1-4 *Domi 81*
UC **FC ZURICH** (a)
Won 2-1 *Maric 50; Shearer 59*
12 **DERBY COUNTY** (h)
Won 2-0 *Eranio 42 (own goal); Shearer 53*
13 **ARSENAL** (a)
Drew 0-0

NOVEMBER
UC **FC ZURICH** (h)
Won 3-1 *Maric 33; Ferguson 58; Speed 61*
14 **EVERTON** (h)
Drew 1-1 *Shearer (penalty) 47*
15 **WATFORD** (h)
Drew 1-1 *Dabizas 59*
UC **AS ROMA** (a)
Lost 0-1
16 **TOTTENHAM HOTSPUR** (h)
Won 2-1 *Ketsbaia 5; Dabizas 57*

DECEMBER
17 **ASTON VILLA** (a)
Won 1-0 *Ferguson 65*
UC **AS ROMA** (h)
Drew 0-0
FA **TOTTENHAM HOTSPUR** (a)
Drew 1-1 *Speed 77*
18 **BRADFORD CITY** (a)
Lost 0-2
FA **TOTTENHAM HOTSPUR** (h)
Won 6-1 *Speed 4; Dabizas 27; Ferguson 44; Dyer 72; Shearer 83, 84*
19 **LIVERPOOL** (h)
Drew 2-2 *Shearer 12; Ferguson 66*
20 **LEICESTER CITY** (a)
Won 2-1 *Ferguson 21; Shearer 53*

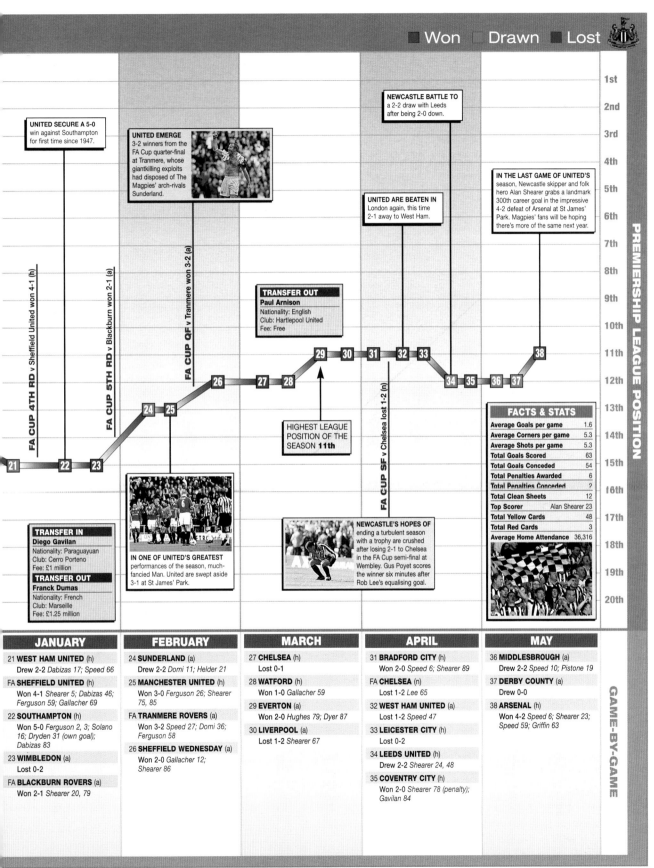

UNITED SECURE A 5-0 win against Southampton for first time since 1947.

UNITED EMERGE 3-2 winners from the FA Cup quarter-final at Tranmere, whose giantkilling exploits had disposed of The Magpies' arch-rivals Sunderland.

NEWCASTLE BATTLE TO a 2-2 draw with Leeds after being 2-0 down.

UNITED ARE BEATEN IN London again, this time 2-1 away to West Ham.

IN THE LAST GAME OF UNITED'S season, Newcastle skipper and folk hero Alan Shearer grabs a landmark 300th career goal in the impressive 4-2 defeat of Arsenal at St James' Park. Magpies' fans will be hoping there's more of the same next year.

TRANSFER OUT
Paul Arnison
Nationality: English
Club: Hartlepool United
Fee: Free

HIGHEST LEAGUE POSITION OF THE SEASON 11th

FA CUP 4TH RD v Sheffield United won 4-1 (h)

FA CUP 5TH RD v Blackburn won 2-1 (a)

FA CUP QF v Tranmere won 3-2 (a)

FA CUP SF v Chelsea lost 1-2 (n)

TRANSFER IN
Diego Gavilan
Nationality: Paraguayuan
Club: Cerro Porteno
Fee: £1 million
TRANSFER OUT
Franck Dumas
Nationality: French
Club: Marseille
Fee: £1.25 million

IN ONE OF UNITED'S GREATEST performances of the season, much-fancied Man. United are swept aside 3-1 at St James' Park.

NEWCASTLE'S HOPES OF ending a turbulent season with a trophy are crushed after losing 2-1 to Chelsea in the FA Cup semi-final at Wembley. Gus Poyet scores the winner six minutes after Rob Lee's equalising goal.

FACTS & STATS

Average Goals per game	1.6
Average Corners per game	5.3
Average Shots per game	5.3
Total Goals Scored	63
Total Goals Conceded	54
Total Penalties Awarded	6
Total Penalties Conceded	2
Total Clean Sheets	12
Top Scorer	Alan Shearer 23
Total Yellow Cards	48
Total Red Cards	3
Average Home Attendance	36,316

PREMIERSHIP LEAGUE POSITION

1st 2nd 3rd 4th 5th 6th 7th 8th 9th 10th 11th 12th 13th 14th 15th 16th 17th 18th 19th 20th

GAME-BY-GAME

JANUARY

21 **WEST HAM UNITED** (h)
Drew 2-2 Dabizas 17; Speed 66

FA **SHEFFIELD UNITED** (h)
Won 4-1 Shearer 5; Dabizas 46; Ferguson 59; Gallacher 69

22 **SOUTHAMPTON** (h)
Won 5-0 Ferguson 2, 3; Solano 16; Dryden 31 (own goal); Dabizas 83

23 **WIMBLEDON** (a)
Lost 0-2

FA **BLACKBURN ROVERS** (a)
Won 2-1 Shearer 20, 79

FEBRUARY

24 **SUNDERLAND** (a)
Drew 2-2 Domi 11; Helder 21

25 **MANCHESTER UNITED** (h)
Won 3-0 Ferguson 26; Shearer 75, 85

FA **TRANMERE ROVERS** (a)
Won 3-2 Speed 27; Domi 36; Ferguson 58

26 **SHEFFIELD WEDNESDAY** (a)
Won 2-0 Gallacher 12; Shearer 86

MARCH

27 **CHELSEA** (h)
Lost 0-1

28 **WATFORD** (h)
Won 1-0 Gallacher 59

29 **EVERTON** (a)
Won 2-0 Hughes 79; Dyer 87

30 **LIVERPOOL** (a)
Lost 1-2 Shearer 67

APRIL

31 **BRADFORD CITY** (h)
Won 2-0 Speed 6; Shearer 89

FA **CHELSEA** (n)
Lost 1-2 Lee 65

32 **WEST HAM UNITED** (a)
Lost 1-2 Speed 47

33 **LEICESTER CITY** (h)
Lost 0-2

34 **LEEDS UNITED** (h)
Drew 2-2 Shearer 24, 48

35 **COVENTRY CITY** (h)
Won 2-0 Shearer 78 (penalty); Gavilan 84

MAY

36 **MIDDLESBROUGH** (a)
Drew 2-2 Speed 10; Pistone 19

37 **DERBY COUNTY** (a)
Drew 0-0

38 **ARSENAL** (h)
Won 4-2 Speed 6; Shearer 23; Speed 59; Griffin 63

AUGUST

"The moment I came to Newcastle, the journalists asked if I understood how big the job was. I thought I knew, but now I know what they really meant." Ruud Gullit

THE MAGPIES SUFFERERED AN AGONISING START TO THE SEASON both on and off the field. Newcastle manager Ruud Gullit, who had guided the team to the FA Cup Final just three months earlier, had invested heavily over the summer, spending over £16 million on Franck Dumas, Kieron Dyer, Alain Goma and Marcelino. However, the former Chelsea boss grabbed the headlines when he announced the squad numbers for the new campaign, choosing to omit highly-respected midfielder Robert Lee from his plans.

The opening match of the Premiership season brought further controversy when skipper Alan Shearer was sent-off for the first time in his career. It was a decision that had Ruud Gullit seething on the sidelines, and the manager's reaction during and after the game led to misconduct charges from the FA. On the field, a third successive league defeat meant Newcastle had made their worse start to a season for 40 years. They scored the first goal in each of their next four games but failed to win any of them. The situation was not helped by a goalkeeping injury crisis that forced Gullit to sign John Karelse from NAC Breda and Tommy Wright on loan from Manchester City.

Without a win going into the fifth game of the season – the home derby against rivals Sunderland – Ruud Gullit dropped captain and leading striker Alan Shearer from the starting line-up. The Magpies started well and took the lead through Kieron Dyer, but Sunderland equalised and went on to win the game 2-1, despite Shearer coming off the bench with 18 minutes to go. Gullit had promised to bring 'sexy football' to Tyneside, but he recognised how badly the side had been playing, so with Newcastle in 19th position in the Premiership, the Dutchman handed in his resignation. With Steve Clarke taking over as caretaker-manager, the month ended with a 5-1 humiliation at Man. United, leaving the team with just one point going into September.

NEWCASTLE UNITED

THE GAMES

Aug. 7 v **Aston Villa** (h)
Aug. 9 v **Tottenham** (a)
Aug. 15 v **Southampton** (a)
Aug. 21 v **Wimbledon** (h)
Aug. 25 v **Sunderland** (h)
Aug. 30 v **Man. United** (a)

TRANSFERS IN

John Karelse
Position: Goalkeeper
Fee: £750,000
From: NAC Breda

Tommy Wright
Position: Goalkeeper
Fee: Loan
From: Manchester City

TRANSFERS OUT

Andreas Andersson
Position: Striker
Fee: Free
To: AIK Stockholm

MATCH facts
Matchman Of The Month

JAMIE McCLEN
Average Rating: 7.00

13

Shearer looks on in amazement as he receives his marching orders from Uriah Rennie.

FROM THE PAGES OF *MATCH*

After a starring role in the Copa America with Peru, **NOLBERTO SOLANO** returned to **NEWCASTLE** raring to start the new season. He told **MATCH** about The Magpies' hopes for the new campaign.

Are Newcastle ready for the season? *"I think we are, yes. We have to improve on last season's performances. It was an up-and-down season and everyone knows that we should be doing a lot better than that. With the squad we have at Newcastle, I certainly think we can do that."*

What do you make of your new boys? *"The early signs of the new players are very encouraging and they've settled in extremely well. We've managed to strengthen the squad in key areas which is important for what we want to achieve."*

What do you make of your opener against Aston Villa? *"We have been working hard towards the start of the season and although we haven't really had the best of results in our pre-season friendlies, as long as we get three points against Villa, it won't matter. Being at home will be a big help."*

What would be a successful season for Newcastle? *"Newcastle haven't won any major trophies for a very long time. We're all here to change that, not only for ourselves but for the fans as well. But we must perform consistently well in the Premiership – that must be our first priority."*

Who is your key player? *"We play as a team here, so there are no key players. It is important that the new players gel into the team quickly, so we don't play as individuals."*

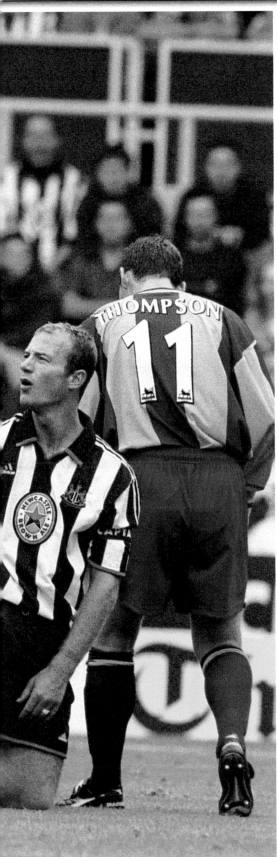

Newcastle United (0) 0
Aston Villa (0) 1

Competition: **FA Carling Premiership**

Date: **Saturday August 7, 1999**

Attendance: **36,376**

Referee: **U Rennie** (Sheffield) 4

Game 1

THE GAME: Alan Shearer was sent-off for the first time in his career as The Magpies lost at home to Aston Villa for the first time in the Premier League. Shearer received a bizarre second yellow card for 'violent conduct' in the 70th minute and Julian Joachim scored five minutes later to put The Villans ahead and leave Newcastle chasing the game with only ten men. It should have been a great day for Shearer, who was making his 100th appearance for The Magpies, but his red card left even the Villa players stunned and summed up a lacklustre opening game for Newcastle. Manager Ruud Gullit couldn't contain his anger at the decision and went on to the pitch at the end of the game to remonstrate with the officials. After the match Gullit was critical of the referee's performance, but also realised that his team would need to improve drastically on this display if they were to make any impact on the Premiership.

ASTON VILLA GOAL: Joachim (75 mins): Met a good cross from Delaney at the near post and scored with a deft header from six yards which caught goalkeeper Harper flat-footed.

MATCH RATING: ★★ **LEAGUE POSITION:** 18th

NEWCASTLE UNITED

Harper	6
Barton ▢	7
Booked: 35 mins (dissent)	
Domi	8
Goma ▢	☆ 8
Booked: 11 mins (foul)	
Marcelino	6
Subbed: 45 mins (Dyer)	
Dumas	6
Speed ▢	6
Booked: 57 mins (foul)	
Solano	6
Subbed: 85 mins (Robinson)	
Serrant	5
Subbed: 76 mins (Maric)	
Shearer ▢ ▢	5
Booked: 37 mins (foul); Sent-off: 70 mins (second bookable offence: foul)	
Ketsbaia	5
sub: Dyer	6
sub: Maric	
sub: Robinson	

Subs not used: Perez, Charvet.

ASTON VILLA

James	7
Delaney ▢	7
Booked: 17 mins (foul)	
Wright	7
Southgate	7
Ehiogu ▢	6
Booked: 66 mins (foul)	
Calderwood	5
Subbed: 87 mins (Stone)	
Taylor	6
Boateng	6
Subbed: 56 mins (Hendrie)	
Thompson ▢	☆ 8
Booked: 30 mins (foul)	
Dublin	5
Joachim ⊕	7
Goal: 75 mins	
sub: Hendrie	6
sub: Stone	

Subs not used: Merson, Oakes, Ghrayib.

MATCH FACTS

Shots On Target
Newcastle 2-1 Aston Villa

Shots Off Target
Newcastle 6-3 Aston Villa

Hit Woodwork
Newcastle 1-0 Aston Villa

Corners
Newcastle 5-4 Aston Villa

HOW THEY LINED UP

Harper

Barton — Marcelino — Goma — Domi

Solano — Dumas — Speed — Serrant

Shearer — Ketsbaia

Dublin — Joachim

Thompson — Taylor — Boateng

Wright — Calderwood — Southgate — Ehiogu — Delaney

James

IN THE NEWS

NEWCASTLE UNITED: German goalkeeper **Mark Ziegler** makes his Newcastle debut while on loan from Stuttgart in a 2-0 pre-season defeat at Celtic. Injuries to **Shay Given** and Steve Harper meant third-choice French goalkeeper **Lionel Perez** had started previous friendly matches… **Ruud Gullit** makes a couple of appearances in pre-season games against Reading and Stoke… Defender **Alessandro Pistone** suffers a knee injury in a friendly at Hartlepool, which ends his hopes of making a quick move to Turkish giants Galatasaray… Midfielder **Stephen Glass** learns that he will not require another operation on his troublesome knee injury, meaning he could be back in action in less than six weeks… Swedish international forward **Andreas Andersson** ends his disappointing spell with the club by signing a three-year deal with Swedish side AIK Stockholm.

PREMIERSHIP: Frank Lampard and Rio Ferdinand agree new deals at West Ham that will keep them under contract until 2005… Arsenal sign Croatian star **Davor Suker** for £2.5 million… Leeds striker **Jimmy Floyd Hasselbaink** joins Spanish club Atletico Madrid for £12 million… Gary Lineker is targeted as the new presenter of the BBC's 'Match Of The Day' after Des Lynam moves to ITV.

THE FINAL SCORE!

AUGUST 7

Arsenal	2-1	Leicester
Chelsea	4-0	Sunderland
Coventry	0-1	**Southampton**
Leeds	0-0	Derby
Middlesbrough	0-1	**Bradford**
Newcastle	0-1	**Aston Villa**
Sheff. Wed.	1-2	**Liverpool**
Watford	2-3	**Wimbledon**
West Ham	1-0	Tottenham

TOP OF THE PREMIERSHIP

	P	W	D	L	Pts
1. Chelsea	1	1	0	0	3
2. Wimbledon	1	1	0	0	3
3. Arsenal	1	1	0	0	3
18. Newcastle	1	0	0	1	0

15

FROM THE PAGES OF *MATCH*

THE NEW RECRUIT

Name: **Kieron Dyer**

Position: **Midfielder**

Signed: **July 14, 1999**

From: **Ipswich Town**

Fee: **£6 million**

Newcastle debut: **v Aston Villa**

How did your move to Newcastle come about? *"I reported back to Ipswich on July 12 and trained for a couple of days. Then the manager, George Burley, asked me to go into his office. He told me to go home, talk to my agent, then book a flight to the north-east because Ipswich had accepted an offer for me from Newcastle United. I was really delighted and signed as soon as I passed my medical. George Burley was disappointed because he wanted me to stay, but I'm thankful to Ipswich. I had three years left on my contract there and they didn't have to let me go."*

Did you join the club mainly because of Ruud Gullit? *"People say Ruud Gullit was the major factor, but it was many things. The Newcastle fans are second to none, it's a massive club and there's plenty of ambition in the transfer market – these are all good reasons as well as the gaffer. Hopefully, these factors will help us to start winning things and become a major force in English football. I really want to be part of a successful Newcastle United team."*

How have the rest of the squad welcomed you? *"I knew quite a few players from the England Under-21s and then I knew Alan Shearer from the full squad. But all of the other players welcomed me from day one. It's a bit different from Ipswich with all the different nationalities at the club, but they all speak good English. Alan Shearer said he was glad I had signed for Newcastle and that I'd love it here because it's such a massive club. That's all the incentive I needed."*

So here's to another rollercoaster year! *"Yeah, you could say I've had an up and down year! We failed to get promoted at Ipswich and I broke my leg as well, but I got my move to Newcastle and I was on the bench when England played Bulgaria. Hopefully I can help England qualify for Euro 2000. I'm enjoying myself here – I feel like a real member of the squad. No disrespect to Ipswich, but I'm playing with better players now and that will help me become a better player."*

Maric was desperate to impress the fans but the game gradually fell away from the visitors.

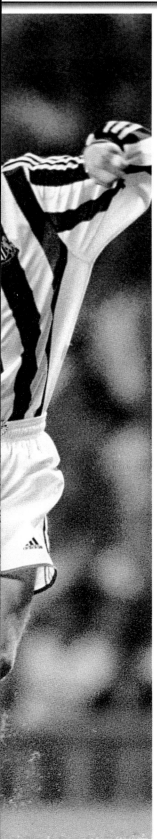

Tottenham Hotspur (2) 3
Newcastle United (1) 1

Game 2

Competition: FA Carling Premiership
Date: Monday August 9, 1999
Attendance: 28,701
Referee: R Harris (Oxford) 6

THE GAME: Ruud Gullit's side lost their second game in just three days in this clash at White Hart Lane. Newcastle started the stronger team, with Temuri Ketsbaia and Alan Shearer both squandering good opportunities before Nolberto Solano put Newcastle ahead after 15 minutes. The Magpies should have stamped their authority on the match to claim their first points of the season, but they let the home side back into the game. After Steffen Iversen equalised, Les Ferdinand and Tim Sherwood added further goals to put Spurs in the driving seat in the second half, with Newcastle never looking like rescuing a point. Shearer and Ketsbaia lacked service up front, while bad marking from set pieces proved crucial for Gullit's side.

TOTTENHAM GOALS: Iversen (28 mins): Met an Anderton cross from a corner and scored with an unstoppable header; **Ferdinand** (44 mins): Taricco exchanged passes with Iversen on the left before sending over a low cross for Ferdinand to tap in past Harper; **Sherwood** (60 mins): Scored with a simple header from Anderton's free-kick to make it 3-1 to Tottenham.
NEWCASTLE GOAL: Solano (15 mins): Harper's goal-kick was flicked to Solano, who crashed a fierce shot into the net.

MATCH RATING: ★★★ LEAGUE POSITION: 19th

MATCH FACTS

Shots On Target
Tottenham 6-5 Newcastle
Shots Off Target
Tottenham 7-3 Newcastle
Hit Woodwork
Tottenham 0-0 Newcastle
Corners
Tottenham 7-2 Newcastle

HOW THEY LINED UP

Walker

Carr Scales Perry Taricco

Anderton Sherwood Leonhardsen Ginola

Ferdinand Iversen

Ketsbaia Shearer

Solano Speed Dumas Dyer

Domi Goma Hughes Barton

Harper

TOTTENHAM HOTSPUR

Walker	6
Scales	6
Perry	7
Carr	6
Taricco	7
Subbed: 89 mins (Young)	
Sherwood ⊕	8
Goal: 60 mins	
Leonhardsen	7
Ginola	7
Iversen ⊕	7
Goal: 20 mins	
Ferdinand ⊕	6
Goal: 44 mins; Subbed: 46 mins (Dominguez)	
Anderton ☆	8
sub: Dominguez	6
Subbed: 78 mins (Freund)	
sub: Freund	
sub: Young	

Subs not used: Baardsen, Fox.

NEWCASTLE UNITED

Harper	5
Barton ▯	5
Booked: 69 mins (foul)	
Domi	☆ 7
Goma ▯	5
Booked: 60 mins (foul)	
Hughes	5
Subbed: 65 mins (Maric)	
Dyer	6
Solano ⊕ ▯	6
Goal: 15 mins; Booked: 27 mins (foul)	
Dumas	5
Subbed: 73 mins (Robinson)	
Speed ▯	6
Booked: 54 mins (foul)	
Ketsbaia	6
Shearer	6
sub: Maric	5
sub: Robinson	

Subs not used: Perez, Serrant, Caldwell.

THE FINAL SCORE!

AUGUST 8		
Everton	1-1	Man. United

AUGUST 9		
Tottenham	3-1	Newcastle

AUGUST 10		
Derby	1-2	**Arsenal**
Sunderland	2-0	Watford
Wimbledon	2-3	**Middlesbrough**

AUGUST 11		
Aston Villa	3-0	Everton
Leicester	1-0	Coventry
Man. United	4-0	Sheff. Wed.
Southampton	0-3	**Leeds**

AUGUST 14		
Bradford	1-1	Sheff. Wed.
Derby	1-3	**Middlesbrough**
Leicester	2-2	Chelsea
Liverpool	0-1	**Watford**
Man. United	2-0	Leeds
Sunderland	0-0	Arsenal
Tottenham	3-2	Everton
Wimbledon	1-1	Coventry

TOP OF THE PREMIERSHIP

	P	W	D	L	Pts
1. Man. United	3	2	1	0	7
2. Arsenal	3	2	1	0	7
3. Aston Villa	2	2	0	0	6
19. Newcastle	2	0	0	2	0

Southampton	(0) 4
Newcastle United	(1) 2

Competition: FA Carling Premiership

Date: Sunday August 15, 1999

Attendance: 15,030

Referee: D Elleray (Harrow) 7

Game 3

THE GAME: A third successive defeat meant Newcastle had made their worst start to a season since 1959 and this result left them rooted at the bottom of the Premiership. In an open and entertaining fixture, The Magpies found themselves on the wrong end of a six-goal thriller. The members of the travelling Toon Army had made the longest journey of the Premiership calendar for no reward, and pressure was already mounting on manager Ruud Gullit even at this stage of the season.

SOUTHAMPTON GOALS: Kachloul (58 mins): A low centre from Ripley was turned in at the far post from close range by Kachloul; **Pahars** (66 mins): Left Karelse with no chance after a powerful left-foot shot from 12 yards; **Kachloul** (68 mins): Pounced on a loose ball in the area to fire home from around 12 yards; **Hughes, M** (78 mins): A trademark right-foot volley into the top right-hand corner from the edge of the area.

NEWCASTLE GOALS: Shearer (penalty 22 mins): Shearer blasted home the spot-kick after Lundekvam had fouled Dyer; **Speed** (84 mins): A right-wing corner by Solano found Speed in space to head home into the top right-hand corner.

MATCH RATING: ★★★★★ **LEAGUE POSITION:** 20th

SOUTHAMPTON		NEWCASTLE UNITED	
Jones	7	Karelse	6
Hiley	7	Barton	7
Benali ☐	6	Domi	6
Booked: 37 mins (foul)		Shearer ⊕	7
Oakley	6	*Goal: 22 mins (pen)*	
Subbed: 46 mins (Ripley)		Ketsbaia	☆ 8
Richards	8	Speed ⊕	6
Lundekvam	7	*Goal: 84 mins*	
Le Tissier	6	Goma	7
Subbed: 46 mins (Soltvedt)		Hughes, A	6
Hughes, M ☐ ⊕	☆ 9	Solano	7
Booked: 8 mins (foul); Goal: 78 mins		Serrant	
Ostenstad	7	*Subbed: 13 mins (Maric)*	
Pahars ⊕	6	Dyer	7
Goal: 66 mins		*sub: Maric*	7
Kachloul ⊕ ⊕	7	*Subbed: 71 mins (Robinson)*	
Goals: 58, 68 mins; Subbed: 88 mins (Bridge)		*sub: Robinson*	
sub: Ripley	7	*Subs not used: Harper, McClen, Caldwell.*	
sub: Soltvedt	7		
sub: Bridge			
Subs not used: Colleter, Moss.			

MATCH FACTS			HOW THEY LINED UP
Shots On Target			Jones
Southampton 8-4 Newcastle			Hiley Richards Lundekvam Benali
Shots Off Target			Oakley Hughes, M Kachloul
Southampton 5-4 Newcastle			Le Tissier
Hit Woodwork			Ostenstad Pahars
Southampton 0-0 Newcastle			Ketsbaia Shearer
Corners			Serrant Speed Dyer Solano
Southampton 7-5 Newcastle			Domi Goma Hughes, A Barton
			Karelse

Dyer was one of the brighter players for Newcastle but he couldn't end their bad run.

The Toon Army celebrations were short-lived as The Dons grabbed a last-gasp equaliser.

Newcastle United (2) 3
Wimbledon (1) 3

Game 4

Competition: FA Carling Premiership
Date: Saturday August 21, 1999
Attendance: 35,809
Referee: M Reed (Birmingham) 8

THE GAME: Newcastle, without the suspended Alan Shearer, finally got their first point of the season, but they should really have sealed all three. Defensive frailties continued to haunt The Magpies as they twice let a two-goal cushion slip in front of the home fans. Newcastle raced into a 2-0 lead with strikes from Gary Speed and Didier Domi in the first half, and looked comfortable despite conceding a sloppy goal on the stroke of half-time. But United got a penalty just two minutes after the interval to regain their two-goal advantage. Nolberto Solano, deputising for regular spot-kick taker Alan Shearer, made no mistake. This should have been Newcastle's first win of the Premiership campaign, but the 3-2 lead was lost in the last minute with another sloppy goal, and the supporters around St James' Park showed their frustration at the end.

NEWCASTLE GOALS: Speed *(8 mins):* Rose unmarked from six yards out to plant a firm header into the net from Solano's free-kick; **Domi** *(29 mins):* Shrugged off Thatcher to squeeze his left-foot shot beyond the reach of the 'keeper at the near post; **Solano** *(penalty 47 mins):* Sent Sullivan the wrong way from the spot after Pedersen had handled Ketsbaia's shot.
WIMBLEDON GOALS: Hughes, M *(45 mins):* Poor marking from Kimble's corner allowed Hughes to crash the ball home from six yards out; **Ainsworth** *(69 mins):* Beharall was caught ball-watching at Hughes' left-wing cross, allowing Ainsworth to score past Karelse. **Ainsworth** *(90 mins):* Hammered in an unstoppable shot from 18 yards for a last-minute equaliser.

MATCH RATING: ★★★★ **LEAGUE POSITION: 18th**

MATCH FACTS	
Shots On Target	
Newcastle 8-7 Wimbledon	
Shots Off Target	
Newcastle 9-5 Wimbledon	
Hit Woodwork	
Newcastle 0-0 Wimbledon	
Corners	
Newcastle 3-8 Wimbledon	

HOW THEY LINED UP

Karelse

Barton Marcelino Goma Domi

Dyer McClen Speed Solano

Robinson Ketsbaia

Gayle

Hughes,M Roberts Andersen Earle Cort

Kimble Cunningham Pedersen Thatcher

Sullivan

NEWCASTLE UNITED

Karelse	5
Barton	7
Marcelino	5
Domi ⊕	7
Goal: 29 mins	
Goma	6
Subbed: 59 mins (Beharall)	
Dyer	6
McClen ▢	7
Booked: 75 mins (foul)	
Speed ⊕	7
Goal: 8 mins	
Robinson	☆ 8
Ketsbaia	6
Subbed: 63 mins (Ferguson)	
Solano ⊕	6
Goal: 47 mins (pen)	
sub: Beharall	5
sub: Ferguson	6

Subs not used: Harper, Kerr, Hughes.

WIMBLEDON

Sullivan	6
Cunningham	6
Kimble	6
Roberts	7
Thatcher	6
Pedersen	5
Earle	6
Subbed: 59 mins (Euell)	
Andersen	5
Subbed: 59 mins (Ainsworth)	
Cort ▢	7
Booked: 86 mins (unsporting behaviour)	
Gayle	6
Hughes, M ⊕	7
Goal: 45 mins; Subbed: 75 mins (Leaburn)	
sub: Euell	6
sub: Ainsworth ⊕⊕▢ ☆ 8	
Goals: 69, 90 mins; Booked: 90 mins (foul)	
sub: Leaburn	6

Subs not used: Davis, Ardley.

IN THE NEWS

NEWCASTLE UNITED: Croatia international **Silvio Maric** admits that he wants to leave the club just five months after his £3.5 million transfer to Newcastle. "I have told the club I am not satisfied and that I want to leave." Maric later says he's been misquoted... Uruguayan star **Daniel Fonseca** has emerged as a potential target for Ruud Gullit as The Magpies boss attempts to strengthen the club's strikeforce... Midfielder **Robert Lee**, who has not been given a squad number, makes his first appearance of the season in Newcastle's reserves.

PREMIERSHIP: Coventry manager Gordon Strachan pips his Midlands rival John Gregory to the signature of highly-rated Wolves frontman **Robbie Keane** for £6 million... Man. United are rumoured to be chasing Aston Villa's **Ugo Ehiogu** following long-term injuries to key Red Devils defenders... Arsenal legend **Ian Wright**, now playing for West Ham, announces he will retire at the end of the season... Several players say they are unhappy at their clubs, even at this early stage of the season, including **Kevin Gallacher** (Blackburn), **Emerson Thome** (Sheff. Wed.), **Michael Hughes** (Wimbledon) and **Don Hutchison** (Everton).

THE FINAL SCORE!

AUGUST 15		
Southampton	4-2	Newcastle

AUGUST 16		
Aston Villa	2-2	West Ham

AUGUST 21		
Chelsea	1-0	Aston Villa
Coventry	2-0	Derby
Everton	4-1	Southampton
Leeds	2-1	Sunderland
Middlesbrough	1-0	Liverpool
Newcastle	3-3	Wimbledon
Sheff. Wed.	1-2	Tottenham
Watford	1-0	Bradford
West Ham	2-1	Leicester

TOP OF THE PREMIERSHIP

		P	W	D	L	Pts
1.	Tottenham	4	3	0	1	9
2.	Middlesbro	4	3	0	1	9
3.	Man United	3	2	1	0	7
18.	Newcastle	4	0	1	3	1

All eyes are on the Newcastle bench as the fans desperately call for their dropped captain.

Newcastle United (1) 1
Sunderland (0) 2

Competition: FA Carling Premiership

Date: Wednesday August 25, 1999

Attendance: 36,500

Referee: G Poll (Tring) 9

Game 5

THE GAME: Ruud Gullit gambled everything for this match by sensationally dropping skipper Alan Shearer, but Newcastle still suffered defeat at the hands of arch-rivals Sunderland in this rain-swept north-east derby. United took the lead for the fourth game in a row but again failed to hold on to it. Kieron Dyer scored his first goal for the club, but second-half strikes from Niall Quinn and Kevin Phillips sealed a 2-1 away win for Sunderland. The miserable weather reflected the disgruntled feelings of the fans at the final whistle, when they called for Gullit to be sacked in just United's fifth game of the season.

NEWCASTLE GOAL: Dyer *(27 mins):* Coolly finished past Sorensen from 15 yards after being put through by Robinson.

SUNDERLAND GOALS: Quinn *(64 mins):* A glancing header from Summerbee's free-kick; **Phillips** *(74 mins):* Wright saved well from Phillips' first attempt, but the ball rebounded straight back to the striker, who duly lofted the ball over the 'keeper.

MATCH RATING: ★★★ **LEAGUE POSITION: 19th**

> "The fans may not agree – but for me, Newcastle losing to Sunderland was the best thing possible because it was my only way back. It feels like years ago now, although it was only at the start of the season." ROBERT LEE

NEWCASTLE UNITED	
Wright	7
Barton	6
Domi ▯	6
Booked: 72 mins (foul)	
Goma ▯	7
Booked: 86 mins (foul)	
Dabizas	7
Dyer ⊕	7
Goal: 27 mins	
McClen ▯	☆ 8
Booked: 90 mins (foul)	
Solano	6
Speed	6
Maric	5
Subbed: 72 mins (Shearer)	
Robinson	6
Subbed: 59 mins (Ferguson)	
sub: Ferguson	6
sub: Shearer	
Subs not used: Harper, Hughes, Green.	

SUNDERLAND	
Sorensen	7
Makin	6
Gray	7
Rae	7
Schwarz	6
Subbed: 59 mins (Ball)	
Bould	7
Butler ▯	7
Booked: 28 mins (dissent)	
Summerbee	7
McCann ▯	7
Booked: 65 mins (foul)	
Quinn ⊕	7
Goal: 64 mins	
Phillips ▯ ⊕	☆ 8
Booked: 28 mins (dissent); Goal: 74 mins	
sub: Ball	6
Subs not used: Oster, Marriott, Dichio, Helmer.	

MATCH FACTS

Shots On Target
Newcastle 2-5 Sunderland

Shots Off Target
Newcastle 2-8 Sunderland

Hit Woodwork
Newcastle 1-0 Sunderland

Corners
Newcastle 4-5 Sunderland

HOW THEY LINED UP

Wright

Barton Dabizas Goma Domi

Solano Dyer McClen Speed Maric

Robinson

Phillips Quinn

McCann Rae Schwarz Summerbee

Gray Butler Bould Makin

Sorensen

It was 1-1 at half-time, but Man. United crushed the visitors in the second half after Dabizas was sent for an early bath.

 Manchester United (1) **5**

Newcastle United (1) **1**

Competition: **FA Carling Premiership**

Date: **Monday August 30, 1999**

Attendance: **55,190**

Referee: **J Winter** (Stockton-on-Tees) 6

 Game 6

THE GAME: Ruud Gullit handed in his resignation after the home defeat by Sunderland, leaving Steve Clarke to assume responsibility as Newcastle travelled to Old Trafford for their biggest test of the campaign. To make matters worse for the disillusioned travelling Toon Army, Man. United tore their side apart. This was one to forget as Nikos Dabizas was sent-off for abusive language after ex-Newcastle forward Andy Cole scored the second of his four-goal blitz. The Magpies did get on the scoresheet, but only through Henning Berg's own goal.

MAN. UNITED GOALS: Cole *(14 mins):* Met a curling cross from Beckham and made no mistake with a low left-foot shot; **Cole** *(46 mins):* Beat Dabizas and rounded 'keeper Wright to score from ten yards; **Cole** *(64 mins):* Ran on to Giggs's pass from the left and blasted home from 12 yards; **Cole** *(71 mins):* Scored with a right-foot shot on the turn from ten yards out following Neville's cross; **Giggs** *(81 mins):* The winger's shot got a deflection en route to goal, giving Wright no chance.

NEWCASTLE GOAL: Berg *(own goal 31 mins):* Sliced Dyer's right-wing cross into the roof of his own net to make it 1-1.

MATCH RATING: ★★★ **LEAGUE POSITION:** 19th

MANCHESTER UNITED		
van der Gouw		6
Neville, G		8
Subbed: 80 mins (Clegg)		
Neville, P		6
Berg ⊕		6
Own Goal: 31 mins		
Stam		7
Beckham		8
Subbed: 74 mins (Sheringham)		
Butt		7
Scholes		6
Subbed: 68 mins (Fortune)		
Cole ⊕⊕⊕⊕	☆	9
Goals: 14, 46, 64, 71 mins		
Yorke		6
Giggs ⊕		7
Goal: 81 mins		
sub: Fortune		5
sub: Sheringham		
sub: Clegg		
Subs not used: *Culkin, Cruyff.*		

NEWCASTLE UNITED		
Wright		6
Barton ▭		6
Booked: 42 mins (dissent)		
Goma		6
Dyer		7
Lee	☆	8
Subbed: 69 mins (McClen)		
Speed		6
Solano ▭		5
Booked: 67 mins (unsporting behaviour)		
Subbed: 74 mins (Beharall)		
Hughes		6
Dabizas ▰		5
Sent-off: 46 mins (foul and abusive language)		
Ferguson		5
Subbed: 78 mins (Robinson)		
Shearer		5
sub: McClen		6
sub: Beharall		
sub: Robinson		
Subs not used: *Harper, Maric.*		

MATCH FACTS	
Shots On Target	
Man. United 10-4 Newcastle	
Shots Off Target	
Man. United 9-4 Newcastle	
Hit Woodwork	
Man. United 0-0 Newcastle	
Corners	
Man. United 6-1 Newcastle	

HOW THEY LINED UP

van der Gouw

Neville, G Berg Stam Neville, P

Beckham Butt Scholes Giggs

Cole Yorke

Ferguson Shearer

Solano Speed Lee Dyer

Hughes Goma Dabizas Barton

Wright

IN THE NEWS

NEWCASTLE UNITED: Ruud Gullit resigns as manager of Newcastle after less than a year in charge. In a statement to the media he said: "I am disappointed by the results, as any other person who loves Newcastle United would be, and therefore I take responsibility for the bad results. The supporters' expectations haven't been fulfilled and I would like to apologise to them. I would also like to thank them for the marvellous support they gave me during this difficult time"… **Tommy Wright**, who played in goal for United between 1988 and 1993, rejoins the club on a month's loan from Man. City as cover for the injured **Steve Harper** and **Shay Given**. Together with **Lionel Perez** and **John Karelse**, Wright is the fifth goalkeeper to be used in the first-team this season.

PREMIERSHIP: Paul Merson says he will retire when his contract expires at Aston Villa in 2002… Danny Wilson blames Sheffield Wednesday's poor start to the season on injuries… Spurs have refused two £21 million bids for **Sol Campbell** from two 'unnamed' Spanish and Italian clubs.

THE FINAL SCORE!

AUGUST 22		
Arsenal	1-2	**Man. United**

AUGUST 23		
Leeds	1-2	**Liverpool**

AUGUST 24		
Middlesbrough	0-3	**Leicester**
Watford	0-1	**Aston Villa**

AUGUST 25		
Arsenal	2-0	Bradford
Coventry	1-2	**Man.United**
Everton	4-0	Wimbledon
Newcastle	1-2	**Sunderland**
Sheff.Wed.	0-2	**Derby**

AUGUST 28		
Aston Villa	1-0	Middlesbrough
Bradford	0-3	**West Ham**
Derby	1-0	Everton
Liverpool	2-0	Arsenal
Southampton	2-0	Sheff.Wed.
Tottenham	1-2	**Leeds**
Wimbledon	0-1	**Chelsea**

AUGUST 29		
Sunderland	1-1	Coventry

AUGUST 30		
Leicester	1-0	Watford
Man. United	5-1	Newcastle

TOP OF THE PREMIERSHIP					
	P	W	D	L	Pts
1. Man. United	6	5	1	0	16
2. Aston Villa	6	4	1	1	13
3. Chelsea	4	3	1	0	10
19. Newcastle	6	0	1	5	1

SEPTEMBER

> "The team desperately needs a victory – that will bring us confidence, but my aim is to instil a bit of enthusiasm, morale and team spirit before then." Bobby Robson

ON SEPTEMBER 2, 1999, BOBBY ROBSON WAS ANNOUNCED AS THE new manager of Newcastle United. It was well known in football circles that Robson held a burning ambition to take over the reigns at St James' Park. In his own words, he had been 'in the wrong place at the right time' when the position had become available in the past, but Robson was welcomed with open arms by the Toon Army. The new manager was soon in the thick of things on Tyneside and faced the massive task of salvaging Newcastle's season. His first target was steering the club away from the relegation zone and avoid being consumed in a battle for Premiership survival.

His presence was felt almost immediately as The Magpies recorded their biggest ever Premiership win – an 8-0 thrashing of Sheffield Wednesday in which Alan Shearer scored five times. It was a good month for Shearer as he also scored a hat-trick for England against Luxembourg in a Euro 2000 qualifier. United also progressed to the second round of the UEFA Cup after beating Bulgarian side CSKA Sofia 4-2 on aggregate. Kieron Dyer offered Robert Lee his number seven shirt back but Lee, who almost left the club under Gullit, declined after thanking Dyer for his gesture.

There were still injury problems to key players, such as Duncan Ferguson, Steve Howey and goalkeeper Shay Given, while Nikos Dabizas was forced to serve a two-match suspension after being sent-off against Manchester United. Bobby Robson also had to discipline Silvio Maric, who reported late for the UEFA Cup trip to Sofia. Although Newcastle were winning games at home and in Europe, they were still languishing in the relegation zone at the bottom of the Premiership. After the euphoria of Robson's homecoming, the Toon Army could clearly see the size of the task ahead of them and the new manager set his sights on winning 40 points to assure top-flight status.

THE GAMES

Sept. 11 v **Chelsea** (a)

Sept. 16 v **CSKA Sofia** (a)

Sept. 19 v **Sheff. Wed.** (h)

Sept. 25 v **Leeds** (a)

Sept. 30 v **CSKA Sofia** (h)

TRANSFERS IN

None

TRANSFERS OUT

None

MATCH facts

Matchman Of The Month

KIERON DYER

Average Rating: 7.66

New boss Bobby Robson greets the Toon Army at Stamford Bridge.

FROM THE PAGES OF *MATCH*

After a dismal start to the season, Newcastle turned to local hero **BOBBY ROBSON** to turn around the club's fortunes. As always, **MATCH** was there to find out just what it meant to him.

How does it feel to be the Newcastle manager at last? *"I'm very proud, honoured and absolutely thrilled. It's great to be back. I thought Barcelona Football Club was quite big, but I think this has just pipped it. It's a great day for me to be announced as the new manager of Newcastle United."*

You've wanted the job for a while, haven't you? *"It didn't sadden me that I couldn't come here two-and-a-half years ago because it was unavoidable. For me, it was the right club at the wrong time. I really thought at that stage, when I couldn't take the position and Newcastle appointed Kenny Dalglish, that my chance to come here had gone."*

How big a job do you have on your hands? *"Well, I have a massive job. You know where we are in the league at the moment, joint bottom. The club needs a victory badly, we certainly haven't had one for some time and I know what happens at football clubs when results are poor. The team desperately needs a victory, and that will bring confidence, but my main aim is to instil a bit of confidence, enthusiasm, morale and team spirit before then."*

What's your chief task for the rest of the season? *"The priority is to bring about a change in the poor results we've had, to stabilise the club on the playing side, and basically to ensure that Newcastle are still in the Premiership next year. We do have a fight on our hands, I'm not going to hide from that. My emphasis to the players is to make sure they know that and understand that. There's no panic. It's very retrievable and I'm confident we'll do it."*

 Chelsea (1) **1**

 Newcastle United (0) **0**

Competition: FA Carling Premiership

Date: Saturday September 11, 1999

Attendance: 35,092

Game 7

Referee: G Poll (Tring) 6

THE GAME: This was Bobby Robson's first game in charge of an English club side for 17 years, but it ended in defeat as he witnessed first-hand the problems that Newcastle have to overcome if they want to retain their Premiership status. The home team made it seven games without conceding a goal in a scrappy match at Stamford Bridge. Chelsea scored the only goal of the game from a controversial Frank Leboeuf penalty. The Magpies had their own appeal for a penalty turned down in the second half after Ed de Goey's clumsy challenge on Kieron Dyer. But little was going right for Newcastle and they had 'keeper Tommy Wright – who was playing his last game for The Magpies – to thank for two brilliant saves to keep out Gianfranco Zola and Tore Andre Flo. Bobby Robson couldn't complain about his side's commitment and passion, but he knows the players will need to display more than these basic qualities to escape the lower reaches of the Premiership.

CHELSEA GOAL: Leboeuf (penalty 37 mins): Dabizas was adjudged to have pushed Babayaro following a Zola free-kick from the left and Leboeuf coolly converted the penalty.

MATCH RATING: ★★ **LEAGUE POSITION:** 19th

CHELSEA		NEWCASTLE UNITED	
de Goey	7	Wright ☆	8
Babayaro	7	Barton ☐	7
Leboeuf ⚽☐	7	*Booked: 36 mins (foul)*	
Goal: 37 mins; Booked: 59 mins (foul)		Domi	6
Desailly ☆	8	Goma	7
Sutton	5	Dyer ☐	7
Subbed: 68 mins (Flo)		*Booked: 60 mins (dissent)*	
Wise ☐	7	Shearer	5
Booked: 32 mins (foul)		Speed	6
Goldbaek	6	Solano ☐	6
Subbed: 46 mins (Petrescu)		*Booked: 12 mins (foul); Subbed: 86 mins (Hughes)*	
Le Saux	7		
Subbed: 57 mins (Poyet)		Ferguson	6
Ferrer ☐	7	*Subbed: 73 mins (Robinson)*	
Booked: 79 mins (dissent)		Dabizas ☐	7
Morris	6	*Booked: 37 mins (foul)*	
Zola	7	Lee	7
sub: Petrescu	7	*Subbed: 77 mins (Maric)*	
sub: Poyet	7	sub: Robinson	
sub: Flo	6	sub: Maric	
		sub: Hughes	
Subs not used: Hogh, Cudicini.			
		Subs not used: Harper, McClen.	

MATCH FACTS	
Shots On Target	
Chelsea	5-1 Newcastle
Shots Off Target	
Chelsea	5-2 Newcastle
Hit Woodwork	
Chelsea	0-0 Newcastle
Corners	
Chelsea	9-3 Newcastle

HOW THEY LINED UP

de Goey

Ferrer   Leboeuf   Desailly   Babayaro

Goldbaek   Wise   Morris   Le Saux

Zola   Sutton

Ferguson   Shearer

Domi   Lee   Speed   Dyer   Solano

Goma   Dabizas   Barton

Wright

IN THE NEWS

NEWCASTLE UNITED: Bobby Robson makes a welcome return to his native north-east by being appointed the new manager of Newcastle after the resignation of Ruud Gullit... **Nikos Dabizas** learns that he'll miss the matches against Sheffield Wednesday and Leeds United later in the month because of his dismissal in the 5-1 drubbing by Man. United... The Magpies are linked with the £20 million-rated Dutch striker **Ruud van Nistelrooy**, who starred under Bobby Robson at Dutch side PSV Eindhoven... Ruud Gullit receives a £250,000 cash bonus for guiding Newcastle to the 1999 FA Cup Final... **Alan Shearer** scores a hat-trick to silence his critics in England's 6-0 thrashing of European minnows Luxembourg at Wembley... **Gary Speed** leads Wales to a 2-1 win in Belarus and **Nikos Dabizas** features in a Greek side beaten 1-0 by Norway in Oslo.

PREMIERSHIP: Twenty-seven players and staff at Leicester are charged by the Football Association in connection with an investigation into black market ticket sales at the Worthington Cup Final last season against Spurs... Prime Minister Tony Blair intervenes to grant **Juninho** a work permit, which will allow the Brazilian star to return to Middlesbrough on loan until the end of June 2000.

THE FINAL SCORE!

SEPTEMBER 11		
Arsenal	3-1	Aston Villa
Chelsea	1-0	Newcastle
Coventry	3-4	**Leeds**
Liverpool	2-3	**Man. United**
Middlesbrough	3-2	Southampton
Sheff. Wed.	0-2	**Everton**
Sunderland	2-0	Leicester
West Ham	1-0	Watford
Wimbledon	2-2	Derby

TOP OF THE PREMIERSHIP

	P	W	D	L	Pts
1. Man. United	7	6	1	0	19
2. Chelsea	5	4	1	0	13
3. West Ham	5	4	1	0	13
19. Newcastle	7	0	1	6	1

Kieron Dyer was instrumental in Newcastle's morale-boosting win in Europe against CSKA Sofia.

FROM THE PAGES OF MATCH

As Newcastle prepared to kick off their campaign in Europe against CSKA Sofia, Magpies defender **WARREN BARTON** spoke to **MATCH** about his hopes for the forthcoming UEFA Cup campaign.

How do you see the first game going? *"It's going to be difficult. CSKA Sofia were playing in the Champions League a couple of years ago and they've won the Bulgarian League something like 23 times in the last 30 years – that's a hell of a record. The good thing is that we've got the second leg at St James' Park – so we'll go out to Bulgaria, hopefully keep a clean sheet and maybe try to nick a goal. Then we can get them back to our place and take it from there."*

How far can you get in Europe this year? *"I think it's very promising. It's a release from the pressure we've been under in the Premiership and a chance to do very well. We've been as far as a quarter-final recently and there's no reason why we can't go further. It's obviously going to be tough but I honestly think we've got a good chance."*

Where does the UEFA Cup fall in your priorities? *"Well, the league is still the priority for us, but a club of this stature has got to be looking to do well in Europe. We should be aiming to qualify for Europe every year, as we have done over the last few seasons, and it's vital we do that, but we also have to get as far as we can in the UEFA Cup now."*

What will be your biggest asset in this competition? *"The experience we've picked up from the last three or four years in Europe, along with our crowd at St James' Park. The Barcelona game, when we beat them, is the one that springs to mind as an example of what we can all expect. Everyone knows how great our fans are. European nights always bring out something extra in everyone."*

 CSKA Sofia (0) **0**

 Newcastle United (0) **2**

Competition: UEFA Cup 1st Rd 1st Leg

Date: Thursday September 16, 1999

Attendance: 25,000

Game 8

Referee: J Rocca (Spain) 7

THE GAME: Newcastle, with an excellent team performance in Sofia that was inspired by England stars Alan Shearer and Kieron Dyer, won their first competitive match since the FA Cup semi-final five months earlier. Steve Harper replaced the ineligible Tommy Wright in goal to keep The Magpies' first clean sheet of the season with a commanding performance. Bobby Robson's men seemed a different side from the team that struggled at the start of the season as they attacked their Bulgarian opponents from the kick-off. They endured several worrying spells in defence as Petkov rattled the crossbar with a ferocious strike from 30 yards, but a fantastic free-kick from Nolberto Solano did wonders for Newcastle's confidence and Temuri Ketsbaia added a second goal to put the team into an excellent position for the return leg at St James' Park.

NEWCASTLE GOALS: Solano *(51 mins):* Following Mrkic's foul on Dyer, Solano curled a superb free-kick around the wall and into the far right-hand corner from 25 yards out; *Ketsbaia (77 mins):* Dyer threaded a diagonal ball to Ketsbaia on the left side of the area. The Georgian turned his marker and chipped the ball over the onrushing Lukic from 12 yards.

MATCH RATING: ★★★★ **LEAGUE POSITION:** 19th

CSKA SOFIA		NEWCASTLE UNITED	
Lukic	7	Harper	6
Sarac	7	Domi ▢	7
Mrkic	6	*Booked: 27 mins (foul)*	
Trentchev	7	Dabizas	7
Subbed: 56 mins (Litera)		Goma	7
Kremenliev	7	Barton ▢	5
Subbed: 61 mins (Ivanov, G)		*Booked: 55 mins (foul)*	
Petkov ▢	☆ 8	Speed	7
Booked: 37 mins (foul)		Lee	7
Velikov	7	Dyer ▢	8
Tchomakov	7	*Booked: 71 mins (unsporting behaviour)*	
Hristov	7	Solano ⚽	6
Subbed: 56 mins (Ivanov, D)		*Goal: 51 mins; Subbed: 84 mins (Hamilton)*	
Berbatov	6	Shearer	☆ 8
Mantchev	7	Ferguson	7
sub: Ivanov, D ▢	7	*Subbed: 18 mins (Ketsbaia)*	
Booked: 90 mins (unsporting behaviour)		*sub: Ketsbaia ⚽*	6
sub: Litera	7	*Goal: 77 mins*	
sub: Ivanov, G	7	*sub: Hamilton*	

Subs not used: Paskov, Kovacevic, Antonov, Ivanov, I.

Subs not used: Beharall, Hughes, Robinson, Karelse, McClen.

MATCH FACTS

Shots On Target
CSKA Sofia 3-5 Newcastle

Shots Off Target
CSKA Sofia 5-10 Newcastle

Hit Woodwork
CSKA Sofia 1-0 Newcastle

Corners
CSKA Sofia 4-7 Newcastle

HOW THEY LINED UP

Lukic

Kremenliev   Mrkic   Trentchev   Sarac

Petkov   Velikov   Tchomakov

Mantchev   Hristov   Berbatov

Ferguson   Shearer

Solano   Speed   Lee   Dyer

Domi   Goma   Dabizas   Barton

Harper

IN THE NEWS

NEWCASTLE UNITED: Midfielder **Robert Lee** has admitted that he almost quit The Magpies under the leadership of **Ruud Gullit** after he was refused a squad number at the start of the 1999-2000 season. **Kieron Dyer** reveals he offered to give Lee his No. 7 shirt when the midfielder returned to first-team training following Gullit's departure from the club... **Silvio Maric** reports late for Newcastle's UEFA Cup trip to CSKA Sofia in Bulgaria. **PREMIERSHIP:** Martin O'Neill's position as Leicester City manager is uncertain as the power struggle in the club's boardroom continues to drag on. O'Neill's future depends on whether his allies – chairman John Elsom and Plc chief executive Sir Rodney Walker – walk away victorious from the battle... Only 250,000 people throughout Britain tune in to watch Man. United and Arsenal open their Champions League campaigns, which are shown on TV channel ONdigital. Man. United, Arsenal and Chelsea earn 0-0 draws with Fiorentina, Croatia Zagreb and AC Milan respectively... Watford manager Graham Taylor smashes the club's transfer record to sign **Nordin Wooter** from Spanish side Real Zaragoza for £975,000... Coventry are trounced 5-1 by First Division outfit Tranmere Rovers in the Worthington Cup... Sunderland's **Kevin Phillips** scores a hat-trick in the 5-0 league win at Derby.

THE FINAL SCORE!

SEPTEMBER 12		
Bradford	1-1	Tottenham

SEPTEMBER 18		
Aston Villa	1-0	Bradford
Derby	0-5	Sunderland
Leicester	2-2	Liverpool
Man. United	1-1	Wimbledon
Southampton	0-1	Arsenal
Watford	1-0	Chelsea

TOP OF THE PREMIERSHIP

	P	W	D	L	Pts
1. Man. United	8	6	2	0	20
2. Arsenal	8	5	1	2	16
3. Aston Villa	8	5	1	2	16
19. Newcastle	7	0	1	6	1

Newcastle United (4) 8
Sheffield Wednesday (0) 0

Competition: FA Carling Premiership

Date: Sunday September 19, 1999

Attendance: 36,619

Referee: N Barry (Scunthorpe) 6

Game 9

THE GAME: Newcastle thrashed Sheffield Wednesday 8-0 with five goals from Alan Shearer in a magnificent display in front of the Toon Army. It was The Magpies' best ever victory in the Premiership, their biggest top-flight win since 1908 and their first league win since April. While the goals were going in at the other end, Bobby Robson's side kept their first league clean sheet for 12 matches. This game was the turning point in Newcastle's season and St James' Park could smile again.

NEWCASTLE GOALS: Hughes (11 mins): Hughes headed in Dyer's cross for his first Newcastle goal; **Shearer** (30 mins): Scored his first goal of the season from open play by poking Solano's cross into the net; **Shearer** (penalty 33 mins): Fired home from the spot after a handball from Thome; **Shearer** (41 mins): Dyer's cross to the far post was knocked in by Shearer; **Dyer** (46 mins): Speed miskicked, allowing Dyer to head the ball in from close range; **Speed** (77 mins): Solano's right-wing corner was converted in style by Speed; **Shearer** (81 mins): A free-kick from Solano was cleared by Pressman but Shearer fired in the rebound; **Shearer** (penalty 84 mins): A jubilant fifth goal after Robinson had been fouled in the area by Haslam.

MATCH RATING: ★★★★ **LEAGUE POSITION:** 19th

NEWCASTLE UNITED		SHEFFIELD WEDNESDAY	
Harper	7	Pressman	4
Barton	8	Thome	4
Domi	8	Nolan	4
Subbed: 82 mins (Glass)		Walker	5
Goma	7	Newsome	4
Hughes ⚽	8	Sonner ☆ 6	
Goal: 11 mins		Booth	4
Dyer ⚽	8	Subbed: 27 mins (Carbone)	
Goal: 46 mins; Subbed: 63 mins (Robinson)		Rudi	4
Solano	8	Subbed: 46 mins (Haslam)	
Lee	8	Alexandersson	5
Speed ⚽	8	Booked: 46 mins (dissent)	
Goal: 77 mins		Donnelly	5
Ketsbaia	8	Subbed: 86 mins (Sibon)	
Subbed: 78 mins (McClen)		de Bilde	5
Shearer ⚽⚽⚽⚽⚽ ☆ 10		sub: Carbone	4
Goals: 30, 33, 41, 81, 84 mins		sub: Haslam	5
sub: Robinson	7	sub: Sibon	
sub: McClen		Subs not used: O'Donnell, Srnicek.	
sub: Glass			
Subs not used: Wright, Beharall.			

MATCH FACTS	
Shots On Target	
Newcastle 11-0 Sheff. Wed.	
Shots Off Target	
Newcastle 4-3 Sheff. Wed	
Hit Woodwork	
Newcastle 0-0 Sheff. Wed.	
Corners	
Newcastle 9-2 Sheff. Wed.	

HOW THEY LINED UP

Harper
Barton Goma Hughes Domi
Dyer Lee Speed Solano
Ketsbaia Shearer
Booth De Bilde
Rudi Alexandersson Sonner Donnelly
Nolan Walker Thome Newsome
Pressman

Kieron Dyer points the way Newcastle are heading after thrashing Wednesday 8-0.

Alan Shearer's double couldn't stop The Magpies from slipping to defeat against Leeds.

Leeds United (2) 3
Newcastle United (1) 2

Competition: FA Carling Premiership

Date: Saturday September 25, 1999

Attendance: 40,192

Referee: B Knight (Orpington) 5

Game 10

THE GAME: England manager and ex-Newcastle boss Kevin Keegan must have been a happy man after watching his No.1 striker score twice for The Magpies, but Alan Shearer's brace wasn't enough to stop United from slipping to defeat against high-flying Leeds. The England captain maintained his recent good form, taking his haul to seven goals in just two games. However, the result didn't go Newcastle's way as Leeds made it five wins in a row with Michael Bridges making amends for a host of missed chances on the day by scoring the winner.

LEEDS GOALS: Bowyer (11 mins): Shot right-footed over Harper from just inside the area after Bakke's fine throughball; **Kewell** (39 mins): Batty sent over a high cross from the right and Kewell ran in to head home powerfully after the ball had bounced; **Bridges** (77 mins): Huckerby's cross from the left was struck into the bottom corner by the in-form Bridges.

NEWCASTLE GOALS: Shearer (42 mins): Shearer jumped above Radebe to head home from Solano's free-kick; **Shearer** (53 mins): Dyer squared the ball perfectly from the left-hand side of the box for Shearer to rifle home from eight-yards.

MATCH RATING: ★★★ LEAGUE POSITION: 19th

MATCH FACTS

Shots On Target
Leeds 7-5 Newcastle

Shots Off Target
Leeds 8-1 Newcastle

Hit Woodwork
Leeds 1-0 Newcastle

Corners
Leeds 4-0 Newcastle

HOW THEY LINED UP

Martyn

Kelly — Woodgate — Radebe — Harte

Bakke — Batty — Bowyer — Kewell

Bridges — Smith

Ketsbaia — Shearer

Solano — Speed — McClen — Dyer

Domi — Marcelino — Goma — Barton

Harper

LEEDS UNITED

Martyn 🟨	6
Booked: 40 mins (foul)	
Kelly 🟨	7
Booked: 79 mins (foul)	
Radebe 🟨	5
Booked: 46 mins (foul)	
Woodgate	6
Harte	6
Bakke	7
Subbed: 78 mins (Haaland)	
Batty 🟨	7
Booked: 83 mins (foul)	
Bowyer ⚽	⭐ 8
Goal: 11 mins	
Kewell ⚽	7
Goal: 39 mins	
Smith 🟨	6
Booked: 60 mins (foul); Subbed: 73 mins (Huckerby)	
Bridges ⚽	6
Goal: 77 mins	
sub: Huckerby	
sub: Haaland	

Subs not used: Mills, Jones, Robinson.

NEWCASTLE UNITED

Harper	7
Barton	7
Marcelino 🟨	6
Booked: 31 mins (foul)	
Goma	6
Domi 🟨	6
Booked: 6 mins (foul)	
Solano	6
McClen	5
Subbed: 73 mins (Charvet)	
Speed 🟨	6
Booked: 75 mins (foul)	
Dyer	⭐ 8
Ketsbaia	6
Shearer ⚽⚽	7
Goals: 42, 53 mins	
sub: Charvet	

Subs not used: Glass, Hughes, Robinson, Wright.

IN THE NEWS

NEWCASTLE UNITED: Croatia midfielder **Silvio Maric** is fined by manager Bobby Robson after missing a team meeting prior to the UEFA Cup trip to Sofia. Maric is also told that his future at the club is up to him... Robson is rumoured to be preparing a £400,000 bid for Granada star **Luca Cominelli**... Striker **Duncan Ferguson** has discovered he will spend another month on the sidelines with a torn hamstring... **Marcelino** is ruled out for a fortnight just three days before the Leeds game.

PREMIERSHIP: David Batty is handed a two-game international ban after being sent-off during the European Championship qualifier with Poland... Former Nottingham Forest manager Brian Clough expresses his displeasure at Manchester United pulling out of the FA Cup to play in Brazil in January and says he hopes they get diarrhoea!... Coventry and Everton are knocked out of the Worthington Cup at the second round stage... Five Premiership players are sent-off during the weekend's games: **Moncur** (West Ham), **Myers** (Bradford), **Fuertes** (Derby), **Southgate** (Aston Villa), and **Gascoigne** (Middlesbrough).

THE FINAL SCORE!

SEPTEMBER 19		
Everton	1-0	West Ham
Leeds	2-0	Middlesbrough
Newcastle	8-0	Sheff. Wed.
Tottenham	3-2	Coventry

SEPTEMBER 25		
Arsenal	1-0	Watford
Coventry	1-0	West Ham
Derby	0-1	**Bradford**
Leeds	3-2	Newcastle
Leicester	3-1	Aston Villa
Man. United	3-3	Southampton
Middlesbrough	0-1	**Chelsea**
Sunderland	1-0	Sheff. Wed.

TOP OF THE PREMIERSHIP

	P	W	D	L	Pts
1. Man. United	9	6	3	0	21
2. Leeds	9	6	1	2	19
3. Arsenal	9	6	1	2	19
19. Newcastle	9	1	1	7	4

The invisible magic carpet came in particularly handy at times last season for Newcastle.

Newcastle United (1) 2
CSKA Sofia (1) 2

Newcastle win 4-2 on aggregate.

Competition: **UEFA Cup 1st Rd 2nd Leg**

Date: **Thursday September 30, 1999**

Attendance: **36,200**

Referee: **L Huyghe** (Belgium) 6

Game 11

THE GAME: Newcastle went through to the second round of the UEFA Cup but had to be content with a 2-2 draw against a side they beat easily in the first leg. CSKA Sofia had nothing to lose at St James' Park and took the lead after 29 minutes, but the goal stirred Newcastle into action and they equalised through Alan Shearer within seven minutes of going behind. The skipper was substituted for Stephen Glass in the dying minutes of the tie and his cross set up the second goal from Paul Robinson to give The Magpies a fine 4-2 aggregate win.

NEWCASTLE GOALS: Shearer *(36 mins):* Domi's left-wing cross was bundled over the line from close range by Shearer; **Robinson** *(87 mins):* A right-wing centre from substitute Glass was forced over the line from three yards by Robinson.

CSKA SOFIA: Litera *(29 mins):* Litera scored with a left-foot shot from 25 yards which dipped into the net; **Simeonov** *(90 mins):* Headed Velikov's cross beyond Harper at the far post.

MATCH RATING: ★★ **LEAGUE POSITION:** 19th

NEWCASTLE UNITED		CSKA SOFIA	
Harper	7	Lukic	7
Barton	☆ 9	Kremenliev ▢	6
		Booked: 34 mins (unsporting behaviour)	
Marcelino	7	Mrkic	6
Goma	7	Velikov ▢	6
Domi	7	*Booked: 73 mins (foul)*	
Dabizas	7	Tomovski	6
Solano	7	Litera ⊕	☆ 8
Lee	7	*Goal: 29 mins; Subbed: 82 mins (Deyanov)*	
Subbed: 90 mins (McClen)		Antonov	6
Speed ▢	8	Ivanov, D	5
Booked: 78 mins (foul)		*Subbed: 54 mins (Simeonov)*	
Maric	6	Berbatov	5
Subbed: 72 mins (Robinson)		Kiofev ▢	6
Shearer ⊕ ▢	8	*Booked: 7 mins (foul)*	
Goal: 36 mins; Booked: 42 mins (foul);		Dukarev	6
Subbed: 86 mins (Glass)		*Subbed: 77 mins (Hristov)*	
sub: Robinson ⊕		sub: Simeonov ⊕	6
Goal: 87 mins		*Goal: 90 mins*	
sub: Glass		sub: Hristov	
sub: McClen		sub: Deyanov	
Subs not used: Karelse, Charvet, Hughes, Pistone.		*Subs not used: Ivanov, G, Paskov, Trentchev, Kutchoukov.*	

MATCH FACTS

Shots On Target
Newcastle 5-3 CSKA Sofia

Shots Off Target
Newcastle 11-4 CSKA Sofia

Hit Woodwork
Newcastle 0-0 CSKA Sofia

Corners
Newcastle 5-0 CSKA Sofia

HOW THEY LINED UP

Harper

Dabizas Goma Marcelino

Solano Barton Lee Speed Domi

Shearer Maric

Berbatov Dukarev

Ivanov, D Kiosev Litera Kremenliev

Tomovski Antonov Mrkic Velikov

Lukic

IN THE NEWS

NEWCASTLE UNITED: Temuri Ketsbaia's injury will rule him out of first-team action for a month... Young defender **Aaron Hughes** earns himself a call-up into the senior Northern Ireland squad.

PREMIERSHIP: Three players are sent-off in the Merseyside derby at Anfield with Liverpool's **Sander Westerveld** and **Steven Gerrard** joined by Everton striker **Francis Jeffers** as The Toffees win 1-0... Wimbledon's **John Hartson** is also red-carded in their encounter with Tottenham... In the Champions League, Manchester United beat Marseille 2-1, Chelsea earn a 1-0 victory against Galatasaray and Arsenal draw 1-1 in Barcelona... Tottenham, Leeds and West Ham join Newcastle in the UEFA Cup second round... Aston Villa skipper **Gareth Southgate** is charged with misconduct by the FA following comments he made after being ordered off at Leicester... **Dan Petrescu** threatens to quit Chelsea unless he's given an improved contract... Derby boss Jim Smith tells transfer-listed **Lars Bohinen** that he still has a future at the club... **Lee Bowyer** signs a new four-year deal with Leeds United... Leicester's **Matt Elliott** is charged with misconduct following his controversial challenge on young Liverpool striker **Michael Owen**... **Paul Gascoigne** gets a two-match ban for his recent sending-off for Middlesbrough... **Benito Carbone** turns down a £1.5 million move to Derby from Sheffield Wednesday ... Tottenham captain **Sol Campbell** is linked with a £15 million move to Italian giants Juventus.

THE FINAL SCORE!

SEPTEMBER 26		
Wimbledon	1-1	Tottenham

SEPTEMBER 27		
Liverpool	0-1	Everton

TOP OF THE PREMIERSHIP

	P	W	D	L	Pts
1. Man. United	9	6	3	0	21
2. Leeds	9	6	1	2	19
3. Arsenal	9	6	1	2	19
19. Newcastle	9	1	1	7	4

OCTOBER

START OF MONTH **19th** END OF MONTH **17th**

"It's a great boost to the club to be out of the bottom three, we have been waiting for a while to say that – too long – but now we're out we aim to stay out." Alan Shearer

IN OCTOBER, KEVIN GALLACHER BECAME BOBBY ROBSON'S FIRST signing in a £500,000 move from Blackburn. Unfortunate injuries to strikers Duncan Ferguson, Temuri Ketsbaia and Paul Robinson meant the new boss needed to delve into the transfer market. Another newcomer was midfielder Jose Rodrigues Alves Antunes – also known as Fumaca – who was signed on loan until the end of the season. On the field, United beat Middlesbrough and Derby in the Premiership and overcame FC Zurich in the UEFA Cup.

Nevertheless, inconsistency was the byword for the month, with even the winning performance in Switzerland provoking criticism from Robson. After beating Middlesbrough at St James' Park, the Tyneside club were knocked out of the Worthington Cup by First Division Birmingham and had 'keeper Steve Harper sent-off. Defender Warren Barton received his marching orders against Coventry in the next game – the third and fourth Newcastle players in 14 games to be shown the red card. With a busy medical room, the loss of key members of the team through suspension was not helping Robson's bid to improve United's confidence and consistency.

However, by the end of October Bobby Robson's side had done enough to lift themselves out of the relegation zone for the first time since the start of the season. The 2-0 win over Derby was their third successive home win in the league, and while the goalless draw at Arsenal may not have been the prettiest performance, it was certainly the most professional. Robson set out a game plan for the visit to Highbury – one of the toughest away trips of the season – and the players did what was asked of them to get the vital point. Alan Shearer was still hounded by the press, though, with the latest round of criticism coming from former Magpies hero Andy Cole, who called Shearer 'the golden boy of English football' in his autobiography.

THE GAMES

Oct. 3 v **Middlesbrough** (h)

Oct. 12 v **Birmingham** (a)

Oct. 16 v **Coventry** (a)

Oct. 21 v **FC Zurich** (a)

Oct. 25 v **Derby** (h)

Oct. 30 v **Arsenal** (a)

TRANSFERS IN

Kevin Gallacher
Position: **Striker**
Fee: **£500,000**
From: **Blackburn Rovers**

Fumaca
Position: **Midfielder**
Fee: **Loan**
From: **Cantuna**

TRANSFERS OUT

None

MATCH facts
Matchman Of The Month

DIDIER DOMI
Average Rating: 7.33

Shearer's brace at home to Middlesbrough took his tally for the season to eleven goals.

Newcastle United (2) 2
Middlesbrough (0) 1

Competition: FA Carling Premiership

Date: Sunday October 3, 1999

Attendance: 36,421

Referee: S Lodge (Barnsley) 5

Game 12

THE GAME: Two strikes from Alan Shearer gave Newcastle victory in this north-east derby, but Brian Deane's 89th minute goal gave the scoreline a rather deceptive look. The Magpies dominated the game at St James' Park from the moment that Middlesbrough centre-back Gary Pallister was stretchered off with concussion. Newcastle should have added more goals after the break, when the in-form Alan Shearer was guilty of missing a number of good chances. Rob Lee and Gary Speed took control of the match in midfield, pulling the strings and feeding wide men Nolberto Solano and Kieron Dyer, who both looked dangerous from the flanks whenever they got the ball.

NEWCASTLE GOALS: Shearer (17 mins): Out-jumped Festa at the far post to head home a pinpoint right-wing cross from Barton; **Shearer** (45 mins): The England captain beat Festa in the air again to head a second from Solano's right-wing cross.

MIDDLESBROUGH GOAL: Deane (89 mins): Forced the ball in from close range following a bending free-kick from Ziege.

MATCH RATING: ★★★ **LEAGUE POSITION:** 19th

MATCH FACTS	HOW THEY LINED UP
Shots On Target	
Newcastle 11-3 Middlesbrough	
Shots Off Target	
Newcastle 9-2 Middlesbrough	
Hit Woodwork	
Newcastle 0-0 Middlesbrough	
Corners	
Newcastle 12-6 Middlesbrough	

HOW THEY LINED UP

Harper

Barton Goma Dabizas Domi

Dyer Lee Speed Solano

Shearer Gallacher

Deane Juninho

Ziege O'Neill Ince Mustoe Fleming

Pallister Cooper Festa

Schwarzer

NEWCASTLE UNITED	
Harper	7
Barton	8
Domi	8
Goma	8
Booked: 88 mins (foul)	
Dabizas	8
Booked: 57 mins (foul)	
Solano	7
Subbed: 89 mins (Glass)	
Lee	8
Speed	8
Dyer	7
Gallacher	7
Subbed: 83 mins (Robinson)	
Shearer ⚽⚽	☆ 9
Goals: 17, 45 mins	
sub: Robinson	
sub: Glass	
Subs not used: Marcelino, Hughes, Karelse.	

MIDDLESBROUGH	
Schwarzer	☆ 8
Fleming	6
Booked: 90 mins (foul)	
Festa	5
Booked: 59 mins (foul)	
Cooper	5
Booked: 20 mins (foul)	
Pallister	6
Subbed: 10 mins (Vickers)	
Mustoe	6
Ince	7
O'Neill	6
Ziege	6
Juninho	5
Subbed: 46 mins (Campbell)	
Deane ⚽	6
Goal: 89 mins	
sub: Vickers	6
sub: Campbell	6
Subs not used: Armstrong, Roberts, Summerbell.	

THIS WEEK...

IN THE NEWS

NEWCASTLE UNITED: Georgian striker **Temuri Ketsbaia** is ruled out for up to six weeks with knee ligament damage... AC Milan forward **Maurizio Ganz** emerges as a possible loan target, although Bobby Robson has also signed Blackburn's **Kevin Gallacher** for £500,000... Brazilian midfielder **Fumaca**, who had been previously touted around the country, joins The Magpies on loan from Crystal Palace... Newcastle are seeded in the UEFA Cup second round draw and paired with Swiss club FC Zurich... Kenny Dalglish agrees an undisclosed settlement with the club as compensation for ending his contract... Long-serving Welsh international **Gary Speed** captains his national side in their 2-0 home defeat by Switzerland at Wrexham.

PREMIERSHIP: Manchester United midfielder **David Beckham** is fined two weeks' wages for attending a party at London Fashion Week just 48 hours before his team's vital Champions League encounter with Sturm Graz... Italian legend **Roberto Baggio** is thought to be on Gianluca Vialli's wanted list at Chelsea... Huddersfield manager **Steve Bruce** announces that he is to hang up his boots after making 737 league appearances.

THE FINAL SCORE!

OCTOBER 2		
Aston Villa	0-0	Liverpool
Bradford	0-4	**Sunderland**
Everton	1-1	Coventry
Sheff. Wed.	5-1	Wimbledon

OCTOBER 3		
Chelsea	5-0	Man. United
Newcastle	2-1	Middlesbrough
Tottenham	2-3	**Leicester**
Watford	1-2	**Leeds**
West Ham	2-1	Arsenal

OCTOBER 4		
Southampton	3-3	Derby

TOP OF THE PREMIERSHIP

	P	W	D	L	Pts
1. Leeds	10	7	1	2	22
2. Man United	10	6	3	1	21
3. Sunderland	10	6	2	2	20
19. Newcastle	10	2	1	7	7

35

Birmingham City	**(1)**	**2**
Newcastle United	**(0)**	**0**

Competition: **Worthington Cup 3rd Rd**

Date: **Tuesday October 12, 1999**

Attendance: **19,795**

Referee: **U Rennie** (Sheffield) 5

Game 13

THE GAME: Newcastle were humbled in the third round of the Worthington Cup against Birmingham at St Andrews, but it could have been very different. Alan Shearer had a penalty saved after just four minutes by goalkeeper Ian Bennett and Newcastle hit the woodwork early on, but the match changed when United conceded a penalty after Steve Harper brought down Andrew Johnson. Harper was sent-off and Birmingham took the lead from the spot through captain Martin O'Connor. Ten-man Newcastle couldn't force an equaliser and the killer blow came when Darren Purse scored a second goal past substitute 'keeper Shay Given. Following the defeat, critics accused Newcastle of not taking the competition seriously – an accusation which boss Bobby Robson vigorously denied.

BIRMINGHAM GOALS: O'Connor *(penalty 44 mins):* United goalkeeper Harper brought down Johnson, who had been put clear by Adebola, to concede the penalty. Harper received his marching orders before O'Connor stepped up to calmly strike the penalty past substitute goalkeeper Given; **Purse** *(59 mins):* Rowett's inswinging corner was headed powerfully into the net by defender Purse to give Birmingham a two-goal lead.

MATCH RATING: ★★★ **LEAGUE POSITION:** 19th

BIRMINGHAM CITY			NEWCASTLE UNITED		
Bennett		7	Harper 🟥		6
Rowett	☆	8	*Sent-off: 45 mins (professional foul)*		
Holdsworth		7	Barton 🟨		6
Purse ⊕		7	*Booked: 12 mins (foul)*		
Goal: 59 mins			Goma		6
Johnson, M		7	Dabizas		6
McCarthy		6	Domi		6
Newton		7	Solano		6
Subbed: 88 mins (Holland)			*Subbed: 44 mins (Given)*		
Hughes, S		6	Glass		6
O'Connor 🟨 ⊕		7	Speed	☆	7
Booked: 38 mins (dissent); Goal: 44 mins;			Lee		6
Subbed: 88 mins (Hyde)			*Subbed: 75 mins (Pistone)*		
Ndlovu			Maric		5
Subbed: 17 mins (Johnson, A)			Shearer		5
Adebola 🟨		6	*Subbed: 77 mins (Robinson)*		
Booked: 25 mins (foul)			**sub:** *Given*		5
sub: *Johnson, A*		6	**sub:** *Pistone* 🟨		
sub: *Holland*			*Booked: 76 mins (foul)*		
sub: *Hyde*			**sub:** *Robinson*		
Subs not used: Poole, Gill.			*Subs not used: McClen, Serrant*		

MATCH FACTS

Shots On Target
Birmingham 6-2 Newcastle

Shots Off Target
Birmingham 2-3 Newcastle

Hit Woodwork
Birmingham 0-1 Newcastle

Corners
Birmingham 8-4 Newcastle

HOW THEY LINED UP

Bennett

Rowett Holdsworth Purse Johnson, M

McCarthy O'Connor Newton Hughes, S

Ndlovu Adebola

Maric Shearer

Glass Speed Lee Solano

Domi Dabizas Goma Barton

Harper

The ten-man Magpies fell at the first hurdle in the Worthington Cup against Birmingham City.

Shearer and Gallacher posed a big threat but Hedman was superb in Coventry's goal.

Coventry City (3) 4
Newcastle United (0) 1

Game 14

Competition: **FA Carling Premiership**

Date: **Saturday October 16, 1999**

Attendance: **23,031**

Referee: **A Wiley** (Burntwood) 6

THE GAME: A second defeat in the space of five days was bad news for Newcastle, who had a player dismissed for the second consecutive match. The Magpies started positively, with Alan Shearer and Didier Domi denied by excellent saves, but while the team was impressive throughout, their inability to score proved costly. The dismissal of Warren Barton, sent-off for violent conduct in an off-the-ball incident with Moroccan midfielder Youssef Chippo, was a punishing body blow from which Newcastle never recovered. By then, United's weakness defending set-pieces already had them trailing by two goals in under half an hour, and worse was to come. Coventry took full advantage of the ten men to record a 4-1 win, but United were disappointed to come away with nothing from Highfield Road.

COVENTRY GOALS: Palmer (13 mins): Headed home from McAllister's well-taken free-kick; **Williams** (21 mins): United's defence was caught watching as defender Williams blasted in a spectacular free-kick from 35 yards; **Keane** (39 mins): Given completely missed the ball, allowing the grateful Keane to tap into the empty net; **Hadji** (90 mins): Hadji's left-foot shot from another free-kick on the edge of Newcastle's area made it 4-1.

NEWCASTLE GOAL: Domi (81 mins): Domi thundered the ball beyond 'keeper Hedman with a cracking left-foot volley.

MATCH RATING: ★★★ **LEAGUE POSITION: 19th**

MATCH FACTS
Shots On Target
Coventry 9-7 Newcastle
Shots Off Target
Coventry 4-7 Newcastle
Hit Woodwork
Coventry 0-0 Newcastle
Corners
Coventry 6-9 Newcastle

HOW THEY LINED UP

Hedman

Edworthy — Shaw — Williams — Hall, M

Telfer — McAllister — Palmer — Chippo

Hadji — Keane

Gallacher — Shearer

Dyer

Speed — Lee — Solano

Domi — Dabizas — Hughes — Barton

Given

COVENTRY CITY
Hedman	☆ 9
Edworthy □	6
Booked: 70 mins (foul); Subbed: 72 mins (Froggatt)	
Williams ⊕	6
Goal: 21 mins	
Shaw	7
Hall, M	6
McAllister	7
Subbed: 85 mins (Roussel)	
Telfer	6
Palmer ⊕ □	7
Goal: 13 mins; Booked: 54 mins (foul)	
Chippo □	7
Booked: 42 mins (foul)	
Keane ⊕	7
Goal: 39 mins	
Hadji ⊕	6
Goal: 90 mins	
sub: Froggatt	
sub: Roussel	

Subs not used: Strachan, G, Nuzzo, Eustace.

NEWCASTLE UNITED
Given	6
Barton ▮	5
Sent-off: 29 mins (violent conduct)	
Domi ⊕	6
Goal: 81 mins	
Hughes	6
Dabizas □	6
Booked: 90 mins (foul)	
Dyer	6
Speed	6
Solano □	☆ 8
Booked: 73 mins (dissent)	
Lee	5
Shearer	5
Gallacher	6

Subs not used: Maric, Harper, Glass, McClen, Pistone.

THE FINAL SCORE!
OCTOBER 16		
Arsenal	4-1	Everton
Coventry	4-1	Newcastle
Derby	0-1	Tottenham
Leeds	2-0	Sheff. Wed.
Leicester	2-1	Southampton
Liverpool	1-0	Chelsea
Man. United	4-1	Watford
Wimbledon	3-2	Bradford

TOP OF THE PREMIERSHIP
	P	W	D	L	Pts
1. Leeds	11	8	1	2	25
2. Man. United	11	7	3	1	24
3. Arsenal	11	7	1	3	22
19. Newcastle	11	2	1	8	7

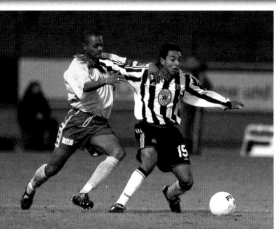

Newcastle held off the threat of FC Zurich to take two away goals back to St James' Park.

FROM THE PAGES OF *MATCH*

ALAN SHEARER is no stranger to criticism and he suffered plenty of abuse during the early part of the season, but the Newcastle captain remained unfazed by it all, as he revealed to **MATCH**.

After all the criticism you had at the start of the season, how enjoyable have your recent performances been?
"I've been pleased, obviously, but I've never lost belief in my own ability. It's important not to do that. It's inevitable that you're going to face criticism at some stage in your career. I've had enough of that. I've had my praise along the way and I'll accept both. I don't believe any of it when it comes along because it can turn the other way so quickly."

People have blamed player power for the resignation of Ruud Gullit. What do you think about that? *"I don't think Ruud resigned because of player power. We had some bad results and the decision was made. Things needed changing at the club and the changes were made."*

How important has the arrival of Bobby Robson been to you? *"From my point of view he's been great. He knew that I was getting a lot of criticism at the time he arrived, but he understood exactly what I was going through because of all the stick he had to take when he was manager of England. He knew I could cope with it."*

Has the new manager got you doing anything different?
"Slightly, yes. He's tinkered with my game, he wants me running towards goal more than I have been, rather than standing with my back to goal and fighting off defenders all the time. At the moment, it's paying dividends. Newcastle and I aren't daft enough to shout our heads off, but we're going along nicely at the moment."

FC Zurich (0) **1**

Newcastle United (0) **2**

Competition: UEFA Cup 2nd Rd 1st Leg

Date: Thursday October 21, 1999

Attendance: 9,500

Referee: J Granat (Poland) 8

Game 15

THE GAME: A second successive UEFA Cup win on foreign soil didn't spare Newcastle's players from a stern lecture after the final whistle from United manager Bobby Robson. Despite watching his side gain the upper hand in the first leg win over Zurich, Robson said the team 'collapsed like a pack of cards' in the last 20 minutes. They had been in the driving seat after transfer-listed Silvio Maric scored his first goal in 21 matches and Alan Shearer powered in a second just before the hour to make it 2-0. But United's problems in defence were exposed yet again as Castillo reduced the deficit following a free-kick. Zurich came close to grabbing a draw by hitting the underside of the crossbar, but The Magpies held on for an important 2-1 win and they return for the second leg of the UEFA Cup tie at St James' Park with two crucial away goals.

ZURICH GOAL: Castillo *(67 mins):* From a free-kick, Castillo cut into the area from the right-hand side to fire past Harper.

NEWCASTLE GOALS: Maric *(50 mins):* Maric intercepted a wayward pass from Kebe and beat the 'keeper with a fine chip; **Shearer** *(59 mins):* Pascolo tipped Hughes' shot onto the crossbar but Shearer finished clinically from the rebound.

MATCH RATING: ★★ **LEAGUE POSITION:** 19th

FC ZURICH	
Pascolo	6
Eydelie	5
Kebe ☐	4
Booked: 26 mins (foul); Subbed: 64 mins (Douglas)	
Sant'Anna	7
Bartlett	7
Frick	7
Subbed: 75 mins (Akale)	
Chassot ☆	8
Subbed: 64 mins (Del Signore)	
Castillo ⚽	5
Goal: 67 mins	
Stocklasa	6
Kavelashvili	6
Djordjevic	6
sub: Del Signore	6
sub: Douglas	6
sub: Akale	

Subs not used: Giannini, Malacarne, Andreoli, Trombini.

NEWCASTLE UNITED	
Harper ☐	6
Booked: 74 mins (foul)	
Barton	7
Dabizas ☆	8
Hughes	7
Domi	6
Solano	7
Subbed: 87 mins (McClen)	
Dyer	6
Subbed: 63 mins (Serrant)	
Lee	6
Speed	6
Shearer ⚽	6
Goal: 59 mins	
Maric ⚽	6
Goal: 50 mins; Subbed: 78 mins (Robinson)	
sub: Serrant	6
sub: Robinson	
sub: McClen	

Subs not used: Given, Pistone, Kerr, Marcelino.

MATCH FACTS

Shots On Target
Zurich 4-6 Newcastle

Shots Off Target
Zurich 7-4 Newcastle

Hit Woodwork
Zurich 0-0 Newcastle

Corners
Zurich 2-3 Newcastle

HOW THEY LINED UP

Pascolo

Castillo — Stocklasa — Djordjevic — Kebe

Chassot — Eydelie — Sant'Anna — Kavelashvili

Bartlett — Frick

Maric — Shearer

Dyer — Speed — Lee — Solano

Domi — Dabizas — Hughes — Barton

Harper

THE FINAL SCORE!

OCTOBER 17		
Middlesbrough	2-0	West Ham

OCTOBER 18		
Sunderland	2-1	Aston Villa

OCTOBER 23		
Aston Villa	1-1	Wimbledon
Bradford	3-1	Leicester
Chelsea	2-3	Arsenal
Southampton	1-1	Liverpool
Tottenham	3-1	Man. United

TOP OF THE PREMIERSHIP

		P	W	D	L	Pts
1.	Leeds	11	8	1	2	25
2.	Arsenal	12	8	1	3	25
3.	Man. United	12	7	3	2	24
19.	Newcastle	11	2	1	8	7

Everything went to plan for United in a comfortable win against Derby.

Newcastle United (1) 2
Derby County (0) 0

Game 16

Competition: **FA Carling Premiership**

Date: **Monday October 25, 1999**

Attendance: **35,614**

Referee: **S Dunn** (Bristol) 8

THE GAME: Bobby Robson's Newcastle side won their third successive home game in the Premiership to move out of the relegation zone for the first time since the start of the season. It helped that Jim Smith's visiting Derby side posed little threat to Shay Given's goal. Stefano Eranio scored the first goal of the game, deflecting the ball into his own net to put United 1-0 up just before half-time. After the break, Newcastle never looked like surrendering their lead with an improved defensive display. The side included full-back Alessandro Pistone – who hadn't played since August 1998 – and Robert Lee, making his 300th appearance for the club. Both players were back to their best after being overlooked by Ruud Gullit. Lee was the driving force behind Newcastle's attacks in the second half and it came as no surprise when Alan Shearer made it 2-0 to secure all three points in an impressive victory for United.

NEWCASTLE GOALS: Eranio *(own goal 42 mins):* Solano curled in a right-wing cross and Eranio mistakenly turned the ball into his own net; **Shearer** *(53 mins):* Shearer side-footed his shot into the net from eight yards after Solano had laid the ball perfectly into the Newcastle captain's path from the right.

MATCH RATING: ★★ **LEAGUE POSITION: 17th**

> "It's a great boost to be out of the bottom three. We've been waiting for a while to say that – too long – but now we're out we aim to stay out." ALAN SHEARER

MATCH FACTS

Shots On Target	
Newcastle	4-1 Derby

Shots Off Target	
Newcastle	7-4 Derby

Hit Woodwork	
Newcastle	0-0 Derby

Corners	
Newcastle	3-5 Derby

NEWCASTLE UNITED

Player	Rating
Given	6
Dabizas	7
Marcelino	7
Solano	7
Lee	☆ 8
Speed	7
Shearer ⊕	7
Goal: 53 mins	
Gallacher	6
Subbed: 80 mins (Ferguson)	
Dyer	6
Subbed: 38 mins (Maric)	
Barton	7
Subbed: 56 mins (Hughes)	
Pistone	7
sub: Maric	6
sub: Hughes	7
sub: Ferguson	

Subs not used: Harper, McClen.

DERBY COUNTY

Player	Rating
Hoult	6
Schnoor	6
Powell ▯	7
Booked: 33 mins (foul)	
Dorigo	6
Subbed: 83 mins (Prior)	
Delap	6
Laursen ▯	☆ 7
Booked: 88 mins (foul)	
Baiano	5
Subbed: 46 mins (Christie)	
Eranio ⊕	5
Own Goal: 42 mins	
Morris	5
Subbed: 57 mins (Burton)	
Johnson	5
Beck	5
sub: Christie	5
sub: Burton ▯	5
Booked: 83 mins (foul)	
sub: Prior	

Subs not used: Carbonari, Knight.

HOW THEY LINED UP

Given

Barton — Dabizas — Marcelino — Pistone

Solano — Lee — Speed — Dyer

Shearer — Gallacher

Beck — Baiano

Johnson — Powell — Eranio — Morris

Dorigo — Schnoor — Laursen — Delap

Hoult

Arsenal struggled to make any impact on Newcastle's much-improved defence.

Arsenal (0) 0
Newcastle United (0) 0

Competition: FA Carling Premiership

Date: Saturday October 30, 1999

Attendance: 38,106

Referee: P Jones (Loughborough) 7

Game 17

THE GAME: Newcastle went to Highbury to defend and did a fantastic job with an assured display that earned them their first away Premiership clean sheet for almost nine months and Bobby Robson's first point away from St James' Park. It might not have been the most entertaining or skilful of matches, but The Magpies chief will take heart form the fact that Arsenal couldn't break down a resilient Newcastle rearguard. Dennis Bergkamp replaced the largely ineffective Thierry Henry in the second half, but nothing changed. The Magpies were content to defend and catch the Arsenal attack offside to earn a point at Highbury – a ground where so many teams have tried but failed to achieve this in the past. The best two chances of the match came when Franck Dumas heroically cleared a Patrick Vieira header off the line and when Suker shot at 'keeper John Karelse from five yards out. In the end it was a satisfying away point, deservedly won by Robson's perfectly executed tactics.

MATCH RATING: ★★ **LEAGUE POSITION:** 17th

> "I went to Arsenal with a defensive plan and it worked. I like to think football is a pleasurable thing to watch but in our situation, where Premiership football is crucial, we just have to fight away from home." BOBBY ROBSON

ARSENAL	
Seaman	7
Winterburn	7
Vieira	7
Keown ▢	6
Booked: 61 mins (foul); Subbed: 65 mins (Upson)	
Adams	7
Ljungberg	5
Suker	6
Henry	6
Subbed: 46 mins (Bergkamp)	
Silvinho	6
Subbed: 60 mins (Overmars)	
Grimandi	7
Luzhny ☆	8
sub: Bergkamp	6
sub: Overmars	6
sub: Upson	6
Subs not used: Manninger, Kanu.	

NEWCASTLE UNITED	
Karelse	7
Marcelino	7
Domi ☆	8
Dumas	7
Shearer	7
Solano	7
Subbed: 90 mins (Ferguson)	
Speed	6
Gallacher	6
Dabizas ▢	8
Booked: 26 mins (foul)	
Pistone	6
Lee ▢	7
Booked: 34 mins (foul)	
sub: Ferguson	
Subs not used: Maric, Charvet, Hughes, Perez.	

MATCH FACTS

Shots On Target
Arsenal 5-2 Newcastle

Shots Off Target
Arsenal 7-1 Newcastle

Hit Woodwork
Arsenal 0-0 Newcastle

Corners
Arsenal 7-4 Newcastle

HOW THEY LINED UP

Seaman

Luzhny Keown Adams Winterburn

Ljungberg Grimandi Vieira Silvinho

Henry Suker

Gallacher Shearer

Speed Lee Solano

Domi Marcelino Dumas Dabizas Pistone

Karelse

IN THE NEWS

NEWCASTLE UNITED: Defender **Marcelino** is linked with a move to Leeds, who are short of defensive options because of a number of injuries... Full-back **Andy Griffin** suffers a back injury and is ruled out for up to two months... **Bobby Robson** is reported to have made a move for Portuguese defender **Helder** of Deportivo La Coruna...

PREMIERSHIP: Arsenal are knocked out of the Champions League at the group stages after a 'home' defeat by Italian side Fiorentina at Wembley... **David Beckham** scores his first goal of the season for Manchester United as they beat Croatia Zagreb 2-1... Arsenal's **Patrick Vieira** receives a six-match ban following his sending-off and spitting incident in the game against West Ham... Middlesbrough make an approach for Arsenal's Ukraine defender **Oleg Luzhny**... Liverpool reveal plans to increase Anfield's capacity to 55,000... **Ian Wright** decides to leave West Ham to join Celtic.

THE FINAL SCORE!

OCTOBER 24		
Everton	4-4	Leeds
Watford	1-2	**Middlesbrough**
West Ham	1-1	Sunderland

OCTOBER 25		
Newcastle	2-0	Derby

OCTOBER 27		
Liverpool	1-0	West Ham

OCTOBER 30		
Arsenal	0-0	Newcastle
Derby	3-1	Chelsea
Leeds	1-0	West Ham
Leicester	3-0	Sheff. Wed.
Man. United	3-0	Aston Villa
Middlesbrough	2-1	Everton
Wimbledon	1-1	Southampton

OCTOBER 31		
Coventry	4-0	Watford
Sunderland	2-1	Tottenham

TOP OF THE PREMIERSHIP

	P	W	D	L	Pts
1. Leeds	13	9	2	2	29
2. Man. United	13	8	3	2	27
3. Sunderland	13	8	3	2	27
17. Newcastle	13	3	2	8	11

NOVEMBER

"The manager Bobby Robson is a very honest man. He told us that we're still behind the likes of Man. United, but we're not as far behind as people think." Kieron Dyer

IN A BIZARRE START TO THE MONTH, BOBBY ROBSON TOOK ROB
Lee off the transfer list – the Newcastle manager hadn't realised that the midfielder was on the list when he arrived at the club. It was an excellent month for Nikos Dabizas, whose outstanding performances and vital goals earnt him the Premiership's Matchman Of The Month award. The Greece international also equalled a 103-year club record by becoming the first United defender in that time to score in three successive matches. But it wasn't such a great month for summer signing Kieron Dyer – surgery meant the England midfield ace would be out of first-team action for four weeks. There were also injury worries in defence, so Robson moved quickly to sign centre-back Helder on loan from Spanish club Deportivo La Coruna.

In the first leg of the UEFA Cup third round, The Magpies flew out to Italy to face AS Roma but were beaten by a controversial Francesco Totti penalty. It was a great performance by Newcastle though, who had to leave almost an entire team at home because of injury, so the makeshift side, with many players in unfamiliar roles, did well to hold out until the decisive spot-kick.

On the domestic front, November was an impressive month for United as Bobby Robson's team completed an unbeaten run of five games that had started in October. Draws with Everton and Watford were followed by a 2-1 win over Spurs and elevated Newcastle to 15th position in the Premiership. There was good news concerning the walking wounded, with Steve Howey and Temuri Ketsbaia returning to action with the reserves. A host of Newcastle players were on international duty around the world in November, including Alan Shearer – who captained England to a crucial 2-1 aggregate win over Scotland in their European Championship play-off to earn Kevin Keegan's side a place at Euro 2000 in Holland and Belgium.

THE GAMES

Nov. 4 v **FC Zurich** (h)

Nov. 7 v **Everton** (h)

Nov. 20 v **Watford** (a)

Nov. 25 v **AS Roma** (a)

Nov. 28 v **Tottenham** (h)

TRANSFERS IN

Helder

Position: **Defender**

Fee: **Loan**

From: **Deportivo La Coruna**

TRANSFERS OUT

None

MATCHfacts

Matchman Of The Month

NIKOS DABIZAS

Average Rating: 8.00

43

Ferguson punches the air as he adds Newcastle's second goal in a Man Of The Match performance.

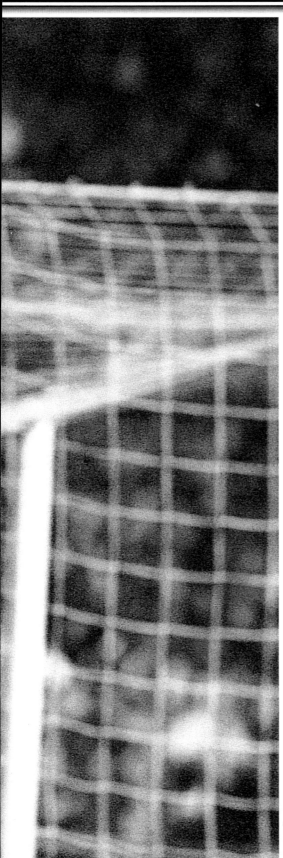

Newcastle United (1) 3

FC Zurich (1) 1

Newcastle win 5-2 on aggregate.

Competition: UEFA Cup 2nd Rd, 2nd Leg

Date: Thursday November 4, 1999

Attendance: 34,502

Referee: D Messina (Italy) 8

Game 18

THE GAME: Newcastle recorded a 3-1 win against Zurich at St James' Park, but The Magpies were not entirely convincing. The visitors, trailing 2-1 from the first leg, must have thought they were in with a chance of rescuing the tie when Jamarauli gave them a 1-0 lead, with United's defence giving the Zurich attack far too much room. But Silvio Maric levelled the scores for Newcastle before Duncan Ferguson put them 2-0 in front, scoring his first goal since his debut in November 1998. Gary Speed scored United's third to give them a good win on paper and send the Toon Army through to the third round.

NEWCASTLE GOALS: Maric *(33 mins):* Shearer's free-kick was deflected onto the bar by Pascolo, leaving Maric to head the rebound into the empty net; **Ferguson** *(58 mins):* Solano's ball found Ferguson, who scored with a left-foot shot from six yards out; **Speed** *(61 mins):* Another assist for Solano, whose left-wing corner from was headed home by Speed.

ZURICH GOAL: Bartlett *(17 mins):* Jamarauli's cross was tucked into the corner by Bartlett to put Zurich 1-0 ahead.

MATCH RATING: ★★ **LEAGUE POSITION:** 18th

NEWCASTLE UNITED		FC ZURICH	
Harper	6	**Pascolo** ▯	6
Barton	6	*Booked: 90 mins (foul)*	
Domi	6	**Giannini**	6
Lee	6	*Subbed: 71 mins (Castillo)*	
Subbed: 80 mins (McClen)		**Fydelie**	6
Marcelino	6	**Kebe**	6
Dabizas	6	*Subbed: 46 mins (Frick)*	
Solano	7	**Sant'Anna**	7
Ferguson ⊕	☆ 8	**Bartlett** ⊕	6
Goal: 58 mins; Subbed: 83 mins		*Goal: 17 mins; Subbed: 46 mins (Chassot)*	
(Robinson)		**Jamarauli**	☆ 8
Shearer	7	**Stocklasa** ▯	6
Maric ⊕	7	*Booked: 19 mins (foul)*	
Goal: 33 mins; Subbed: 86 mins (Glass)		**Quentin**	7
Speed ⊕	6	**Djordjevic**	6
Goal: 61 mins		**Kavelashvili**	6
sub: McClen		*sub: Chassot*	6
sub: Robinson		*sub: Frick*	6
sub: Glass		*sub: Castillo*	

Subs not used: Karelse, Charvet, Hughes, Pistone. | *Subs not used: Trombini, Kanga, Andreoli, Douglas.*

MATCH FACTS	
Shots On Target	
Newcastle 8-5 Zurich	
Shots Off Target	
Newcastle 6-2 Zurich	
Hit Woodwork	
Newcastle 0-0 Zurich	
Corners	
Newcastle 13-3 Zurich	

HOW THEY LINED UP

Harper

Barton — Dabizas — Marcelino — Domi

Solano — Lee — Speed

Maric

Shearer — Ferguson

Jamarauli — Bartlett — Kavelashvili

Sant'Anna — Eydelie — Kebe

Quentin — Djordjevic — Stocklasa — Giannini

Pascolo

IN THE NEWS

NEWCASTLE UNITED: England international **Kieron Dyer** could be out of action for up to six weeks after undergoing an operation to clear up the pain he's experienced in his calf... The Magpies decide to take Portuguese international defender **Rodrigues Helder** on loan from Spanish club Deportivo La Coruna until the end of the season... **Rob Lee** has finally been taken off the transfer list by Bobby Robson. ... Robson joins Leeds boss David O'Leary in criticising the format of this season's UEFA Cup, which allows losers from the European Champions League into the competition at the third round.

PREMIERSHIP: Sir Alex Ferguson hints that his Manchester United captain, **Roy Keane**, could still sign a new contract at the club despite months of speculation regarding the Irishman's future. Ferguson's former assistant at Old Trafford, Brian Kidd, is sacked as the boss of Blackburn Rovers after just eleven months in charge at Ewood Park with the Lancashire club struggling in Division One... Leicester City defender **Matt Elliott** is handed a one match ban for his challenge on Liverpool's **Michael Owen**, which went unpunished at the time by referee Uriah Rennie... Former England boss Graham Taylor signs a new three-year contract with Watford as The Hornets try to climb away from the foot of the Premiership.

THE FINAL SCORE!

NOVEMBER 1		
Liverpool	3-1	Bradford

NOVEMBER 6		
Aston Villa	0-1	Southampton
Bradford	1-1	Coventry
Liverpool	2-0	Derby
Man. United	2-0	Leicester
Middlesbrough	1-1	Sunderland
Sheff. Wed.	2-2	Watford

TOP OF THE PREMIERSHIP

	P	W	D	L	Pts
1. Man. United	14	9	3	2	30
2. Leeds	13	9	2	2	29
3. Sunderland	14	8	4	2	28
18. Newcastle	13	3	2	8	11

Newcastle United	(0) 1
Everton	(0) 1

Competition: FA Carling Premiership

Date: Sunday November 7, 1999

Attendance: 36,164

Game 19

Referee: M Reed (Birmingham) 8

THE GAME: Battling Everton prevented United from making it four Premiership wins in a row at a rain-drenched St James' Park. While The Magpies had the bulk of possession, nobody could deny Everton their point for a spirited defensive display. Inspired by striker Duncan Ferguson, Newcastle controlled the first-half but it wasn't until another former Toffees player, Gary Speed, was brought down in the area that The Magpies had something to show for their dominance. Alan Shearer tucked away the penalty to claim his 12th goal of the season, but it never looked as though it would be enough and Everton soon grabbed an equaliser from Kevin Campbell to earn themselves a point. Kevin Gallacher almost clinched a winner, but Gerrard turned his shot against the post and United were left to reflect on a first-half where they failed to turn possession into goals.

NEWCASTLE GOAL: Shearer (penalty 47 mins): Put United 1-0 ahead from the spot after Gerrard had fouled Speed.

EVERTON GOAL: Campbell (61 mins): Campbell squeezed between two Newcastle defenders and scored past Harper with a diving header from Barmby's right-wing cross.

MATCH RATING: ★★★ **LEAGUE POSITION: 16th**

NEWCASTLE UNITED		EVERTON		
Harper	6	Gerrard ☐		6
Pistone	6	Booked: 46 mins (foul)		
Domi	6	Cleland ☐		6
Dumas ☐	7	Booked: 20 mins (foul)		
Booked: 76 mins (foul)		Dunne ☐		6
Dabizas	7	Booked: 38 mins (foul)		
Lee	7	Ball		5
Solano	6	Subbed: 46 mins (Johnson)		
Speed ☐	☆ 8	Unsworth ☐	☆ 8	
Booked: 68 mins (foul)		Booked: 88 mins (unsporting behaviour)		
Gallacher	5	Weir		7
Ferguson	6	Collins		6
Subbed: 85 mins (Maric)		Hutchison		6
Shearer ⊕	6	Pembridge		6
Goal: 47 mins		Barmby ☐		6
sub: Maric		Booked: 31 mins (foul)		
Subs not used: Karelse, Marcelino, Glass, Hughes.		Campbell ⊕		7
		Goal: 61 mins		
		sub: Johnson ☐		6
		Booked: 82 mins (unsporting behaviour)		
		Subs not used: Simonsen, Ward, Jevons, Clarke.		

MATCH FACTS

Shots On Target
Newcastle 8-1 Everton

Shots Off Target
Newcastle 0-2 Everton

Hit Woodwork
Newcastle 1-0 Everton

Corners
Newcastle 9-5 Everton

HOW THEY LINED UP

Harper

Pistone Dabizas Dumas Domi

Solano Lee Speed

Gallacher

Shearer Ferguson

Campbell

Pembridge Cleland Collins Hutchison Barmby

Ball Unsworth Weir Dunne

Gerrard

Referee Mike Riley had a busy afternoon in this 1-1 battle, issuing eight yellow cards.

The Magpies did well to get back into the game at Vicarage Road but only came away with a point.

Watford (0) 1
Newcastle United (0) 1

Game 20

Competition: FA Carling Premiership

Date: Saturday November 20, 1999

Attendance: 19,539

Referee: S Dunn (Bristol) 6

THE GAME: There was controversy in the second half of this match at Vicarage Road when Watford took the lead through Michel Ngonge, heading home from what seemed an obvious offside position. Bobby Robson's side stepped up a gear after going 1-0 down, determined not to lose to one of the weaker sides in the Premiership, quickly equalised, and then looked the more likely winners in the second half. The Hornets felt aggrieved after 79 minutes when Marcelino seemed to handle and Watford captain Robert Page received a booking for his protests. A late effort by substitute Stephen Glass was clawed around the post by Watford goalkeeper Alex Chamberlain.

WATFORD GOAL: Ngonge *(53 mins):* Headed home at the second attempt after his first effort was saved by Harper.

NEWCASTLE GOAL: Dabizas *(59 mins):* Scored his first goal of the season with a tremendous curling shot.

MATCH RATING: ★★★ **LEAGUE POSITION:** 16th

> "We didn't deserve that. Given that we didn't play very well, they scored with an offside goal and didn't even deserve a point. Steve Harper only had a couple of saves to make, but they still got a point." **NIKOS DABIZAS**

WATFORD

Player		
Chamberlain		7
Page ▢		☆ 9
Booked: 79 mins (dissent)		
Palmer		7
Robinson		7
Ngonge ⊕		6
Goal: 53 mins; Subbed: 63 mins (Wooter)		
Hyde		6
Noel-Williams ▢		7
Booked: 56 mins (foul)		
Easton		6
Subbed: 44 mins (Bakalli)		
Gravelaine		7
Millor		7
Cox		6
sub: Bakalli		6
sub: Wooter		6

Subs not used: Day, Smith, Gibbs.

NEWCASTLE UNITED

Player		
Harper		7
Marcelino ▢		5
Booked: 11 mins (handball)		
Dumas		6
Shearer		6
Maric		5
Subbed: 81 mins (Glass)		
Speed		7
Hughes		6
Gallacher		
Subbed: 8 mins (Ketsbaia)		
Dabizas ⊕		☆ 8
Goal: 59 mins		
Pistone		6
Lee ▢		7
Booked: 67 mins (foul)		
sub: Ketsbaia		7
sub: Glass		

Subs not used: Fumaca, Kareise, Solano.

MATCH FACTS

Shots On Target
Watford 4-9 Newcastle

Shots Off Target
Watford 6-8 Newcastle

Hit Woodwork
Watford 0-1 Newcastle

Corners
Watford 3-6 Newcastle

HOW THEY LINED UP

Chamberlain

Cox   Palmer   Page   Robinson

Hyde   Miller   Easton

Ngonge   Noel-Williams   Gravelaine

Gallacher   Shearer

Maric

Speed   Dumas   Lee

Pistone   Marcelino   Dabizas   Hughes

Harper

IN THE NEWS

NEWCASTLE UNITED: The arrival of centre-back **Rodrigues Helder** from Deportivo La Coruna sparks interest from Marseille and Paris St Germain for defender **Alain Goma**... **Steve Howey** returns to action in the reserve team after a long-term Achilles injury, as does **Temuri Ketsbaia**... **Carl Serrant** is declared fit and ready for first-team selection... **Alan Shearer** captains England to a 2-1 aggregate victory over a Scotland side including **Kevin Gallacher** to qualify for Euro 2000... Bobby Robson is said to be considering a £3 million move for top Benfica midfielder **Jose Calado** after being told he has money to spend. The United manager has also cast his eye over Turkish midfield stars **Sergen Yalcin** and **Abdullah Ercan**... **Duncan Ferguson** is ruled out for two more weeks with a torn calf muscle... **Nolberto Solano** scores the winner in Peru's 2-1 friendly win over Slovakia... **Nikos Dabizas** plays in Greece's 1-0 friendly win over Bulgaria.

PREMIERSHIP: Leeds' **Harry Kewell** is banned from playing against Bradford by FIFA after he decides not to travel to Australia for the friendly match with Brazil.

THE FINAL SCORE!

NOVEMBER 7		
Chelsea	0-0	West Ham
Newcastle	1-1	Everton
Tottenham	2-1	Arsenal
Wimbledon	2-0	Leeds

NOVEMBER 20		
Arsenal	5-1	Middlesbrough
Derby	1-2	Man. United
Everton	1-1	Chelsea
Leeds	2-1	Bradford
Leicester	2-1	Wimbledon
Southampton	0-1	Tottenham
Sunderland	0-2	Liverpool
Watford	1-1	Newcastle

TOP OF THE PREMIERSHIP

	P	W	D	L	Pts
1. Man. United	15	10	3	2	33
2. Leeds	15	10	2	3	32
3. Arsenal	15	9	2	4	29
16. Newcastle	15	3	4	8	13

Shearer couldn't score in the Italian capital, but the tie was still wide open going into the second leg.

 AS Roma (0) **1**

 Newcastle United (0) **0**

Competition: **UEFA Cup 3rd Rd 1st Leg**

Date: **Thursday November 25, 1999**

Attendance: **45,655**

Referee: **C Colombo** (France) 5

Game 21

THE GAME: Despite being depleted by injuries, The Magpies deserved a draw in Rome after putting on a brave display, but they lost the first leg of this tie to a disputed penalty. Defender Laurent Charvet was judged to have fouled Marco Delvecchio and Francesco Totti scored from the spot. Totti then appeared to claw at Nolberto Solano's face but the referee didn't take any action. Despite losing, it was an encouraging, disciplined performance by United and Temuri Ketsbaia almost levelled the tie late on, forcing a good save from the Roma 'keeper.

ROMA GOAL: Totti *(penalty 50 mins):* Struck the ball inside Harper's post after Charvet's challenge on Delvecchio.

MATCH RATING: ★★★★ **LEAGUE POSITION:** 16th

> "We put square pegs in square holes against the Roma players, closed them down, gave no room. I think they're worried about coming to our place." **BOBBY ROBSON**

AS ROMA	
Antonioli	7
Cafu	7
Zago	7
Booked: 24 mins (foul)	
Assuncao	7
Aldair	7
Booked: 65 mins (foul)	
Montella	7
Totti	☆ 8
Goal: 50 mins; Booked: 90 mins (violent conduct)	
Di Francesco	6
Delvecchio	7
Candela	6
Rinaldi	6

Subs not used: Lupatelli, Zanetti, Bartelt, Alenitchev, Tommasi, Fabio Junior, Gurenko.

NEWCASTLE UNITED	
Harper	8
Barton	8
Charvet	7
Dabizas	8
Hughes	☆ 9
Pistone	7
Lee	8
Speed	8
Solano	7
Shearer	7
Booked: 69 mins (foul)	
Ketsbaia	6
Subbed: 81 mins (Robinson)	

sub: Robinson

Subs not used: Maric, Glass, McClen, Serrant, Caldwell, Karelse.

MATCH FACTS		
Shots On Target		
AS Roma	4-3	Newcastle
Shots Off Target		
AS Roma	7-6	Newcastle
Hit Woodwork		
AS Roma	0-0	Newcastle
Corners		
AS Roma	6-3	Newcastle

HOW THEY LINED UP

Antonioli

Zago Aldair Rinaldi Cafu

Assuncao Di Francesco Candela

Totti

Montella Delvecchio

Ketsbaia Shearer

Pistone Speed Lee Solano

Hughes Charvet Dabizas Barton

Harper

Man Of The Match Nikos Dabizas showed his ability from set-pieces to score the winner against Spurs.

 Newcastle United (1) **2**

 Tottenham Hotspur (1) **1**

Competition: FA Carling Premiership
Date: Sunday November 28, 1999
Attendance: 36,460
Referee: P Alcock (Halstead) 5

Game 22

THE GAME: Bobby Robson's side took their unbeaten run in the Premiership to seven league matches since the new boss arrived at St James' Park in September. But they were pushed all the way by Spurs in this explosive clash at St James' Park. There were three changes from the Roma game, with United debuts for Helder and Fumaca and a start for long-term injury victim Stephen Glass. Helder, playing in his first game for over nine months, was particularly impressive. But Nikos Dabizas, who scored the equalising goal at Watford in the Premiership the week before, was again the hero for the Toon Army as he grabbed a second-half winner to maintain Newcastle's recent good run and impressive form in front of their home fans.

NEWCASTLE GOALS: Glass *(5 mins):* Fired in a header from Solano's right-wing cross which Walker fumbled into the goal; **Dabizas** *(57 mins):* Solano's left-wing corner set up Dabizas to score with a stooping header at the far post to make it 2-0.
TOTTENHAM GOAL: Armstrong *(43 mins):* Forced the ball home at Newcastle's far post after Dabizas had failed to cut out a Tottenham corner from the right.

MATCH RATING: ★★★★ **LEAGUE POSITION:** 15th

NEWCASTLE UNITED		TOTTENHAM HOTSPUR	
Harper	7	Walker	6
Hughes	8	Taricco ▢	7
Charvet	7	*Booked: 83 mins (foul)*	
Dabizas ⊕	★9	Edinburgh ▢	7
Goal: 57 mins		*Booked: 64 mins (foul)*	
Lee	8	Campbell	7
Solano ▢	7	Perry	7
Booked: 29 mins (foul); Subbed: 85 mins (Maric)		*Booked: 90 mins (foul)*	
Glass ⊕	6	Freund	6
Goal: 5 mins		*Subbed: 84 mins (Clemence)*	
Ketsbaia	6	Sherwood ▢	★8
Subbed: 75 mins (Ferguson)		*Booked: 29 mins (foul)*	
Shearer	8	Leonhardsen	7
Helder	8	Ginola ▢	7
Fumaca	6	*Booked: 41 mins (foul)*	
Subbed: 81 mins (McClen)		Armstrong ⊕▢	6
sub: Ferguson		*Goal: 43 mins; Booked: 64 mins (unsporting behaviour); Subbed: 68 mins (Dominguez)*	
sub: McClen		Iversen	6
sub: Maric		**sub:** Dominguez	7
Subs not used: Given, Beharall.		**sub:** Clemence	6
		Subs not used: Baardsen, Vega, Young.	

MATCH FACTS
Shots On Target
Newcastle 7-4 Tottenham
Shots Off Target
Newcastle 4-1 Tottenham
Hit Woodwork
Newcastle 0-0 Tottenham
Corners
Newcastle 6-3 Tottenham

HOW THEY LINED UP

Harper

Charvet Helder Dabizas Hughes

Solano Fumaca Lee Glass

Ketsbaia Shearer

Armstrong Iversen

Ginola Sherwood Freund Leonhardsen

Edinburgh Campbell Perry Taricco

Walker

IN THE NEWS

NEWCASTLE UNITED: Nikos **Dabizas** is rumoured to be on his way to Fiorentina in a £2 million move when the Italian transfer window opens in January... **Steve Howey** comes through his first 90 minutes of action in a County Cup tie after his injury problems... **Kevin Gallacher** and **Franck Dumas** are both ruled out for two weeks through injury... **Nolberto Solano** is suspended following his latest booking against Tottenham.

PREMIERSHIP: England defender **Gareth Southgate** finds himself on an FA misconduct charge after his first ever red card in Aston Villa's game against Leicester... Derby County's Argentina striker **Esteban Fuertes** is banned from returning to England after his passport is found to be a fake... Arsenal are looking at three sites in London on which to build a new £100 million stadium... Leicester City abandon plans to sign Sheffield Wednesday striker **Andy Booth** for £2.7 million because of a dispute over payment of the transfer fee... Nigerian star **Nwankwo Kanu** is expected to sign a new, four-year contract at Arsenal in a deal that is worth an estimated £4 million.

THE FINAL SCORE!

NOVEMBER 21		
West Ham	4-3	Sheff. Wed.

NOVEMBER 22		
Coventry	2-1	Aston Villa

NOVEMBER 27		
Coventry	0-1	Leicester
Everton	0-0	Aston Villa
Middlesbrough	0-0	Wimbledon
Watford	2-3	Sunderland
West Ham	1-0	Liverpool

NOVEMBER 28		
Arsenal	2-1	Derby
Chelsea	1-0	Bradford
Leeds	1-0	Southampton
Newcastle	2-1	Tottenham

TOP OF THE PREMIERSHIP

		P	W	D	L	Pts
1.	Leeds	16	11	2	3	35
2.	Man. United	15	10	3	2	33
3.	Arsenal	16	10	2	4	32
15.	Newcastle	16	4	4	8	16

DECEMBER

"Fans don't boo bad players. That's the way I have always looked at it. Beckham and Ginola get booed all the time and they're not bad players, are they?" Alan Shearer

THE FA CUP KICKED OFF EARLIER THAN USUAL, MEANING THE TOP clubs entered the competition just before Christmas. Newcastle, who were the losing Wembley finalists in 1998 under Kenny Dalglish and in 1999 under Ruud Gullit, were paired against Premiership rivals Tottenham. After forcing a draw at White Hart Lane, Bobby Robson expected a close encounter but his improving side recorded one of their best performances of the season to thrash Spurs 6-1. Gary Speed was outstanding on the night and it was a great result for Bobby Robson in his first FA Cup campaign since 1982.

To counter the FA Cup win, there was disappointment in the UEFA Cup as The Magpies were knocked out in the third round after Italian club AS Roma forced a goalless draw at St James' Park to win the tie on aggregate after their narrow 1-0 victory in Rome. December opened with a win at Villa Park, Newcastle's first away triumph for eight months, thanks to Duncan Ferguson scoring his first Premiership goal for 372 days. By the end of 1999, the Toon Army were up to 14th place and the club was boosted by the news that ntl had increased their share in the club to 9.9 per cent, with the media giants guaranteeing United an interest-free loan of £25 million.

Franck Dumas impressed with his return to the team until injury curtailed his run. The Frenchman looked set for a bright future at the club, but there was a real sense of disappointment when it was revealed that Dumas was set for a move to Marseille. Carl Serrant was set for a loan move to Sheffield United but picked up an unfortunate injury, while there was good news from defender Marcelino, who pledged his future to the club after overtures from Spanish giants Real Madrid. Meanwhile, England coach and ex-Newcastle boss Kevin Keegan expressed his desire to stage an international game at St James' Park in the future because of the redevelopment at Wembley.

THE GAMES

Dec. 4 v **Aston Villa** (a)
Dec. 9 v **AS Roma** (h)
Dec. 12 v **Tottenham** (a)
Dec. 18 v **Bradford** (a)
Dec. 22 v **Tottenham** (h)
Dec. 26 v **Liverpool** (h)
Dec. 28 v **Leicester** (a)

TRANSFERS IN

None

TRANSFERS OUT

None

MATCHfacts

Matchman Of The Month

WARREN BARTON
Average Rating: 7.33

51

Dion Dubin tried everything to beat the United defence, but the visitors held firm.

Shearer and his team-mates battled hard but couldn't score against the Italians.

Aston Villa	(0)	**0**
Newcastle United	(0)	**1**

Competition: FA Carling Premiership

Date: Saturday December 4, 1999

Attendance: 34,531

Game 23

Referee: M Riley (Leeds) 6

THE GAME: Duncan Ferguson earned The Magpies their first away win for eight months at Villa Park. Bobby Robson made an inspired decision to bring on Ferguson after United 'keeper Steve Harper had put in a Man Of The Match display to keep Villa at bay. Ferguson's winner – scored within seven minutes of coming on for Silvio Maric – was his first Premiership goal for 372 days. Torrential rain hampered the quality of a match which offered few clear chances, although Harper was called upon to deny Villa's Benito Carbone with a great save to help his side grab all three points. It was a game in which the result mattered more than the drab performance in poor conditions.

NEWCASTLE GOAL: Ferguson *(65 mins):* Ketsbaia crossed from the right wing and Ferguson forced his way in front of the Villa defence to power a trademark header into the net.

MATCH RATING: ★★★ **LEAGUE POSITION:** 14th

"Since we have adopted the policy of giving nothing away, scrambling for some points, picking up the odd one point away and three points at home, we have made some kind of progress." BOBBY ROBSON

MATCH FACTS

Shots On Target
Aston Villa 5-2 Newcastle

Shots Off Target
Aston Villa 2-1 Newcastle

Hit Woodwork
Aston Villa 0-0 Newcastle

Corners
Aston Villa 9-5 Newcastle

HOW THEY LINED UP

James

Calderwood Southgate Barry

Delaney Taylor Boateng Hendrie Wright

Joachim Dublin

Ketsbaia Shearer

Maric

Pistone Speed Lee Solano

Helder Dumas Dabizas

Harper

ASTON VILLA	
James	6
Wright 🟨	6
Booked: 67 mins (foul)	
Delaney 🟨	7
Booked: 11 mins (foul)	
Southgate	☆8
Calderwood	7
Barry	6
Hendrie	
Subbed: 9 mins (Thompson)	
Dublin	6
Subbed: 51 mins (Carbone)	
Joachim	6
Boateng 🟨	7
Booked: 37 mins (foul)	
Taylor	7
sub: Thompson 🟨	6
Booked: 47 mins (foul); Subbed: 73 mins (Merson)	
sub: Carbone	6
Subs not used: Stone, Enckelman.	

NEWCASTLE UNITED	
Harper	☆8
Helder	7
Dumas	6
Dabizas 🟨	7
Booked: 90 mins (foul)	
Solano	6
Subbed: 85 mins (Barton)	
Lee	7
Speed 🟨	6
Booked: 44 mins (foul)	
Pistone 🟨	6
Booked: 40 mins (dissent)	
Maric	6
Subbed: 58 mins (Ferguson)	
Shearer	6
Ketsbaia	6
Subbed: 84 mins (Hughes)	
sub: Ferguson ⚽	7
Goal: 65 mins	
sub: Hughes	
sub: Barton	
Subs not used: Given, Glass.	

Newcastle United	**(0)**	**0**
AS Roma	**(0)**	**0**

AS Roma win 1-0 on aggregate.

Competition: **UEFA Cup 3rd Rd 2nd Leg**

Date: **Thursday December 9, 1999**

Attendance: **35,739**

Referee: **H Strampe** (Germany) 6

 Game 24

THE GAME: The Magpies bowed out of the UEFA Cup in this second leg at St James' Park, but only after the team put up a glorious fight against Serie A leaders AS Roma. But Bobby Robson's side couldn't get the goal which would have taken the game into extra-time, and in the end they lost to Totti's controversial penalty from the first leg in Rome. Newcastle battled hard but Temuri Ketsbaia was unable to put away the chances that came to him, denied both times by saves from 'keeper Antonioli. Roma were under intense pressure in the final stages but the goal never came. Their celebrated coach, Fabio Capello, was so relieved at the final whistle that he ran on to the pitch with his arms held high, and Newcastle were out of the competition by the narrowest of margins.

MATCH RATING: ★ ★ ★ LEAGUE POSITION: 14th

> "Newcastle fans really are the best supporters in the world. They are second to none. They treat football like a religion and everything that happens in Newcastle is to do with football." **KIERON DYER**

NEWCASTLE UNITED			AS ROMA		
Harper		7	Antonioli		7
Dumas		6	Cafu		7
Subbed: 28 mins (Hughes)			Zago ☐		7
Charvet		7	*Booked: 89 mins (foul)*		
Dabizas		7	Assuncao		7
Pistone		7	Aldair	☆	9
Dyer		6	Tommasi ☐		6
Subbed: 73 mins (Ferguson)			*Booked: 88 mins (foul)*		
Speed		7	Mangone		6
Solano		6	Candela		6
Lee ☐	☆	9	Delvecchio ☐		6
Booked: 52 mins (foul)			*Booked: 27 mins (unsporting behaviour)*		
Shearer		6	Montella		6
Ketsbaia		5	*Subbed: 64 mins (Di Francesco)*		
Subbed: 73 mins (Glass)			Totti		7
sub: Hughes		7	**sub:** Di Francesco ☐		6
sub: Ferguson			*Booked: 85 mins (foul)*		
sub: Glass					

Subs not used: Given, Barton, Maric, McClen.

Subs not used: Lupatelli, Alenitchev, Choutos, Tomic, Gurenko, Rinaldi.

MATCH FACTS

Shots On Target
Newcastle 3-3 AS Roma

Shots Off Target
Newcastle 10-7 AS Roma

Hit Woodwork
Newcastle 0-0 AS Roma

Corners
Newcastle 9-4 AS Roma

HOW THEY LINED UP

Harper

Charvet Dabizas Dumas

Solano Lee Dyer Speed Pistone

Shearer Ketsbaia

Delvecchio Montella

Totti

Candela Assuncao Tommasi Cafu

Mangone Aldair Zago

Antonioli

IN THE NEWS

NEWCASTLE UNITED: Magpies defender **Marcelino** says he has no intention of quitting Tyneside despite interest from clubs in Spain, saying: "I intend to stay and prove my worth"... Nikos Dabizas wins the November Premiership Matchman Of The Month award... Newcastle confirm they'd love to host one of England's international games after Kevin Keegan said he'd like to see the World Cup qualifying game against Germany played at an intimidating ground like St James' Park or Anfield... Media giants ntl have increased their holding in Newcastle United to 9.9 per cent after guaranteeing a £25 million interest-free loan... Real Madrid cool their interest in Magpies defender **Marcelino**.

PREMIERSHIP: Manchester United win the World Club Cup by beating Palmeiras of Brazil 1-0 in Tokyo... **Thierry Henry** says that he is in paradise at Highbury after media reports insist he is still finding it difficult to adjust since moving to England... **Roy Keane** signs an improved contract with Manchester United worth £52,000 a week... Leicester sign Norwich City striker **Darren Eadie** for £3 million... Middlesbrough, Watford and West Ham become the first Premiership casualties of this season's FA Cup, being knocked out by Wrexham, Birmingham and Tranmere Rovers respectively at the third round stage... Darlington, knocked out in the second round, gain the 'lucky losers' spot in Manchester United's absence and are rewarded with a draw against Aston Villa... Spurs striker **Steffen Iversen** admits that he would like to sign a long-term deal to stay at White Hart Lane.

THE FINAL SCORE!

DECEMBER 4		
Aston Villa	0-1	**Newcastle**
Bradford	1-1	Middlesbrough
Leicester	0-3	**Arsenal**
Man. United	5-1	Everton
Southampton	0-0	Coventry
Sunderland	4-1	Chelsea
Wimbledon	5-0	Watford

DECEMBER 5		
Derby	0-1	**Leeds**
Liverpool	4-1	Sheff. Wed.

DECEMBER 6		
Tottenham	0-0	West Ham

TOP OF THE PREMIERSHIP

	P	W	D	L	Pts
1. Leeds	17	12	2	3	38
2. Man. United	16	11	3	2	36
3. Arsenal	17	11	2	4	35
14. Newcastle	17	5	4	8	19

Tottenham Hotspur	(0)	**1**
Newcastle United	(0)	**1**

The Toon Army went wild when Speed powered in Newcastle's equaliser.

Competition: FA Cup 3rd Rd

Date: Sunday December 12, 1999

Attendance: 33,116

Referee: G Poll (Tring) 7

Game 25

THE GAME: Bobby Robson's first FA Cup tie since 1982 ended level at White Hart Lane. After Tottenham took the lead, Robson decided to gamble by changing the shape of the side, pulling off one of his defenders and opting for three forwards. The tactical switch worked a treat, while Gary Speed gave an inspirational performance in midfield to earn United a replay at St James' Park. Speed capped his display with a headed equaliser even though Spurs dominated early on, with David Ginola, Allan Nielsen and Steffen Iversen all being denied by Newcastle 'keeper Steve Harper. George Graham's side, with Ginola pulling the strings, forced themselves ahead in the 57th minute, but with midfielders Speed, Robert Lee and Stephen Glass pushing them back, Tottenham failed to hold on to their advantage. The Magpies could have won the tie in injury-time with a chance for Kevin Gallacher, but he steered Alessandro Pistone's cross into the arms of Spurs 'keeper Ian Walker.

TOTTENHAM GOAL: Iversen *(56 mins):* Iversen beat Harper in Newcastle's goal with an outstanding diving header, beating Charvet to Ginola's right-wing cross.

NEWCASTLE GOAL: Speed *(77 mins):* A corner from Glass was headed in by Man Of The Match Speed from six yards.

MATCH RATING: ★★★ **LEAGUE POSITION:** 14th

TOTTENHAM HOTSPUR		NEWCASTLE UNITED	
Walker	6	Harper	7
Freund ▢	7	Barton	6
Booked: 85 mins (foul)		Dyer	6
Campbell	7	*Subbed: 76 mins (Ketsbaia)*	
Perry	7	Shearer	6
Iversen ⚽	6	Speed ⚽	☆ 8
Goal: 56 mins		*Goal: 77 mins*	
Edinburgh	6	Charvet	6
Subbed: 81 mins (Vega)		Ferguson	6
Ginola	7	*Subbed: 64 mins (Glass)*	
Fox	6	Dabizas	7
Dominguez	6	Pistone	6
Subbed: 81 mins (Armstrong)		Lee	7
Young	☆ 8	Helder ▢	6
Nielsen ▢	7	*Booked: 45 mins (foul); Subbed: 64 mins (Gallacher)*	
Booked: 76 mins (foul)			
sub: Armstrong		*sub:* Gallacher	6
sub: Vega		*sub:* Ketsbaia	6
Subs not used: Baardsen, Clemence, Gower.		*sub:* Glass	6
		Subs not used: Given, Hughes.	

MATCH FACTS	
Shots On Target	
Tottenham 11-8 Newcastle	
Shots Off Target	
Tottenham 5-5 Newcastle	
Hit Woodwork	
Tottenham 0-0 Newcastle	
Corners	
Tottenham 8-9 Newcastle	

HOW THEY LINED UP

Walker

Young Perry Campbell Edinburgh

Fox Freund Nielsen Dominguez

Ginola Iversen

Shearer Ferguson

Speed Lee Dyer

Charvet

Pistone Helder Dabizas Barton

Harper

Despite playing with three strikers, The Magpies couldn't convert their goalscoring chances at Bradford.

Bradford City (0) 2
Newcastle United (0) 0

Game 26

Competition: **FA Carling Premiership**

Date: **Saturday December 18, 1999**

Attendance: **18,276**

Referee: **N Barry** (Scunthorpe) 7

THE GAME: Bobby Robson's side suffered their first defeat in seven Premiership games in front of a full house at Valley Parade. The lively crowd was treated to an entertaining match in which Newcastle looked the stronger team in the first half. Duncan Ferguson and Nolberto Solano both had shots saved by Bantams 'keeper Matt Clarke, while Ferguson hit the bar and Kevin Gallacher also went close. The missed chances in the first half were to haunt United as Bradford scored twice in the second period – one from a cross and another, inevitably, from a free-kick. Towards the end of the game, Solano had a penalty appeal turned down by referee Neale Barry which would have given Newcastle a fighting chance for a draw, but he waved the strong appeals away. This was a disappointing result for The Magpies in an entertaining match, with both sides created goalscoring opportunities – the difference was that Bradford took their chances and scored two goals.

BRADFORD GOALS: Saunders (55 mins): Saunders rifled in a left-foot shot from seven yards to beat 'keeper Harper after a clever lay-off from Mills inside the Newcastle box; **Wetherall** (71 mins): From Sharpe's floated free-kick, Wetherall managed to out-jump the entire Magpies defence and direct a six-yard header into the bottom left-hand corner of the net.

MATCH RATING: ★★★★ LEAGUE POSITION: 15th

MATCH FACTS

Shots On Target
Bradford 5-6 Newcastle

Shots Off Target
Bradford 3-10 Newcastle

Hit Woodwork
Bradford 0-1 Newcastle

Corners
Bradford 4-7 Newcastle

HOW THEY LINED UP

Clarke

Halle   Wetherall   O'Brien   Myers

Lawrence   Windass   McCall   Sharpe

Saunders   Mills

Ferguson   Shearer

Gallacher

Speed   Lee   Solano

Pistone   Helder   Hughes   Barton

Harper

BRADFORD CITY

Clarke	6
Myers	6
McCall	7
Wetherall ⚽	7
Goal: 71 mins	
Lawrence 🟨	6
Booked: 41 mins (foul)	
Mills	7
O'Brien	8
Windass	7
Sharpe	6
Subbed: 78 mins (Beagrie)	
Halle	6
Saunders ⚽🟨 ☆	9
Goal: 55 mins; Booked: 83 mins (dissent)	
sub: Beagrie	

Subs not used: Davison, Westwood, Blake, Whalley.

NEWCASTLE UNITED

Harper	7
Barton	6
Shearer ☆	7
Speed	6
Solano	6
Subbed: 70 mins (Dyer)	
Hughes	6
Ferguson	6
Gallacher	6
Subbed: 73 mins (Glass)	
Pistone	6
Lee	6
Subbed: 84 mins (Fumaca)	
Helder 🟨	6
Booked: 35 mins (handball)	
sub: Dyer	4
sub: Glass	
sub: Fumaca	

Subs not used: Given, Ketsbaia.

THE FINAL SCORE!

DECEMBER 18

Arsenal	1-1	Wimbledon
Aston Villa	2-1	Sheff. Wed.
Bradford	2-0	Newcastle
Leicester	0-1	Derby
Liverpool	2-0	Coventry
Middlesbrough	2-1	Tottenham
Sunderland	2-0	Southampton
Watford	1-3	Everton
West Ham	2-4	Man. United

TOP OF THE PREMIERSHIP

	P	W	D	L	Pts
1. Man. United	17	12	3	2	39
2. Leeds	17	12	2	3	38
3. Sunderland	18	11	4	3	37
15. Newcastle	18	5	4	9	19

Newcastle's skipper completes the rout with two late goals in the 6-1 drubbing of Tottenham.

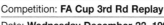

Newcastle United   (3) 6
Tottenham Hotspur   (1) 1

Competition: **FA Cup 3rd Rd Replay**

Date: **Wednesday December 22, 1999**

Attendance: **35,415**

Referee: **G Poll** (Tring) 8

Game 27

THE GAME: Newcastle humiliated Tottenham in this FA Cup replay. Alan Shearer predicted it would be a tight game, but the Magpies put on a commanding display to secure a fourth round tie against Sheffield United. Spurs were outclassed by the black and whites, with Gary Speed and Rob Lee dominant in midfield and the attacking football a joy to watch. It could have been even worse for the visitors, with Sol Campbell and Ian Walker preventing the score from reaching double figures.

NEWCASTLE GOALS: Speed *(4 mins):* Barton's cross was headed down by Ferguson for Speed to score; **Dabizas** *(27 mins):* Solano's fine corner was headed past Walker at the far post; **Ferguson** *(44 mins):* Walker dropped Barton's cross and Ferguson lashed in a left-foot drive; **Dyer** *(72 mins):* Made no mistake in front of goal after Shearer's pass; **Shearer** *(penalty 83 mins):* Converted from the spot after being fouled by Vega; **Shearer** *(84 mins):* Headed in Ketsbaia's cross to make it 6-1.
TOTTENHAM GOAL: Ginola *(33 mins):* The consolation goal came from a 20-yard shot that was deflected past Harper.

MATCH RATING: ★★★★ LEAGUE POSITION: 15th

NEWCASTLE UNITED	
Harper	7
Barton	8
Hughes	7
Helder	7
Subbed: 46 mins (Marcelino)	
Dabizas ⊕	7
Goal: 27 mins	
Lee ▢	8
Booked: 8 mins (foul)	
Speed ⊕	☆ 9
Goal: 4 mins	
Solano	8
Gallacher	8
Subbed: 65 mins (Dyer)	
Ferguson ⊕ ▢	8
Goal: 44 mins; Booked: 76 mins (foul);	
Subbed: 76 mins (Ketsbaia)	
Shearer ⊕ ⊕	8
Goals: 83, 84 mins	
sub: Marcelino	7
sub: Dyer ⊕	8
Goal: 72 mins	
sub: Ketsbaia	
Subs not used: *Given, Glass.*	

TOTTENHAM HOTSPUR	
Walker	5
Young	5
Subbed: 22 mins (Fox)	
Taricco	5
Campbell	☆ 7
Perry	5
Sherwood	5
Vega ▢	5
Booked: 88 mins (foul)	
Ginola ⊕	7
Goal: 33 mins; Subbed: 75 mins	
(Dominguez)	
Clemence ▢	5
Booked: 77 mins (foul)	
Nielsen	5
Iversen	5
sub: Fox	6
Subbed: 71 mins (Armstrong)	
sub: Armstrong	
sub: Dominguez	
Subs not used: *Baardsen, Gower.*	

MATCH FACTS

Shots On Target
Newcastle 8-1 Tottenham

Shots Off Target
Newcastle 6-3 Tottenham

Hit Woodwork
Newcastle 1-0 Tottenham

Corners
Newcastle 6-4 Tottenham

HOW THEY LINED UP

Harper
Barton — Dabizas — Helder — Hughes
Solano — Lee — Speed — Gallacher
Shearer — Ferguson
Iversen — Ginola
Nielsen
Taricco — Sherwood — Young — Clemence
Campbell — Vega — Perry
Walker

THE FINAL SCORE!

DECEMBER 19

Chelsea   0-2   Leeds

TOP OF THE PREMIERSHIP					
	P	W	D	L	Pts
1. Leeds	18	13	2	3	41
2. Man. United	17	12	3	2	39
3. Sunderland	18	11	4	3	37
15. Newcastle	18	5	4	9	19

Newcastle United (1) 2
Liverpool (1) 2

Competition: FA Carling Premiership

Date: Sunday December 26, 1999

Attendance: 36,445

Referee: D Elleray (Harrow) 8

Game 28

THE GAME: Defensive errors by Alessandro Pistone and Nikos Dabizas gifted two goals to Liverpool's Michael Owen and cost United maximum points. After taking an early lead through Alan Shearer, The Magpies had to be content with salvaging a point through Duncan Ferguson's equaliser after going 2-1 behind. Both teams came into this match on the back of impressive runs, with Liverpool winning eight of their previous ten matches and Newcastle losing only twice in 13 games. In an entertaining game at St James' Park, both sides played with confidence, never doubting that they would take something from the game. Warren Barton was in superb form, but he couldn't make up for the errors of his fellow defenders that gifted the visitors their goals.

NEWCASTLE GOALS: Shearer *(12 mins):* Shearer beat Westerveld with a glancing header from Solano's free-kick; **Ferguson** *(66 mins):* Barton's right-wing cross was headed home from 12 yards by Ferguson to bring United level.

LIVERPOOL GOALS: Owen *(31 mins):* Pistone failed to cut out Hamann's throughball, allowing Owen to rifle a shot past Harper from eight yards; **Owen** *(53 mins):* Dabizas hit a terrible backpass that allowed Owen to intercept and score.

MATCH RATING: ★★★ LEAGUE POSITION: 15th

NEWCASTLE UNITED		LIVERPOOL	
Harper	6	Westerveld	6
Barton	☆ 9	Song	7
Pistone	6	Matteo	7
Hughes	7	Hyypia	7
Dabizas	6	Carragher	7
Solano	6	Hamann	6
Subbed: 73 mins (Gallacher)		Gerrard	7
Speed	6	Murphy	6
Lee	7	*Subbed: 82 mins (Fowler)*	
Dyer	6	Camara	7
Subbed: 53 mins (Glass)		*Subbed: 69 mins (Heggem)*	
Shearer ⊕	7	Owen ⊕ ⊕	☆ 9
Goal: 12 mins		*Goals: 31, 53 mins*	
Ferguson ⊕	7	Berger	6
Goal: 66 mins; Subbed: 90 mins (Ketsbaia)		*sub: Heggem*	6
sub: Glass	7	*sub: Fowler*	
sub: Gallacher		*Subs not used: Staunton, Friedel, Traore.*	
sub: Ketsbaia			
Subs not used: Given, Marcelino.			

MATCH FACTS

Shots On Target

Newcastle 4-6 Liverpool

Shots Off Target

Newcastle 8-0 Liverpool

Hit Woodwork

Newcastle 0-0 Liverpool

Corners

Newcastle 3-5 Liverpool

HOW THEY LINED UP

Harper

Barton　Dabizas　Hughes　Pistone

Solano　Lee　Speed

Dyer

Shearer　Ferguson

Camara　Owen

Berger　Hamann　Gerrard　Murphy

Matteo　Carragher　Hyypia　Song

Westerveld

Hughes beats Owen to the ball, but the England striker continued his good record against Newcastle.

Rob Lee was instrumental in winning the crucial midfield battle at Filbert Street.

Leicester City (0) 1
Newcastle United (1) 2

Competition: FA Carling Premiership

Date: Tuesday December 28, 1999

Attendance: 21,225

Referee: P Durkin (Portland) 7

Game 29

THE GAME: Newcastle's second Premiership away victory of the season came courtesy of their £22 million strikeforce, Duncan Ferguson and Alan Shearer, with the United skipper netting his 14th Premiership goal of the season. It was the perfect antidote to the booing Shearer received from some of the Leicester supporters around Filbert Street. It was also a magnificent midfield performance from The Magpies, with Rob Lee, Nolberto Solano and Gary Speed impressing for the visitors. Leicester had plenty of the ball, but Magpies 'keeper Steve Harper was largely untroubled, although he was called upon to deny Emile Heskey from close range just before the break. A third goal nearly came from Ferguson, but his header hit the post and Kevin Gallacher put the rebound over the bar.

LEICESTER GOAL: Zagorakis (83 mins): Scored with a low, powerful 20-yard shot set up by a Leicester free-kick routine.

NEWCASTLE GOALS: Ferguson (21 mins): Shearer centred to Ferguson at the far post to sidefoot home from close range; **Shearer** (53 mins): Solano played the ball behind the defence for Shearer to score the winning goal with an angled shot.

MATCH RATING: ★★★ **LEAGUE POSITION:** 14th

MATCH FACTS

Shots On Target
Leicester 8-6 Newcastle

Shots Off Target
Leicester 2-5 Newcastle

Hit Woodwork
Leicester 0-2 Newcastle

Corners
Leicester 2-8 Newcastle

HOW THEY LINED UP

Flowers

Sinclair Elliott Taggart Gilchrist

Savage Zagorakis Izzet Eadie

Cottee Heskey

Shearer Ferguson

Gallacher

Pistone Speed Lee Solano

Marcelino Dabizas Barton

Harper

LEICESTER CITY

Flowers	7
Sinclair	6
Taggart ▢	6
Booked: 33 mins (foul)	
Izzet	6
Subbed: 32 mins (Campbell)	
Heskey	7
Eadie	6
Savage ▢	☆ 8
Booked: 71 mins (foul)	
Gilchrist	6
Elliott	7
Cottee	6
Subbed: 60 mins (Thomas)	
Zagorakis ⊕	6
Goal: 83 mins	
sub: Campbell	6
sub: Thomas	7

Subs not used: Gunnlaugsson, Fenton, Arphexad.

NEWCASTLE UNITED

Harper	7
Barton	7
Marcelino	6
Shearer ⊕	7
Goal: 53 mins	
Speed	7
Solano	☆ 8
Ferguson ⊕	7
Goal: 21 mins	
Gallacher	7
Dabizas	7
Pistone	7
Lee	7

Subs not used: Given, Ketsbaia, Glass, Hughes, Fumaca.

THE FINAL SCORE!

DECEMBER 26		
Coventry	3-2	Arsenal
Derby	0-2	**Aston Villa**
Everton	5-0	Sunderland
Leeds	2-1	Leicester
Man. United	4-0	Bradford
Newcastle	2-2	Liverpool
Sheff. Wed.	1-0	Middlesbrough
Southampton	1-2	**Chelsea**
Tottenham	4-0	Watford
Wimbledon	2-2	West Ham

DECEMBER 28		
Arsenal	2-0	Leeds
Bradford	0-0	Everton
Leicester	1-2	**Newcastle**
Liverpool	3-1	Wimbledon
Sunderland	2-2	Man. United
Watford	3-2	Southampton
West Ham	1-1	Derby

DECEMBER 29		
Aston Villa	1-1	Tottenham
Chelsea	3-0	Sheff. Wed.

TOP OF THE PREMIERSHIP

	P	W	D	L	Pts
1. Leeds	20	14	2	4	44
2. Man. United	19	13	4	2	43
3. Arsenal	20	12	3	5	39
14. Newcastle	20	6	5	9	23

59

JANUARY

"Even at the start I thought this club was too big to be involved in relegation. Everybody knows we have too many good players to go down." Nikos Dabizas

NEWCASTLE'S FA CUP RUN CONTINUED DURING JANUARY AS THEY went through to the last eight of the competition after beating First Division sides Sheffield United and Blackburn Rovers. The 2-1 win against Blackburn was particularly satisfying for Alan Shearer, who was subjected to a barrage of boos and jeers at his old stamping ground, but the captain scored both of the goals to seal a place in the quarter-finals. It was the perfect response to the Blackburn fans who seemed to forget that Shearer helped their team to win the Premiership title in 1995 and left Rovers with a bulging bank balance after his record £15 million move home to The Magpies.

The New Year began with Newcastle fielding an unchanged side against West Ham for the first time since October 1998, a sure sign that stability and consistency was returning to the team. A 5-0 thrashing of Southampton was the highlight of the month on the field and the final score could easily have reached double figures. Off the field, there was speculation that Newcastle wanted to sign Argentina international Christian Bassedas of Velez Sarsfield. However, it was another South American – the Paraguay international Diego Gavilan – who became Bobby Robson's second permanent signing for the club in a £1 million deal from Cerro Porteno.

Leaving St James' Park was Franck Dumas in a £1.25 million move to Olympique Marseille after just six months on Tyneside, but Gavilan gladly took the number eight shirt from the Frenchman. Silvio Maric, who had also been with The Magpies for less than year, was not endearing himself to the management team, being substituted after 15 minutes of a reserve match for lack of effort. In stark contrast, Steve Howey was giving everything to get back to his best and the former England defender, who was recovering from a long-term injury, was also beginning to attract interest from other clubs.

NEWCASTLE UNITED

THE GAMES

Jan. 3 v **West Ham** (h)

Jan. 8 v **Sheffield United** (h)

Jan. 16 v **Southampton** (h)

Jan. 22 v **Wimbledon** (a)

Jan. 31 v **Blackburn** (a)

TRANSFERS IN

Diego Gavilan

Position: **Midfielder**

Fee: **£1 million**

From: **Cerro Porteno**

TRANSFERS OUT

Franck Dumas

Position: **Defender**

Fee: **£1.25 million**

To: **Olympique Marseille**

MATCH facts

Matchman Of The Month

NOLBERTO SOLANO

Average Rating: 8.00

61

Speed crashes in a volley to put Newcastle 2-0 up against West Ham.

 Newcastle United (1) **2**

 West Ham United (0) **2**

Competition: FA Carling Premiership

Date: Monday January 3, 2000

Attendance: 36,314

Referee: R Harris (Oxford) 6

 Game 30

THE GAME: The Magpies fielded an unchanged team for the first time in 68 games in this first game of the new millennium. The last time it had happened was – coincidentally – against West Ham in October 1998. But Bobby Robson wasn't happy at the end of this game after his team squandered a two-goal lead against The Hammers and lost two valuable points. Nikos Dabizas and Robert Lee put the Toon Army 2-0 up and Kevin Gallacher almost scored a third in the second half, but he was denied by a spectacular save from Shaka Hislop. The Magpies also had a penalty claim ignored when Scott Minto appeared to play the ball with his arm inside the West Ham area. So after failing to convert any of these chances, the game was decided by two defensive lapses from Newcastle in the last six minutes. From a comfortable position, Robson's side let West Ham back into the game and claim a share of the spoils.

NEWCASTLE GOALS: Dabizas (17 mins): Hislop could only punch Gallacher's right-wing cross to Pistone, whose shot was blocked, allowing Dabizas to poke the ball into the net from six yards; **Speed** (66 mins): Volleyed home impressively from eight yards following Solano's right-wing cross.

WEST HAM GOALS: Lampard (84 mins): Sent a thundering 25-yard shot in off the post; **Stimac** (87 mins): A right-wing free-kick from Sinclair was headed past Harper by Stimac.

MATCH RATING: ★★ **LEAGUE POSITION:** 15th

MATCH FACTS
Shots On Target
Newcastle 9-3 West Ham
Shots Off Target
Newcastle 5-4 West Ham
Hit Woodwork
Newcastle 0-1 West Ham
Corners
Newcastle 3-7 West Ham

HOW THEY LINED UP
Harper
Barton Dabizas Marcelino Pistone
Solano Lee Speed
Gallacher
Shearer Ferguson

Sinclair Cole
Keller Lampard Foe Carrick
Minto Stimac Ferdinand Potts
Hislop

NEWCASTLE UNITED
Harper	6
Barton	7
Pistone	7
Marcelino	7
Dabizas ⚽	★8
Goal: 17 mins	
Lee	7
Subbed: 51 mins (Fumaca)	
Solano	7
Speed ⚽	7
Goal: 66 mins	
Gallacher	7
Subbed: 75 mins (Glass)	
Shearer	7
Ferguson	7
Subbed: 78 mins (Ketsbaia)	
sub: Fumaca	6
sub: Glass	
sub: Ketsbaia	

Subs not used: Given, Hughes.

WEST HAM UNITED
Hislop	7
Potts 🟨	7
Booked: 72 mins (foul)	
Minto	6
Ferdinand	7
Stimac ⚽	7
Goal: 87 mins	
Lampard ⚽	7
Goal: 84 mins	
Foe	6
Keller	6
Subbed: 79 mins (Byrne)	
Sinclair	7
Cole	★8
Carrick	6
sub: Byrne	

Subs not used: Forrest, Newton, Defoe, Iriekpen.

Newcastle eased into the fifth round of the competition with a superb win over The Blades.

Newcastle United (1) 4
Sheffield United (1) 1

Competition: FA Cup 4th Rd
Date: Saturday January 8, 2000
Attendance: 36,220
Referee: M Halsey (Welwyn) 7

Game 31

THE GAME: Kevin Gallacher scored his first goal for his new club to round off an entertaining 4-1 win over Sheffield United. The Magpies got off to an ideal start with a goal from captain Alan Shearer, but the First Division side equalised to make it 1-1 at the break. Newcastle were less charitable in the second half, showing their Premiership class to score a further three times through Nikos Dabizas, Duncan Ferguson and Gallacher. With the home team comfortably ahead, the game petered out in an array of substitutions, but there was a welcome return to the team for Didier Domi – who had been out for two months with ankle ligament damage – as The Magpies shut up shop.

NEWCASTLE GOALS: Shearer (5 mins): Volleyed home from six yards after a left-wing Solano corner; **Dabizas** (46 mins): Speed hit the bar from a Solano cross and Dabizas headed home the rebound; **Ferguson** (59 mins): Lashed the ball home from 14 yards after Pistone had set him up with a simple pass; **Gallacher** (69 mins): Fired home after Shearer's chest down.
SHEFFIELD UNITED GOAL: Smith (17 mins): Smith beat his marker to sidefoot an equaliser past 'keeper Harper.

MATCH RATING: ★★★★ **LEAGUE POSITION:** 15th

NEWCASTLE UNITED		SHEFFIELD UNITED	
Harper	6	Tracey	5
Barton	6	Ford	6
Marcelino	6	Sandford ⬜	6
Dyer ☆ 8		Booked: 72 mins (foul)	
Subbed: 86 mins (Fumaca)		Kozluk	6
Shearer ⊕⬜	7	Derry	6
Goal: 5 mins; Booked: 42 mins (foul)		Subbed: 82 mins (Hamilton)	
Speed ⬜	7	Woodhouse	6
Booked: 38 mins (foul)		Hunt	6
Solano	8	Bent ☆ 8	
Ferguson ⊕	7	Subbed: 82 mins (Katchuro)	
Goal: 59 mins		Smith ⊕	7
Gallacher ⊕	7	Goal: 17 mins	
Goal: 69 mins; Subbed: 82 mins (Ketsbaia)		Gysbrechts	6
Dabizas ⊕	8	Quinn	5
Goal: 46 mins		Subbed: 66 mins (Ribeiro)	
Pistone	6	sub: Ribeiro	6
Subbed: 82 mins (Domi)		sub: Hamilton	
sub: Ketsbaia		sub: Katchuro	
sub: Domi		**Subs not used:** Smeets, Doane.	
sub: Fumaca			
Subs not used: Given, Hughes.			

MATCH FACTS
Shots On Target
Newcastle 11-2 Sheff. United
Shots Off Target
Newcastle 7-2 Sheff. United
Hit Woodwork
Newcastle 1-0 Sheff. United
Corners
Newcastle 5-3 Sheff. United

HOW THEY LINED UP

Harper

Barton Dabizas Marcelino Pistone

Solano Dyer Speed

Gallacher

Shearer Ferguson

Bent

Smith Woodhouse Ford Derry Hunt

Quinn Sandford Gysbrechts Kozluk

Tracey

IN THE NEWS

NEWCASTLE UNITED: £4 million Argentina international **Christian Bassedas** is wanted to strengthen the squad with Marseille-bound **Franck Dumas** leaving after coach Gordon Milne saw him in action for Velez Sarsfield in the Argentinian League… Newcastle learn that **Nolberto Solano** will miss games against Sheffield Wednesday and Manchester United after being told that he must play for Peru in the Gold Cup… Promising striker **Paul Robinson**, citing lack of first-team opportunities, puts in a transfer request. First Division trio Charlton, Birmingham and Norwich are all linked with the youngster who is valued at around £500,000.

PREMIERSHIP: Nigerian coach Amodu Shaibu calls for Arsenal to be thrown out of the FA Cup if they do not release **Kanu** to play in the African Nations Cup… Man. United fail to beat both Rayos Del Necaxa and Vasco Da Gama in the World Club Championship in Brazil… Wimbledon are knocked out of the FA Cup by Fulham while Sunderland bow out to Tranmere… In an all-Premiership tie, Aston Villa defeat Southampton with a **Gareth Southgate** goal… Leeds' **David Batty** visits a French specialist in a bid to cure a tendon injury.

THE FINAL SCORE!

JANUARY 3		
Derby	2-0	Watford
Everton	2-2	Leicester
Leeds	1-2	**Aston Villa**
Newcastle	2-2	West Ham
Sheff. Wed.	1-1	Arsenal
Southampton	1-0	Bradford
Tottenham	1-0	Liverpool
Wimbledon	1-0	Sunderland

JANUARY 4		
Coventry	2-2	Chelsea

JANUARY 8		
Bradford	1-1	Chelsea

TOP OF THE PREMIERSHIP

	P	W	D	L	Pts
1. Leeds	21	14	2	5	44
2. Man. United	19	13	4	2	43
3. Arsenal	21	12	4	5	40
15. Newcastle	21	6	6	9	24

Newcastle United	(4) 5
Southampton	(0) 0

Competition: FA Carling Premiership

Date: Sunday January 16, 2000

Attendance: 35,623

Referee: N Barry (Scunthorpe) 8

 Game 32

United turned on the style against Southampton with Kieron Dyer in inspired form.

THE GAME: The last time that Newcastle beat Southampton 5-0 was back in 1947 – but this time the scoreline could have reached double figures as the unchanged Magpies hit the woodwork five times. Amazingly, Alan Shearer failed to score, but he did have an eventful game – making two goals, hitting the woodwork three times and seeing his 35th minute penalty crash off the underside of the bar. Duncan Ferguson headed against the bar after Shearer's spot-kick and Nolbert Solano's shot from the second rebound went for a corner! The Magpies weren't to be denied though, and led 4-0 at the break before Dabizas scored the fifth for a superb win.

NEWCASTLE GOALS: Ferguson *(2 mins):* Shearer headed Solano's left-wing cross against the bar but Ferguson nodded home the rebound; **Ferguson** *(3 mins):* Dyer laid the ball into the path of Ferguson, who shot home right-footed from the edge of the penalty area; **Solano** *(16 mins):* Solano played a one-two with Shearer before sliding the ball home from ten yards; **Dryden** *(own goal 31 mins):* Dyer cut inside and hit a low cross which Dryden deflected into his own net; **Dabizas** *(83 mins):* Defender Dabizas mis-hit a right-foot shot into the ground and the ball bounced over Jones and into the net.

MATCH RATING: ★★★★ **LEAGUE POSITION: 15th**

NEWCASTLE UNITED		SOUTHAMPTON	
Harper	8	Jones	5
Barton	7	Tessem	6
Subbed: 84 mins (Hughes)		Colleter	5
Pistone	7	*Subbed: 46 mins (Benali)*	
Marcelino	7	Richards	5
Dabizas ⊕	8	Dryden ⊕	5
Goal: 83 mins		*Own Goal: 31 mins; Subbed: 72 mins (Beresford)*	
Solano ⊕	☆ 9		
Goal: 16 mins; Subbed: 81 mins (Ketsbaia)		Hughes, M ▯	5
Speed	8	*Booked: 49 mins (foul)*	
Dyer	8	Ripley	4
Gallacher	8	Soltvedt	☆ 7
Subbed: 76 mins (Domi)		Boa Morte	4
Shearer	8	*Subbed: 24 mins (Monk)*	
Ferguson ⊕ ⊕	8	Davies	5
Goals: 2, 3 mins		Beattie	5
sub: *Domi*		**sub:** *Monk*	5
sub: *Ketsbaia*		**sub:** *Benali*	5
sub: *Hughes*		**sub:** *Beresford*	
Subs not used: Given, Fumaca.		*Subs not used: Moss, Pahars.*	

MATCH FACTS	
Shots On Target	
Newcastle 11-2 Southampton	
Shots Off Target	
Newcastle 4-6 Southampton	
Hit Woodwork	
Newcastle 5-0 Southampton	
Corners	
Newcastle 8-6 Southampton	

HOW THEY LINED UP

Harper

Barton · Marcelino · Dabizas · Pistone

Solano · Dyer · Speed

Gallacher

Shearer · Ferguson

Davies · Beattie

Boa Morte · Soltvedt · Hughes · Ripley

Colleter · Dryden · Richards · Tessem

Jones

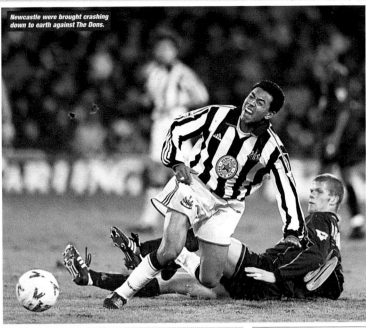

Newcastle were brought crashing down to earth against The Dons.

Wimbledon (0) 2
Newcastle United (0) 0

Competition: FA Carling Premiership
Date: Saturday January 22, 2000
Attendance: 22,118
Referee: D Gallagher (Banbury) 8

Game 33

THE GAME: After lining up with the same team that was so impressive at home to Southampton the week before, United lost to a Wimbledon side that had only won five of their last 22 Premiership games. Bobby Robson's Newcastle dominated the first half but couldn't convert their possession into goals, with Kieron Dyer, Gary Speed and Alan Shearer squandering chances they really should have put away. Dons 'keeper Neil Sullivan was the Man Of The Match as Newcastle failed to find a way past the Scottish No.1 and were punished by two Wimbledon strikes in the second half to condemn United to their tenth Premiership defeat of the season.

WIMBLEDON GOALS: Earle *(47 mins):* Harper's weak punch from Alan Kimble's left-wing free kick sent the ball onto Earle's knee and into the net; **Gayle** *(69 mins):* Cunningham's cross from the right wing picked out the unmarked Gayle perfectly and the striker beat Harper with a well-timed header.

MATCH RATING: ★★★★ **LEAGUE POSITION:** 15th

MATCH FACTS

Shots On Target
Wimbledon 4-2 Newcastle

Shots Off Target
Wimbledon 3-3 Newcastle

Hit Woodwork
Wimbledon 0-0 Newcastle

Corners
Wimbledon 2-5 Newcastle

HOW THEY LINED UP

Sullivan

Cunningham Hreidarsson Andersen Kimble

Badir Earle Euell

Cort Leaburn Gayle

Ferguson Shearer

Gallacher

Speed Dyer Solano

Pistone Dabizas Marcelino Barton

Harper

WIMBLEDON

Sullivan	☆	9
Cunningham		7
Kimble		7
Cort		7
Earle ⚽		8
Goal: 47 mins		
Euell		7
Gayle ⚽		8
Goal: 69 mins		
Leaburn		7
Subbed: 60 mins (Ardley)		
Badir		6
Andersen		6
Hreidarsson		7
sub: Ardley		7

Subs not used: Heald, Anderson, Willmott, Francis.

NEWCASTLE UNITED

Harper		6
Barton		7
Marcelino		7
Dyer	☆	8
Shearer		8
Speed		8
Solano		8
Ferguson		7
Subbed: 74 mins (Domi)		
Gallacher		6
Dabizas		7
Pistone		7
sub: Domi		

Subs not used: Given, Ketsbaia, Hughes, Helder.

THIS WEEK...

IN THE NEWS

NEWCASTLE UNITED: Silvio **Maric** looks destined to leave the club after being substituted just 15 minutes into a reserve match for lack of effort... Bobby Robson's long-term future at the club looks secure as Magpies chiefs prepare to offer the former England boss a new contract... Robson expects to complete a deal for Paraguay midfielder **Diego Gavilan** after his club Cerro Porteno dropped their asking price from £1.8 million to just £1 million... Some bizarre speculation suggests American television giants ntl want to bring Kevin Keegan back to the club. Although the company are likely to offer a new contract to current manager Bobby Robson, it is rumoured that ntl would wait until after the World Cup in 2002 to bring Keegan back to Tyneside.

PREMIERSHIP: Arsenal have been linked with Juventus striker **Daniel Fonseca**... Aston Villa could make a move for Galatasaray's **Hakan Sukur**... Inter Milan deny they have made a £10 million bid for Coventry City's **Robbie Keane**... Germany international defender **Markus Babbel** signs for Liverpool on a free transfer... Leeds United learn they are likely to face a clash with FIFA if **Harry Kewell** is not released for Australia's Olympic team in September 2000...

THE FINAL SCORE!

JANUARY 12		
Chelsea	1-0	Tottenham

JANUARY 15		
Arsenal	4-1	Sunderland
Chelsea	1-1	Leicester
Coventry	2-0	Wimbledon
Everton	2-2	Tottenham
Middlesbrough	1-4	**Derby**
Sheff. Wed.	2-0	Bradford
Watford	2-3	**Liverpool**
West Ham	1-1	Aston Villa

JANUARY 16		
Newcastle	5-0	Southampton

JANUARY 22		
Aston Villa	0-0	Chelsea
Bradford	3-2	Watford
Derby	0-0	Coventry
Leicester	1-3	**West Ham**
Liverpool	0-0	Middlesbrough
Southampton	2-0	Everton
Tottenham	0-1	**Sheff. Wed.**
Wimbledon	2-0	Newcastle

TOP OF THE PREMIERSHIP

	P	W	D	L	Pts
1. Leeds	21	14	2	5	44
2. Man. United	19	13	4	2	43
3. Arsenal	22	13	4	5	43
15. Newcastle	23	7	6	10	27

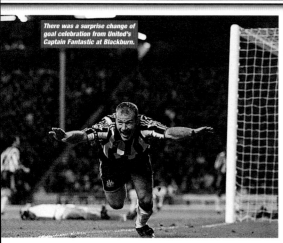

There was a surprise change of goal celebration from United's Captain Fantastic at Blackburn.

FROM THE PAGES OF *MATCH*

KEVIN GALLACHER was Bobby Robson's first signing for **NEWCASTLE UNITED**. **MATCH** asked the striker about his big move to the Premiership and being re-united with Alan Shearer.

What do you see as your role at Newcastle? *"Well, Bobby Robson didn't have to pull the wool over my eyes. He said he wanted me as cover for Duncan and Alan, but there have been a lot of injuries and I've found myself playing just in behind the front two. To be honest, I'm loving every minute of it now that I'm used to that position."*

How did your move actually come about then? *"I was surprised with the move to Newcastle. I knew there was an offer in the pipeline and I never considered that I wouldn't play in the top-flight again because I thought I would get a chance playing with Blackburn. But now Newcastle have given me that chance and I'm very happy to have taken it."*

So what do you make of the slightly different role you've been playing in? *"Well, I've been playing a bit deeper in midfield, just behind the front two of Alan and Duncan, and I've been very happy with the way I've been playing."*

What's it like playing with Alan Shearer again? *"It's been very good to line up with Alan again because I know how he plays. We played together for a few seasons at Blackburn so we learned to work well together and we were successful there. It's always nice to move to a new club and know someone who's there."*

It's karaoke party time as Shearer scores his second in the 2-1 FA Cup victory.

Blackburn Rovers	(1)	**1**
Newcastle United	(1)	**2**

Competition: FA Cup 5th Rd

Date: Monday January 31, 2000

Attendance: 29,946

Referee: P Durkin (Portland) 8

Game 34

THE GAME: After this match, Bobby Robson said Blackburn had given Newcastle their toughest away examination of the season, even though Alan Shearer silenced the Ewood Park boo boys after scoring his 15th goal in his last 16 FA Cup ties to put The Magpies 2-1 up. Blackburn had done well to come back from a goal down, but they rarely looked threatening in front of Steve Harper's goal. Robson wisely substituted Helder in the 50th minute after the defender – who had already been cautioned earlier in the game – came close to being sent-off for a bad challenge on Matt Jansen. Robson brought on Didier Domi for Kevin Gallacher with 20 minutes left and switched to a more solid 4-4-2 formation – ensuring that the tie was safe and that Newcastle made the quarter-finals of the FA Cup.

BLACKBURN GOAL: Jansen (25 mins): Beat the 'keeper to Frandsen's pass from the centre circle to bring Rovers level.

NEWCASTLE GOALS: Shearer (20 mins): Shearer managed to beat the offside trap and shoot home as the defence was caught napping by Ferguson's defence-splitting flick. **Shearer** (79 mins): McAteer lost possession, allowing Domi to cross for Shearer to slide the ball into the Blackburn net at the far post.

MATCH RATING: ★★★★ **LEAGUE POSITION:** 15th

BLACKBURN ROVERS	
Kelly	7
Grayson ▢	7
Booked: 15 mins (foul)	
Peacock	★ 8
Dailly	7
Davidson	7
McAteer	7
Carsley	7
Subbed: 46 mins (Johnson)	
Frandsen	7
Duff	7
Jansen ⊕	7
Goal: 25 mins	
Blake	7
sub: Johnson ▢	7
Booked: 90 mins (foul)	

Subs not used: Ostenstad, Gillespie, Fettis, Harkness.

NEWCASTLE UNITED	
Harper	7
Barton	7
Helder ▢	7
Booked: 32 mins (foul); Subbed: 50 mins (Hughes)	
Dabizas	7
Pistone	7
Speed	7
Dyer	7
Subbed: 89 mins (Maric)	
Gallacher	7
Subbed: 68 mins (Domi)	
Lee	7
Shearer ⊕ ▢ ⊕	★ 8
Goals: 20, 79 mins; Booked: 70 mins (foul)	
Ferguson	7
sub: Hughes	7
sub: Domi	7
sub: Maric	

Subs not used: Fumaca, Given.

MATCH FACTS

Shots On Target
Blackburn 7-9 Newcastle

Shots Off Target
Blackburn 9-8 Newcastle

Hit Woodwork
Blackburn 0-0 Newcastle

Corners
Blackburn 5-5 Newcastle

HOW THEY LINED UP

Kelly

Grayson — Peacock — Dailly — Davidson

McAteer — Carsley — Frandsen — Duff

Jansen — Blake

Shearer — Ferguson

Gallacher

Speed — Lee — Dyer

Pistone — Dabizas — Helder — Barton

Harper

IN THE NEWS

NEWCASTLE UNITED: Steve Howey is reassured about his future at St James' Park despite a lengthy lay-off after snapping his Achilles tendon last April. Magpies boss Bobby Robson tells interested clubs the former England defender is not available... Meanwhile, the club is rumoured to be showing an interest in bringing former Everton midfielder **Olivier Dacourt** back to England, although the Frenchman's club, Lens, would want a fee in the region of £5 million.

PREMIERSHIP: Manchester United midfielder **David Beckham** comes second in the World Player Of The Year awards. He is beaten into the runners-up spot by Barcelona star **Rivaldo**... Persistent injury forces former Sheffield Wednesday and England star **David Hirst** to retire from the game. The Southampton striker had been struggling to play for the past 18 months... Sheffield Wednesday fans vent their anger at local MPs who had called for the dismissal of Owls manager Danny Wilson... Liverpool boss Gerrard Houllier, keen to add to his forward line following injuries to **Michael Owen** and **Robbie Fowler**, has reportedly failed in a bid to sign Vitesse Arnhem's Dutch striker **Pierre Van Hooijdonk** on loan. Houllier has also been linked with bringing Italian stars **Fabrizio Ravanelli** and **Roberto Baggio** to Anfield as cover for The Reds until the end of the season... Coventry, Leicester, Sheffield Wednesday and Leeds are all knocked out in the fifth round of the FA Cup.

THE FINAL SCORE!

JANUARY 23		
Sunderland	1-2	Leeds

JANUARY 24		
Man. United	1-1	Arsenal

JANUARY 29		
Man. United	1-0	Middlesbrough

TOP OF THE PREMIERSHIP

		P	W	D	L	Pts
1. Man. United		21	14	5	2	47
2. Leeds		22	15	2	5	47
3. Arsenal		23	13	5	5	44
15. Newcastle		23	7	6	10	27

FEBRUARY

"This is the first time for so long that I'm working at the wrong end of the league table. It must be the first time since 1970 in my early days with Ipswich." Bobby Robson

THERE MAY HAVE BEEN VICTORIES OF GREATER MARGINS DURING 1999-2000, but Newcastle recorded one of the most satisfying wins of the season in February when they beat Manchester United 3-0. The overall team performance rattled the defending Premiership champions, with goals from Duncan Ferguson and Alan Shearer, who scored a brace. It was a result that was achieved without Nolberto Solano, who was on international duty with Peru at the CONCACAF Gold Cup. Bobby Robson had told Solano not to play after picking up an injury, but the winger passed himself fit and could not have been surprised when he was fined two weeks' wages on his return.

England skipper Alan Shearer shocked the world by announcing he would retire from international football after Euro 2000 to concentrate on his club career with The Magpies, which was fantastic news for the Toon Army. But there was some bad news for 13 players who were put on the club's transfer list – either at their own request or by Bobby Robson – after being told they had no future at the club. The list included first-team squad members like Stephen Glass, Des Hamilton, John Karelse, Silvio Maric and Carl Serrant.

Newcastle reached the FA Cup semi-finals for the third successive year, defeating First Division Tranmere Rovers 3-2 in the quarter-finals where the team had to defend against Dave Challinor's devastatingly accurate long throws – a tactic that Bobby Robson suggested were more dangerous than David Beckham's crosses. In the Premiership, Newcastle's progression up the league table saw them finish the month in 12th position, with the results and performances earning Bobby Robson the Carling Premiership Manager Of The Month award for February. Steve Howey returned to first-team action in the game against Sheffield Wednesday for the first time since playing in the 1999 FA Cup semi-final against Tottenham at Old Trafford.

69

Dyer completed the whole game after injury but couldn't inspire his Newcastle team to victory.

 Sunderland (1) **2**

 Newcastle United (2) **2**

Competition: FA Carling Premiership

Date: Saturday February 5, 2000

Attendance: 42,192

Referee: D Gallagher (Banbury) 7

 Game 35

THE GAME: Newcastle were guilty of squandering another two-goal advantage as the 118th Tyne and Wear derby ended level. A record crowd at the Stadium Of Light saw United race into a deserved two-goal lead, but Sunderland battled back in a pulsating game in which Steve Harper was the busier of the two 'keepers. After going 2-0 ahead, The Magpies' lead was halved within a minute by Kevin Phillips and they held out until just eight minutes before the end when Phillips volleyed in his second. There was more bad news for Newcastle as defender Alessandro Pistone had to be stretchered off with a broken leg after a collision with Nicky Summerbee. But Bobby Robson did have some good news, with Kieron Dyer looking back to his best after recovering from an injury he suffered in October, Robert Lee back in action for the first time since the turn of the year, and new signing Diego Gavilan making his debut.

SUNDERLAND GOALS: Phillips (22 mins): Latched on to Quinn's flick-on to blast his shot under the body of Harper; **Phillips** (82 mins): Beat the Newcastle 'keeper with a volley from the edge of the six-yard box following Kilbane's cross.

NEWCASTLE GOALS: Domi (11 mins): Ferguson set up Domi, who cracked home a deflected left-foot shot from 12 yards; **Helder** (21 mins): Dyer whipped in a free-kick from the left wing and Helder raced past two Sunderland defenders to head past Sorensen and into the net from close range.

MATCH RATING: ★★★ LEAGUE POSITION: 13th

SUNDERLAND	
Sorensen	6
Makin	8
Gray	6
Craddock	8
Butler, P	7
Summerbee	5
Subbed: 75 mins (Reddy)	
Schwarz ▢	7
Booked: 57 mins (foul)	
McCann	7
Quinn	7
Phillips ⊕⊕	☆ 9
Goals: 22, 82 mins	
Kilbane	6
sub: Reddy	

Subs not used: Marriott, Rae, Roy, Holloway.

NEWCASTLE UNITED	
Harper	☆ 9
Barton	8
Domi ⊕	7
Goal: 11 mins; Subbed: 88 mins (Gallacher)	
Dyer	8
Shearer	5
Speed	7
Ferguson	6
Dabizas ▢	7
Booked: 46 mins (foul)	
Pistone	6
Subbed: 36 mins (Hughes)	
Lee ▢	7
Booked: 86 mins (foul); Subbed: 88 mins (Gavilan)	
Helder ⊕	8
Goal: 21 mins	
sub: Hughes	6
sub: Gallacher	
sub: Gavilan	

Subs not used: Given, Fumaca.

MATCH FACTS	
Shots On Target	
Sunderland 9-9 Newcastle	
Shots Off Target	
Sunderland 4-5 Newcastle	
Hit Woodwork	
Sunderland 0-0 Newcastle	
Corners	
Sunderland 8-9 Newcastle	

HOW THEY LINED UP

Sorensen

Makin — Craddock — Butler, P — Gray

Summerbee — McCann — Schwarz — Kilbane

Quinn — Phillips

Ferguson — Shearer

Domi — Speed — Lee — Dyer

Pistone — Dabizas — Helder — Barton

Harper

IN THE NEWS

NEWCASTLE UNITED: Paraguay international ace Diego Gavilan officially signs for The Magpies from Cerro Porteno for an initial fee of £1 million... Toon defender **Andrew Griffin** comes back into contention for a first-team place after an eight-month lay-off due to a stress fracture of his lower spine. The 20-year-old full-back has not played since the 1999 FA Cup Final... **Temuri Ketsbaia** leaves England to play for Georgia in the Cyprus Tournament.

PREMIERSHIP: Arsenal are linked with Barcelona's **Patrick Kluivert** and Coventry goalkeeper **Magnus Hedman**... Aston Villa sign Roma's Argentinian **Gustavo Bartelt** on loan until the end of the season... AC Milan defender **Paolo Maldini** is quoted as saying he wants to join Chelsea... Coventry's **Youssef Chippo** sustains a hip injury while playing for Morocco in the African Nations Cup... Derby County pay Conference side Nuneaton Borough another £25,000 for **Malcolm Christie** after the striker makes his tenth first-team appearance... Leicester's **Steve Walsh** learns he will miss the Worthington Cup Final against Tranmere Rovers through suspension after being sent-off in the FA Cup fifth round clash at Chelsea last month.

THE FINAL SCORE!

FEBRUARY 2		
Sheff. Wed.	0-1	**Man. United**

FEBRUARY 5		
Aston Villa	4-0	Watford
Bradford	2-1	Arsenal
Derby	3-3	Sheff. Wed.
Leicester	2-1	Middlesbrough
Liverpool	3-1	Leeds
Man. United	3-2	Coventry
Southampton	2-1	West Ham
Sunderland	2-2	Newcastle
Tottenham	0-1	**Chelsea**

TOP OF THE PREMIERSHIP

	P	W	D	L	Pts
1. Man. United	23	16	5	2	53
2. Leeds	23	15	2	6	47
3. Arsenal	24	13	5	6	44
13. Newcastle	24	7	7	10	28

Big Dunc terrorised Man. United and scored a cracker in the enthralling 3-0 victory at St James' Park.

| Newcastle United | (1) 3 |
| Manchester United | (0) 0 |

Competition: FA Carling Premiership

Date: Saturday February 12, 2000

Attendance: 36,470

Referee: S Lodge (Barnsley) 6

Game 36

THE GAME: This was surely the most satisfying result of the season for Newcastle as they comfortably beat Man. United at St James' Park. The Magpies outplayed their opponents, who became increasingly frustrated with themselves before boiling over and having captain Roy Keane sent-off. Newcastle never allowed their trophy-laden opponents to settle, and they were helped by good fortune when Warren Barton went unpunished for handling in his own box and when Andy Cole's goalbound effort hit the post and rebounded off Harper's back. But The Magpies certainly deserved the win. Duncan Ferguson opened the scoring with a brilliant volley which even Sir Alex Ferguson admitted was a worthy winner and Alan Shearer bagged two more goals in the second half for a famous Toon Army victory.

NEWCASTLE GOALS: Ferguson *(26 mins):* Shearer knocked the ball down for Ferguson, who let the ball bounce and then struck a stunning left-foot volley from the edge of the box into the roof of the net; **Shearer** *(75 mins):* Left Bosnich sprawling with a 22-yard curling shot from the left; **Shearer** *(85 mins):* Domi advanced at speed before crossing from the edge of the penalty area for Shearer to fire home from eight yards.

MATCH RATING: ★★★★ **LEAGUE POSITION:** 13th

NEWCASTLE UNITED	
Harper	7
Barton	8
Hughes	8
Dabizas	8
Helder	7
Dyer	7
Subbed: 83 mins (Gavilan)	
Speed	7
Lee	7
Gallacher ☆	9
Subbed: 83 mins (Domi)	
Ferguson ⚽	8
Goal: 26 mins; Subbed: 62 mins (Ketsbaia)	
Shearer ▢ ⚽ ⚽	8
Booked: 55 mins (dissent); Goals: 75, 85 mins	
sub: Ketsbaia	7
sub: Domi	
sub: Gavilan	
Subs not used: Given, Furnaca.	

MANCHESTER UNITED	
Bosnich	6
Neville, G	6
Irwin	7
Subbed: 69 mins (Butt)	
Silvestre	6
Stam ▢	7
Booked: 84 mins (dissent)	
Beckham	6
Scholes ▢ ☆	8
Booked: 66 mins (foul)	
Keane ▢ ▢	6
Booked: 44 mins (dissent); Sent-off: 64 mins (second bookable offence: foul)	
Sheringham	6
Subbed: 74 mins (Solskjaer)	
Cole ▢	6
Booked: 64 mins (dissent)	
Giggs	6
sub: Butt	6
sub: Solskjaer	
Subs not used: Neville, P, Berg, van der Gouw.	

MATCH FACTS

Shots On Target
Newcastle 7-2 Man. United

Shots Off Target
Newcastle 11-5 Man. United

Hit Woodwork
Newcastle 1-0 Man. United

Corners
Newcastle 3-3 Man. United

HOW THEY LINED UP

Harper

Barton · Helder · Dabizas · Hughes

Dyer · Lee · Speed · Gallacher

Shearer · Ferguson

Sheringham · Cole

Giggs · Scholes · Keane · Beckham

Irwin · Silvestre · Stam · Neville, G

Bosnich

IN THE NEWS

NEWCASTLE UNITED: Italian defender **Alessandro Pistone** is expected to be out of action for three months after breaking his leg against Sunderland... The Magpies are reportedly casting their eye over Feyenoord skipper and Holland international **Paul Bosvelt**, a midfielder rated at £4 million... Bobby Robson's potential deal to lure Argentina midfielder **Christian Bassedas** to St James' Park is put on hold... **Stephen Glass** hands in a transfer request, unhappy about his lack of first-team opportunities... **Temuri Ketsbaia** helps Georgia to third place at the Cyprus Tournament.

PREMIERSHIP: Former England coach Glenn Hoddle takes over the reigns at Southampton... Man. United finalise a four-year sponsorship deal with Vodafone worth £30 million... Chelsea's **Frank Leboeuf** has been handed a two-match ban on top of the two game suspension that he received for stamping on **Harry Kewell** in Chelsea's 2-0 defeat by Leeds last December... **Stan Collymore** joins Leicester City from Aston Villa for £500,000... Wimbledon sign **Andreas Lund** from Molde for £2.5 million... Tottenham's injury crisis leaves them with only one fit striker at White Hart Lane, former Newcastle hitman **Les Ferdinand.**

THE FINAL SCORE!

FEBRUARY 6		
Wimbledon	0-3	**Everton**

FEBRUARY 12		
Chelsea	3-1	Wimbledon
Coventry	3-2	Sunderland
Everton	2-1	Derby
Leeds	1-0	Tottenham
Newcastle	3-0	Man. United
Sheff. Wed.	0-1	**Southampton**
Watford	1-1	Leicester
West Ham	5-4	Bradford

TOP OF THE PREMIERSHIP

	P	W	D	L	Pts
1. Man. United	24	16	5	3	53
2. Leeds	24	16	2	6	50
3. Arsenal	24	13	5	6	44
13. Newcastle	**25**	**8**	**7**	**10**	**31**

Tranmere Rovers (1) 2
Newcastle United (2) 3

Competition: FA Cup Quarter-Final
Date: Sunday February 20, 2000
Attendance: 15,776
Referee: S Dunn (Bristol) 8

Game 37

THE GAME: The Toon Army opened this FA Cup quarter-final tie with a rendition of 'Happy Birthday' for Bobby Robson and ended the day singing 'Que Sera Sera' as Newcastle reached their third successive semi-final in the competition. First-half goals from Gary Speed and Didier Domi put United 2-0 ahead, but First Division Tranmere refused to lie down. Wayne Allison pulled a goal back on the stroke of half-time before Duncan Ferguson scored his tenth of the season to put Newcastle 3-1 up. With Dave Challinor's throw-ins causing problems, Rovers grabbed a second goal, but it turned out to be a consolation strike as The Magpies held on to progress to the semi-finals.

TRANMERE GOALS: Allison *(45 mins):* Headed the ball in at the far post after Challinor's huge throw-in; **Jones, G** *(76 mins):* Scored from close range after Allison's blocked shot.
NEWCASTLE GOALS: Speed *(27 mins):* Powered a header past 'keeper Murphy from Gallacher's right-wing cross; **Domi** *(36 mins):* Gallacher put in a right-wing cross which fell to Domi, who sent his shot crashing into the net to put United 2-0 ahead; **Ferguson** *(58 mins):* Dyer's cross from the right found Ferguson, who finished convincingly from seven yards.

MATCH RATING: ★★★★ **LEAGUE POSITION:** 13th

TRANMERE ROVERS		NEWCASTLE UNITED	
Murphy	☆ 8	Given	8
Hazell	6	Barton	8
Challinor ▢	7	Dabizas	7
Booked: 81 mins (foul)		Helder	7
Babb	7	Hughes	7
Roberts	7	Dyer	8
Subbed: 89 mins (Thompson)		Speed ⊕	7
Parkinson	6	*Goal: 27 mins*	
Subbed: 32 mins (Taylor, S)		Gallacher ☆	9
Henry	6	Domi ⊕	8
Jones, G ⊕	7	*Goal: 36 mins*	
Goal: 76 mins		Shearer	7
Mahon	6	Ferguson ⊕	7
Subbed: 52 mins (Morgan)		*Goal: 58 mins*	
Allison ⊕	7	*Subs not used: Karelse, Howey, Ketsbaia, Glass, Fumaca.*	
Goal: 45 mins			
Kelly	7		
sub: Taylor, S	6		
sub: Morgan	6		
sub: Thompson			
Subs not used: Achterberg, Black.			

MATCH FACTS	
Shots On Target	
Tranmere 6-10 Newcastle	
Shots Off Target	
Tranmere 7-4 Newcastle	
Hit Woodwork	
Tranmere 0-1 Newcastle	
Corners	
Tranmere 2-4 Newcastle	

HOW THEY LINED UP

Murphy
Hazell — Challinor — Babb — Roberts
Parkinson — Jones — Henry — Mahon
Allison — Kelly

Shearer — Ferguson
Domi — Speed — Dyer — Gallacher
Hughes — Helder — Dabizas — Barton
Given

Kieron Dyer gets the praise after his cross from the right is turned in by Duncan Ferguson for United's third.

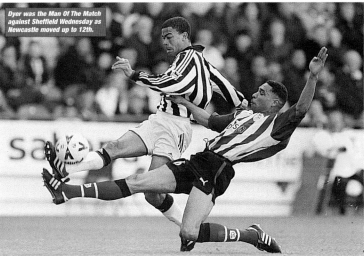

Dyer was the Man Of The Match against Sheffield Wednesday as Newcastle moved up to 12th.

Sheffield Wednesday (0) 0
Newcastle United (1) 2

Competition: FA Carling Premiership

Date: Saturday February 26, 2000

Attendance: 29,212

Referee: M Riley (Leeds) 7

Game 38

THE GAME: Newcastle completed their first league double of the season with this deserved away victory against Sheffield Wednesday. United were in control for most of the game but they gave The Owls several chances to equalise in the second half. Fortunately, the struggling home team couldn't make the most of the defensive lapses and Newcastle kept a rare clean sheet before adding a second goal late on. Steve Howey made his first appearance for United since the 1999 FA Cup semi-final against Spurs, replacing the injured Helder. The result at Hillsborough was never really in doubt, but it never looked like living up to the 8-0 massacre that heralded Bobby Robson's arrival at St James' Park back in September. Taking the shine off this win was Duncan Ferguson's withdrawal at half-time with a back problem. The injury didn't seem too serious, but the prospect of losing one of his strikers was the last thing Bobby Robson needed at this stage of the season.

NEWCASTLE GOALS: Gallacher *(12 mins):* Atherton's back header fell well short of his 'keeper, ex-Magpie Pavel Srnicek, allowing Gallacher to race in to score convincingly; **Shearer** *(86 mins):* Lee hit a long ball forward for Shearer, who took it in his stride and beat Srnicek with a low shot from 15 yards, tucking the ball just inside the far post to seal the points.

MATCH RATING: ★★★ LEAGUE POSITION: 12th

MATCH FACTS

Shots On Target
Sheff. Wed. 2-5 Newcastle

Shots Off Target
Sheff. Wed. 3-5 Newcastle

Hit Woodwork
Sheff. Wed. 1-0 Newcastle

Corners
Sheff. Wed. 1-5 Newcastle

SHEFFIELD WEDNESDAY

Srnicek	7
Nolan	6
Atherton	6
Walker	6
Hinchcliffe	☆ 8
Alexandersson	7
Quinn	6
Sonner	6
Subbed: 85 mins (Rudi)	
Haslam	6
de Bilde	6
Subbed: 57 mins (Cresswell)	
Sibon	6
sub: *Cresswell*	6
sub: *Rudi*	

Subs not used: Pressman, Briscoe, Staniforth.

NEWCASTLE UNITED

Given	7
Barton 🟨	7
Booked: 16 mins (foul)	
Dabizas	7
Helder	7
Subbed: 69 mins (Howey)	
Hughes	7
Gallacher ⚽	7
Goal: 12 mins; Subbed: 76 mins (Domi)	
Lee	7
Speed	7
Dyer	☆ 8
Ferguson	7
Subbed: 46 mins (Ketsbaia)	
Shearer ⚽	7
Goal: 86 mins	
sub: *Ketsbaia*	7
sub: *Howey*	6
sub: *Domi*	

Subs not used: Karelse, Gavilan.

HOW THEY LINED UP

Srnicek

Nolan — Atherton — Walker — Hinchcliffe

Alexandersson — Haslam — Sonner — Quinn

Sibon — de Bilde

Ferguson — Shearer

Gallacher — Speed — Lee — Dyer

Hughes — Helder — Dabizas — Barton

Given

IN THE NEWS

NEWCASTLE UNITED: Newcastle tell Inter Milan that **Kieron Dyer** is not for sale after the Italians are linked with a £10 million move for the England star... Bobby Robson has agreed a 12-month extension to his contract... Four youth team players – **Ryan Hogg, Paul Dunn, Johnny Mann** and **Kev Weallans** – are injured in a car crash... **Steve Howey,** who impressed in several reserve team games, returns to the squad for the first time since the 1999 FA Cup semi-final... Newcastle place 13 players on the transfer list – **Paul Arnison, Garry Brady, Stephen Caldwell, James Coppinger, Stuart Elliott, Stephen Glass, Des Hamilton, John Karelse, Ian Martin, Silvio Maric, Lionel Perez, Carl Serrant** and **Paul Talbot... Nol Solano** is fined £30,000 – the equivalent of two weeks' wages – for defying orders to play for Peru while still struggling with a hamstring injury. He helped his country to reach the semi-finals of the Gold Cup before they were beaten by Colombia... **Alan Shearer** announces that he will quit international football after Euro 2000... Transfer-listed **Stuart Elliott** moves to Hartlepool United on a month's loan... **Kieron Dyer** plays at right-back for England in their promising 0-0 draw against Argentina at Wembley.

PREMIERSHIP: Leicester City beat First Division Tranmere Rovers 2-1 in the Worthington Cup Final with two goals from captain Matt Elliott.

THE FINAL SCORE!

FEBRUARY 13		
Arsenal	0-1	**Liverpool**

FEBRUARY 14		
Middlesbrough	0-4	**Aston Villa**

FEBRUARY 19		
Middlesbrough	2-0	Coventry

FEBRUARY 20		
Leeds	0-1	**Man. United**

FEBRUARY 26		
Arsenal	3-1	Southampton
Bradford	1-1	Aston Villa
Chelsea	2-1	Watford
Coventry	0-1	**Tottenham**
Middlesbrough	0-0	Leeds
Sheff. Wed.	0-2	**Newcastle**
Sunderland	1-1	Derby
West Ham	0-4	**Everton**
Wimbledon	2-2	Man. United

TOP OF THE PREMIERSHIP

	P	W	D	L	Pts
1. Man. United	26	17	6	3	57
2. Leeds	26	16	3	7	51
3. Arsenal	26	14	5	7	47
12. Newcastle	26	9	7	10	34

MARCH

"There really is nothing to be mournful about this season. We set out to maintain our status in the Premier League and we have gone on to do that." Bobby Robson

BOBBY ROBSON REACHED HIS ORIGINAL TARGET OF 40 POINTS IN March to assure Newcastle's place in the Premiership. United won two and lost two games in the league to leave the team in the security of mid-table. That left The Magpies in the difficult position of being clear of the relegation battle but too distant from the sides jostling for European places. However, the situation allowed the Magpies boss to experiment.

With one eye on the FA Cup semi-final clash against Chelsea, scheduled for April, Robson fielded a five-man defence to face Gianluca Vialli's side in the Premiership. The strategy didn't work, though, and Newcastle lost by a single goal. After this setback, wins against Watford and Everton, followed by defeat to Liverpool, gave The Magpies six points from a possible 12 for the month. Several of Newcastle's stars flew out of Tyneside on international duty, with Nolberto Solano of Peru and Paraguay's Diego Gavilan having the longest journeys of the month – to South America – to start their 2002 World Cup qualifying campaigns with their respective countries.

The medical team at St James' Park was discharging more of the playing staff from its care and back towards the Newcastle first team. Alain Goma's long rehabilitation from Achilles tendon trouble was complete, Marcelino had recovered from hip and ankle injuries and the unlucky Carl Serrant was back after surgery on his knee. The defenders were all training again and making themselves available to manager Bobby Robson. Several players went out on loan, including James Coppinger (to Hartlepool United), Lionel Perez (to Cambridge United), Garry Brady and Des Hamilton (both to Norwich City). Paul Arnison, who had previously been on loan to Hartlepool, signed for the Third Division side on a free transfer while Steve Caldwell was taken off the transfer list and given a new one year contract with the club.

THE GAMES

Mar. 4 v **Chelsea** (h)

Mar. 11 v **Watford** (h)

Mar. 19 v **Everton** (a)

Mar. 25 v **Liverpool** (a)

TRANSFERS IN

None

TRANSFERS OUT

Paul Arnison

Position: **Midfielder**

Fee: **Free**

To: **Hartlepool United**

MATCH facts

Matchman Of The Month

KEVIN GALLACHER
Average Rating: 7.00

United were outclassed by Chelsea, who went into the match unbeaten in 2000.

Newcastle United (0) 0
Chelsea (1) 1

Competition: FA Carling Premiership

Date: Saturday March 4, 2000

Attendance: 36,448

Referee: M Riley (Leeds) 7

Game 39

THE GAME: Newcastle were defeated at St James' Park for the first time since Bobby Robson's arrival on Tyneside in this rehearsal for the FA Cup semi-final against Chelsea. United's line-up included Steve Howey for his first Premiership start in almost a year after Helder was ruled out of the match through injury. Bobby Robson's plan was to stop Chelsea's galaxy of foreign stars by using five men in defence with Aaron Hughes marking Gianfranco Zola, but The Magpies lost the battle in midfield and their strikers rarely troubled Chelsea goalkeeper Ed de Goey on a disappointing afternoon for the Toon Army.

CHELSEA GOAL: Poyet *(21 mins):* Given was beaten by the simplest of moves when Poyet headed in a cross from Morris.

MATCH RATING: ★★ **LEAGUE POSITION: 12th**

> "We were poor against Chelsea, everything was flat. We started off poorly and couldn't raise our game. We owe it to our fans to get the performance against Chelsea out of our system." ALAN SHEARER

NEWCASTLE UNITED

Player	Rating
Given	6
Barton	7
Domi	5
Subbed: 46 mins (Solano)	
Howey	6
Dyer	5
Shearer	6
Speed	6
Hughes	6
Ferguson	5
Dabizas	☆ 8
Lee	5
Subbed: 75 mins (Ketsbaia)	
sub: Solano	6
sub: Ketsbaia	

Subs not used: Harper, Gavilan, Fumaca.

CHELSEA

Player	Rating
de Goey	7
Babayaro	6
Leboeuf	9
Poyet ⊕	☆ 9
Goal: 21 mins	
Sutton	6
Subbed: 72 mins (Flo)	
Wise	6
Di Matteo	7
Subbed: 48 mins (Petrescu)	
Ferrer	6
Morris	7
Zola	7
Thome	7
sub: Petrescu	7
sub: Flo	

Subs not used: Ambrosetti, Cudicini, Terry.

MATCH FACTS

Shots On Target
Newcastle 5-5 Chelsea

Shots Off Target
Newcastle 0 3 Chelsea

Hit Woodwork
Newcastle 0-0 Chelsea

Corners
Newcastle 4-3 Chelsea

HOW THEY LINED UP

Given

Barton Dabizas Howey Hughes Domi

Dyer Lee Speed

Ferguson Shearer

Zola Sutton

Poyet Wise Morris Di Matteo

Babayaro Leboeuf Thome Ferrer

de Goey

Operating on the left of midfield, Gallacher opens his account for Newcastle to beat Watford.

Newcastle United	(0)	**1**
Watford	(0)	**0**

Competition: FA Carling Premiership

Date: Saturday March 11, 2000

Attendance: 36,433

Referee: A Wiley (Burntwood) 8

Game 40

THE GAME: It was a memorable day for Bobby Robson as he collected February's Manager Of The Month Award before the game and a well-deserved three points at the end of the afternoon. Gallacher scored the winner against Watford with his first goal for Newcastle at St James' Park, but the winning margin should have been much greater after a good first half for the home side. United dominated the second half as well, with Alan Shearer hitting the post and squandering two good chances to extend Newcastle's lead. Duncan Ferguson, Nikos Dabizas and Gary Speed all forced superb saves from Watford 'keeper Alec Chamberlain. But despite United's possession, their midfield failed to provide enough service to Alan Shearer and Duncan Ferguson, while United 'keeper Shay Given made two valuable saves to deny the visitors an equaliser.

NEWCASTLE GOAL: Gallacher (59 mins): Domi's low cross set up Gallacher to score from six yards past Chamberlain.

MATCH RATING: ★★ **LEAGUE POSITION:** 12th

> "My last Manager Of The Month Award would have been back in my days at Ipswich. In fact, I had several of them because I built a good team there over a number of years, so yes, it is very pleasurable. I'm flattered by it, but it's thanks to the players." **BOBBY ROBSON**

NEWCASTLE UNITED

Given	6
Barton	☆ 8
Hughes	6
Subbed: 46 mins (Domi)	
Howey	7
Dabizas	6
Solano	6
Lee	6
Speed	6
Gallacher ⊕	7
Goal: 59 mins	
Shearer	6
Ferguson	6
sub: Domi	7

Subs not used: Harper, Fumaca, Ketsbaia, Gavilan.

WATFORD

Chamberlain	☆ 9
Kennedy	7
Page	7
Palmer	7
Robinson	6
Hyde	6
Johnson	6
Subbed: 87 mins (Bonnot)	
Smart	6
Wooter	7
Subbed: 79 mins (Williams)	
Cox	6
Helguson	6
sub: Williams	
sub: Bonnot	

Subs not used: Day, Ngonge, Smith.

MATCH FACTS

Shots On Target
Newcastle 6-5 Watford

Shots Off Target
Newcastle 14-2 Watford

Hit Woodwork
Newcastle 1-0 Watford

Corners
Newcastle 11-2 Watford

HOW THEY LINED UP

Given

Barton   Howey   Dabizas   Hughes

Solano   Lee   Speed   Gallacher

Ferguson   Shearer

Helguson   Smart

Kennedy   Hyde   Johnson   Wooter

Robinson   Palmer   Page   Cox

Chamberlain

IN THE NEWS

NEWCASTLE UNITED: After playing for Peru while carrying an injury, **Nolberto Solano** is linked with a £5 million move to Spanish club Real Madrid. The 26-year-old ignored the club's instructions not to play and has apparently rejected a new deal at St James' Park... Bobby Robson wins February's Carling Manager Of The Month award after beating Man. United and Sheffield Wednesday and drawing away to Sunderland... Newcastle's on-loan Portuguese defender **Helder** says he wants to stay on at St James' Park when his current contract expires... Transfer listed **James Coppinger** and **Paul Arnison** go to Hartlepool on loan. **PREMIERSHIP:** Leicester City striker **Emile Heskey** becomes one of the most wanted men in football after his inspiring performance for England against Argentina.

THE FINAL SCORE!

MARCH 4		
Derby	4-0	Wimbledon
Everton	1-1	Sheff. Wed.
Man. United	1-1	Liverpool
Newcastle	0-1	**Chelsea**
Southampton	1-1	Middlesbrough
Tottenham	1-1	Bradford
Watford	1-2	West Ham

MARCH 5		
Aston Villa	1-1	Arsenal
Leeds	3-0	Coventry
Leicester	5-2	Sunderland

MARCH 8		
West Ham	2-0	Southampton

MARCH 11		
Aston Villa	1-0	Coventry
Chelsea	1-1	Everton
Liverpool	1-1	Sunderland
Man. United	3-1	Derby
Newcastle	1-0	Watford
Sheff. Wed.	3-1	West Ham
Tottenham	7-2	Southampton
Wimbledon	2-1	Leicester

TOP OF THE PREMIERSHIP

		P	W	D	L	Pts
1.	Man. United	28	18	7	3	61
2.	Leeds	27	17	3	7	54
3.	Chelsea	28	14	8	6	50
12.	Newcastle	28	10	7	11	37

Everton	(0) **0**
Newcastle United	(0) **2**

Competition: **FA Carling Premiership**

Date: **Sunday March 19, 2000**

Attendance: **32,512**

Referee: **G Barber** (Tring) 6

Game 41

THE GAME: Aaron Hughes and Kieron Dyer were on target as Newcastle inflicted a rare home defeat on Everton. Former Evertonian Duncan Ferguson, who only passed a fitness test on a thigh injury in the morning, received a standing ovation from the home supporters. But it was the Newcastle fans who were cheering at the end as Aaron Hughes' 79th minute strike broke the deadlock before Dyer wrapped up the game late on to give Newcastle their highest league position of the season.

NEWCASTLE GOALS: Hughes (79 mins): Everton failed to clear Domi's left-wing cross and Hughes fired the ball from eight yards past 'keeper Gerrard; **Dyer** (87 mins): Lobbed the ball over first Weir and then Xavier before racing forward and chipping goalkeeper Gerrard for a stunning individual goal.

MATCH RATING: ★★★ **LEAGUE POSITION:** 11th

> "I've been getting into some great positions lately but missing the target, so it was extra sweet when it hit the back of the net. Apart from Manchester United at home, this is the best result of the season for us." KIERON DYER

EVERTON		NEWCASTLE UNITED	
Gerrard	6	Given	6
Unsworth	6	Barton	6
Weir	6	Howey ▢	☆7
Gough	7	*Booked: 34 mins (foul)*	
Xavier ▢	6	Dabizas	7
Booked: 69 mins (foul)		Hughes, A ⚽	7
Pembridge	5	*Goal: 79 mins*	
Hughes, S	5	Solano	6
Subbed: 77 mins (Ball)		*Subbed: 77 mins (Dyer)*	
Collins	☆7	Lee	6
Barmby	6	Speed ▢	7
Subbed: 85 mins (Dunne)		*Booked: 25 mins (foul)*	
Hughes, M ▢	6	Gallacher	7
Booked: 90 mins (foul)		*Subbed: 68 mins (Domi)*	
Moore	5	Shearer	6
Subbed: 66 mins (Cadamarteri)		Ferguson ▢	6
sub: Cadamarteri	5	*Booked: 28 mins (foul)*	
sub: Ball		*sub:* Domi	6
sub: Dunne		*sub:* Dyer ⚽	
		Goal: 87 mins	
Subs not used: Myhre, Gemmill.		*Subs not used: Goma, Harper, Ketsbaia.*	

MATCH FACTS

Shots On Target

Everton 0-2 Newcastle

Shots Off Target

Everton 4-5 Newcastle

Hit Woodwork

Everton 0-0 Newcastle

Corners

Everton 9-3 Newcastle

HOW THEY LINED UP

Gerrard

Xavier — Gough — Weir — Unsworth

Barmby — Pembridge — Collins — Hughes, S

Hughes, M — Moore

Shearer — Ferguson

Gallacher — Speed — Lee — Solano

Hughes, A — Dabizas — Howey — Barton

Given

Total concentration as Aaron Hughes strikes to put United 1-0 up at Goodison Park.

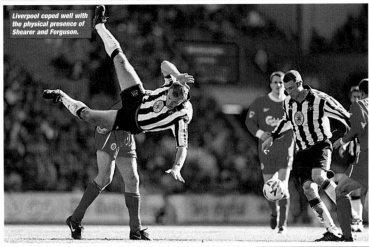

Liverpool coped well with the physical presence of Shearer and Ferguson.

Liverpool (0) **2**
Newcastle United (0) **1**

Competition: **FA Carling Premiership**

Date: **Saturday March 25, 2000**

Attendance: **44,743**

Referee: **P Durkin** (Portland) 7

Game 42

THE GAME: Newcastle were denied a well-deserved point at Anfield by a late winner from substitute Jamie Redknapp. The Magpies contained the home side for most of this match, with Warren Barton, Gary Speed and Rob Lee doing good marking jobs to thwart Liverpool's attack and leaving goalkeeper Shay Given to deal with mostly long-range efforts. Alan Shearer and Duncan Ferguson had little to work with in attack, but Shearer grabbed an equaliser and Kieron Dyer hit a post. The Magpies thought they'd done enough for a draw until Gerrard Houllier's side snatched their dramatic win with just two minutes left.

LIVERPOOL GOALS: Camara *(51 mins):* Gerrard sent over a cross for striker Camara to blast a rising shot past Given; **Redknapp** *(88 mins):* From Murphy's corner, Redknapp rose higher than The Magpies' defence to score the winning goal.

NEWCASTLE GOAL: Shearer *(67 mins):* Beat Matteo to Hughes' cross to send a looping header over Westerveld.

MATCH RATING: ★★★★ **LEAGUE POSITION:** 11th

> "I think Newcastle now have a team which can compete at a high level in the Premier League. In my opinion, they are now a side which can take on anyone in the league."
> **DIETMAR HAMANN (LIVERPOOL)**

MATCH FACTS

Shots On Target
Liverpool 6-2 Newcastle

Shots Off Target
Liverpool 6-2 Newcastle

Hit Woodwork
Liverpool 0-1 Newcastle

Corners
Liverpool 8-2 Newcastle

HOW THEY LINED UP

Westerveld

Carragher Henchoz Hyypia Matteo

Thompson Gerrard Hamann Berger

Heskey Camara

Ferguson Shearer

Hughes, A Speed Lee Dyer Barton

Dabizas Howey Goma

Given

LIVERPOOL

Westerveld	6
Matteo	7
Henchoz	7
Hyypia	☆ 8
Carragher	6
Berger	6
Subbed: 86 mins (Murphy)	
Hamann	6
Gerrard	7
Subbed: 78 mins (Redknapp)	
Thompson	6
Subbed: 75 mins (Meijer)	
Camara ⚽	6
Goal: 51 mins	
Heskey	6
sub: Meijer	
sub: Murphy	
sub: Redknapp ⚽	
Goal: 88 mins	

Subs not used: Song, Friedel.

NEWCASTLE UNITED

Given	☆ 7
Hughes	6
Dabizas	6
Goma 🟨	6
Booked: 36 mins (foul); Subbed: 57 mins (Domi)	
Howey	6
Barton	5
Speed	6
Lee	6
Subbed: 65 mins (Gallacher)	
Dyer	7
Ferguson	5
Shearer ⚽	6
Goal: 67 mins	
sub: Domi	5
sub: Gallacher	7

Subs not used: Harper, Ketsbaia, Fumaca.

81

🦅 START OF MONTH **11th** 🦅 END OF MONTH **12th** 🦅

"We have to win things. The sign of a good side is how many pieces of silverware you have. At this moment Newcastle haven't had any for a very long time." Alan Shearer

NEWCASTLE CAPTAIN ALAN SHEARER SAID THAT THE SOONER THEY knocked down Wembley the better after his team lost at the Twin Towers for the third time in as many years. The Magpies got on the scoresheet through Rob Lee, but it was to no avail as another FA Cup dream was ended at the semi-final stage by two strikes from Chelsea's Gustavo Poyet. The match had become the focus of Newcastle's entire season and failing to reach the final left the club with an uncertain run-in to the rest of the campaign.

After the disappointment at Wembley, Bobby Robson's side lost to West Ham and Leicester City in the Premiership – a sequence of three successive defeats in six days – and it looked like United's season would peter out with a series of uninspiring performances. But the players didn't give up, earning a fighting draw with Leeds and a victory against Coventry at St James' Park. The Toon Army still expected passion and commitment and that was exactly what they were getting. The injury list, which had been a persistent handicap to Newcastle's season, still featured a number of first-teamers, with Laurent Charvet, Nikos Dabizas, Kevin Gallacher, Helder, Temuri Ketsbaia and Silvio Maric all needing attention. Maric's future on Tyneside looked bleak though when the club discovered that the Croatian's work permit was unlikely to be renewed for 2000-2001 because of his lack of first-team appearances.

Alan Shearer reached a landmark in April as he played his 150th game for The Magpies against Coventry, where he also scored his 299th career goal. Bobby Robson suggested that Kevin Keegan should not forget Rob Lee as the England manager began to finalise his squad for Euro 2000. Alessandro Pistone returned to match fitness by playing in the reserves, but all this was merely news from the periphery. Despite securing their Premiership status, Newcastle's chance of silverware had disappeared for another season.

NEWCASTLE UNITED

THE GAMES

Apr. 1 v **Bradford** (h)

Apr. 9 v **Chelsea** (n)

Apr. 12 v **West Ham** (a)

Apr. 15 v **Leicester** (h)

Apr. 23 v **Leeds** (h)

Apr. 29 v **Coventry** (h)

TRANSFERS IN

None

TRANSFERS OUT

None

MATCHfacts

Matchman Of The Month

ROBERT LEE
Average Rating: 7.00

83

Warren Barton starts another attacking move in United's 2-0 victory over Bradford.

FROM THE PAGES OF *MATCH*

During a rollercoaster season that started badly but improved dramatically after Bobby Robson's appointment, **ALAN SHEARER** told **MATCH** about the highs and lows of the 1999-200 campaign.

Was it heartbreaking to see the club doing so badly earlier in the season? *"It wasn't nice, but I'm part of the club so I've had to take my responsibilities as the captain as well. It's not nice when you're losing games and the longer it is you get beaten, the harder it becomes to win games – and that's how it was at the start of the season."*

So did you ever consider leaving the club? *"No. I signed for Newcastle United for a number of different reasons and the most important reason was to win things. We haven't done that yet, but I'm not going to quit the club. I'm not going to give up until we've won something."*

Is success now expected at St James' Park? *"We have to win things. The sign of any good side is how many pieces of silverware you have at the end of the season. At the moment Newcastle haven't had any for a very long time but we're all here to make that change."*

People really sat up and took notice after the win over Manchester United, but was that a one-off? *"I wouldn't say it was a one-off performance. I think we're capable of putting in a performance like that every week, but it was nice to know that we'd beaten the best team in Europe – and deservedly beaten them, too."*

Newcastle United (1) 2
Bradford City (0) 0

Competition: **FA Carling Premiership**

Date: **Saturday April 1, 2000**

Attendance: **36,572**

Referee: **A D'Urso** (Billericay) 5

Game 43

THE GAME: Gary Speed's ninth goal of the season and Alan Shearer's 26th strike were enough to seal a 2-0 win in front of the Toon Army against Bradford City. This wasn't a convincing performance, but the partnership of Helder and Alain Goma in defence looked impressive. Newcastle were guilty of missing a host of chances in front of goal, with Kieron Dyer, Duncan Ferguson, Robert Lee, Didier Domi and Shearer going close. Thankfully, at the other end, Steve Harper was in good form in goal and made a number of vital saves. The victory finally assured the club's Premiership status and took some of the pressure off the side before their FA Cup semi-final.

NEWCASTLE GOALS: Speed (6 mins): Headed home a Dyer corner from six yards out; **Shearer** (89 mins): Blasted a shot into the top right-hand corner from the edge of the area after being set up by Speed.

MATCH RATING: ★★ **LEAGUE POSITION:** 11th

"Steve Harper did very well making the save of the match while Alan Shearer scored a goal with a brilliant strike. But I was especially pleased with my central defenders Helder and Alain Goma. The whole team has left me with a nice selection problem for the FA Cup." BOBBY ROBSON

NEWCASTLE UNITED	
Harper	6
Barton	7
Hughes	7
Goma	7
Helder	☆8
Speed ⚽	7
Goal: 6 mins	
Lee	7
Dyer	6
Subbed 73 mins (Ketsbaia)	
Domi	7
Shearer ⚽	7
Goal: 89 mins	
Ferguson	6
sub: *Ketsbaia*	
Subs not used: Given, Marcelino, Maric, Fumaca.	

BRADFORD CITY	
Clarke	6
Halle ▯	6
Booked: 62 mins (foul)	
Jacobs	7
Wetherall	☆8
O'Brien	7
McCall	6
Windass	6
Sharpe	6
Subbed (66 mins) (Blake)	
Dreyer	6
Subbed 70 mins (Cadete)	
Beagrie	6
Saunders	6
sub: *Blake*	6
sub: *Cadete*	6
Subs not used: Westwood, Todd, Davison.	

MATCH FACTS

Shots On Target
Newcastle 7-3 Bradford

Shots Off Target
Newcastle 11-1 Bradford

Hit Woodwork
Newcastle 0-0 Bradford

Corners
Newcastle 9-2 Bradford

HOW THEY LINED UP

Harper

Barton — Goma — Helder — Hughes

Dyer — Lee — Speed — Domi

Shearer — Ferguson

Saunders — Windass

Sharpe — Dreyer — McCall — Beagrie

Jacobs — O'Brien — Wetherall — Halle

Clarke

Rob Lee equalised, but Chelsea regained the lead within six minutes to book their place in the final against Aston Villa.

United's miserable week continued with defeat at a rain-swept Upton Park.

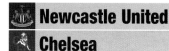

Newcastle United (0) 1
Chelsea (1) 2

Competition: FA Cup Semi-Final

Game 44

Date: **Sunday April 9, 2000**

Attendance: **73,876**

Referee: **D Gallagher** (Banbury) 6

NEWCASTLE UNITED

Given	7
Barton	7
Hughes	6
Subbed: 79 mins (Ketsbaia)	
Howey	7
Dabizas	7
Solano	8
Speed	7
Lee ⚽	7
Goal: 65 mins	
Dyer	8
Shearer	⭐ 8
Ferguson	6
Subbed: 38 mins (Domi)	
sub: *Domi*	7
sub: *Ketsbaia*	
Subs not used: Harper, Goma, Gavilan.	

CHELSEA

de Goey	8
Ferrer	7
Subbed: 74 mins (Petrescu)	
Harley	7
Leboeuf	7
Desailly	7
Di Matteo	6
Deschamps 🟨	7
Booked: 75 mins (foul)	
Wise	8
Poyet ⚽⚽	⭐ 9
Goals: 16, 71 mins	
Sutton	5
Subbed: 46 mins (Flo)	
Weah	7
Subbed: 79 mins (Zola)	
sub: *Flo*	0
sub: *Petrescu*	
sub: *Zola*	
Subs not used: Cudicini, Hogh.	

THE GAME: Rob Lee scored United's first goal at Wembley since the 1976 League Cup Final but it wasn't enough to take his team through to their third successive FA Cup Final. The Magpies, who recalled Shay Given, Nikos Dabizas, Nolberto Solano and Steve Howey to the starting line-up, dominated the game for long spells and created more chances than their semi-final opponents, but it was the superior finishing power of Gianluca Vialli's side that won the match. Solano was the main culprit, missing several chances, while Gustavo Poyet was Chelsea's two-goal hero. The Magpies took control of the midfield and were effective out wide with Solano and Didier Domi, but they couldn't score the goals to take them through to the final. The fact that Newcastle had 14 shots at goal to Chelsea's nine told its own story. To add to the pain, this was Alan Shearer's sixth Wembley defeat at club level.

NEWCASTLE GOAL: Lee *(65 mins):* Shearer sent in a good cross from the right which Lee headed powerfully into the top corner from seven yards.

CHELSEA GOALS: Poyet *(16 mins):* Weah chipped the ball forward to Poyet, who lobbed the ball over goalkeeper Given; **Poyet** *(71 mins):* As Dyer lay injured, Harley raced forward and swung in a looping cross for Poyet to head in from six yards.

MATCH RATING: ★★★★ **LEAGUE POSITION:** 11th

MATCH FACTS

Shots On Target
Newcastle 8-4 Chelsea

Shots Off Target
Newcastle 0-5 Chelsea

Hit Woodwork
Newcastle 0-0 Chelsea

Corners
Newcastle 11-2 Chelsea

HOW THEY LINED UP

Given

Barton · Howey · Dabizas · Hughes

Solano · Lee · Speed · Dyer

Shearer · Ferguson

Weah · Sutton

Poyet · Wise · Deschamps · Di Matteo

Harley · Leboeuf · Desailly · Ferrer

de Goey

West Ham United (0) 2
Newcastle United (0) 1

Competition: FA Carling Premiership

Game 45

Date: **Wednesday April 12, 2000**

Attendance: **25,817**

Referee: **P Alcock** (Halstead) 7

THE GAME: Bobby Robson's side were defeated in London for the second time in four days against West Ham, meaning they hadn't won a game in the capital since 1997. Newcastle started brightly at Upton Park despite their FA Cup hangover, with Kieron Dyer and Alan Shearer hitting the post. They took the lead through Gary Speed shortly after the break, but then conceded their advantage and ended the match without even a share of the points. The arrival of Hammers substitute Paulo Wanchope in the second half proved United's undoing as he scored both of West Ham's goals. The Costa Rican striker had been subjected to criticism from his own supporters before this game but scored the winning goal in the 89th minute.

WEST HAM GOALS: Wanchope *(60 mins):* Charles set off on a run down the right wing and crossed for Wanchope to head past Given; **Wanchope** *(89 mins):* Wanchope fired home after the Newcastle defence was completely wrong-footed by Di Canio's neat backheel in the United area.

NEWCASTLE GOAL: Speed *(47 mins):* Speed gave United the lead with a 15-yard left-foot shot past 'keeper Forrest.

MATCH RATING: ★★★ **LEAGUE POSITION:** 11th

> "I know the fans have got frustrated with us sometimes this season. We understand, but we never go out not to play football. Some days it doesn't happen, but at least on those days now we battle and get results where maybe that wasn't happening before." **AARON HUGHES**

Newcastle United (0) 0
Leicester City (1) 2

Competition: FA Carling Premiership
Date: Saturday April 15, 2000
Attendance: 36,426
Referee: U Rennie (Sheffield) 8

Game 46

THE GAME: The Toon Army expressed its dissatisfaction as Newcastle put in a poor, disjointed performance on their way to a third successive defeat in six days, but their cause wasn't helped by injuries to Duncan Ferguson, Nikos Dabizas, Kevin Gallacher, Helder, Silvio Maric and Temuri Ketsbaia. It could have been a completely different story if Didier Domi's effort hadn't hit the woodwork or if Gary Speed's shot hadn't been superbly blocked on the line by Phil Gilchrist – it just wasn't Newcastle's day. The service to the front two was particularly poor, with Domi and Nol Solano strangely off-form. Goals from Leicester's Tony Cottee and Robbie Savage sealed the points for The Foxes and ended a miserable week for The Magpies and their disappointed black and white fans.

LEICESTER GOALS: Cottee (7 mins): Newcastle's defence failed to clear Impey's low cross and allowed Cottee to shoot past Given; **Savage** (52 mins): Savage's free run across the area ended with a powerful 16-yard shot into the net.

MATCH RATING: ★★ **LEAGUE POSITION:** 11th

> "Gerry Taggart did well against Alan Shearer, but I know how much respect he has for him because he spent an hour and a half in the toilet." MARTIN O'NEILL

WEST HAM UNITED

Forrest	6
Ferdinand	7
Ruddock	6
Subbed: 53 mins (Wanchope)	
Stimac ▯	6
Booked: 66 mins (foul); Subbed: 78 mins (Margas)	
Keller	5
Subbed: 53 mins (Charles)	
Minto ▯	6
Booked: 57 mins (foul)	
Lampard	6
Cole	7
Foe	7
Kanoute	7
di Canio	7
sub: Charles	6
sub: Wanchope ⊕ ⊕ ☆	8
Goals: 60, 89 mins	
sub: Margas	
Subs not used: Feuer, Newton.	

NEWCASTLE UNITED

Given	7
Barton	7
Goma	7
Hughes	6
Dabizas	7
Subbed: 49 mins (Howey)	
Domi	6
Solano ▯	☆ 8
Booked: 80 mins (foul)	
Lee ▯	7
Booked: 64 mins (foul)	
Speed ⊕	7
Goal: 47 mins	
Dyer	7
Subbed: 86 mins (Ketsbaia)	
Shearer	6
sub: Howey	5
sub: Ketsbaia	
Subs not used: Harper, Gavilan, Marcelino.	

NEWCASTLE UNITED

Given	5
Barton	5
Hughes	5
Subbed: 68 mins (Robinson)	
Goma	5
Howey	5
Solano	5
Subbed: 68 mins (Gavilan)	
Lee	☆ 6
Speed	5
Domi	5
Dyer	5
Subbed: 80 mins (Fumaca)	
Shearer	5
sub: Gavilan	5
sub: Robinson	5
sub: Fumaca	
Subs not used: Harper, Griffin.	

LEICESTER CITY

Flowers	8
Sinclair	5
Taggart	8
Gilchrist	8
Lennon	7
Guppy	6
Savage ⊕	☆ 9
Goal: 52 mins; Subbed: 81 mins (Zagorakis)	
Impey	8
Oakes	6
Subbed: 68 mins (Marshall)	
Cottee ⊕	7
Goal: 7 mins	
Elliott	8
sub: Marshall	6
sub: Zagorakis	
Subs not used: Walsh, Arphexad, Dudfield.	

WEST HAM / MATCH FACTS

Shots On Target
West Ham 3-4 Newcastle
Shots Off Target
West Ham 5-4 Newcastle
Hit Woodwork
West Ham 0-2 Newcastle
Corners
West Ham 3-4 Newcastle

HOW THEY LINED UP

Forrest

Ferdinand · Ruddock · Stimac · Minto

Cole · Foe · Lampard · Keller

Kanoute · di Canio

Dyer · Shearer

Domi · Speed · Lee · Solano

Hughes · Dabizas · Goma · Barton

Given

NEWCASTLE / MATCH FACTS

Shots On Target
Newcastle 2-2 Leicester
Shots Off Target
Newcastle 6-1 Leicester
Hit Woodwork
Newcastle 1-0 Leicester
Corners
Newcastle 6-3 Leicester

HOW THEY LINED UP

Given

Barton · Goma · Howey · Hughes

Solano · Lee · Speed · Domi

Dyer

Shearer

Cottee · Elliott

Oakes · Lennon · Savage

Guppy · Gilchrist · Taggart · Sinclair · Impey

Flowers

Newcastle United (1) 2
Leeds United (2) 2

Competition: FA Carling Premiership

Date: Sunday April 23, 2000

Attendance: 36,460

Referee: D Elleray (Harrow) 5

Game 47

THE GAME: A partially-fit Alan Shearer was the only striker available to Bobby Robson for this game against Leeds, but the captain still managed to score both goals to earn United a draw at St James' Park. Kieron Dyer hit the post after just 45 seconds, but Leeds – who were without a victory in seven games – were 2-0 ahead by the 17th minute and things were looking bleak for the Toon Army. Shearer came to the rescue though, netting twice to level the scores. Ian Harte missed the chance to put Leeds back in front from the penalty spot, but by end of the game both sides were content with a point.

NEWCASTLE GOALS: Shearer (24 mins): Domi beat Wilcox to a clearance from a corner and sent over a cross for Shearer to head in from six yards; **Shearer** (48 mins): Leeds 'keeper Martyn was at fault as he dropped Domi's corner, allowing Shearer to pounce on the ball and score from close range.

LEEDS GOALS: Bridges (12 mins): Dabizas' sliced clearance from Wilcox's cross fell into the path of Bridges, who thumped the ball in from 12 yards; **Wilcox** (17 mins): A free-kick from Wilcox evaded everyone and ended up in the back of the net.

MATCH RATING: ★★★★ **LEAGUE POSITION: 12th**

NEWCASTLE UNITED	
Given	6
Barton	6
Hughes	7
Helder	6
Subbed: 65 mins (Marcelino)	
Howey	5
Lee	7
Dabizas	6
Gavilan	6
Subbed: 86 mins (Fumaca)	
Domi	8
Dyer	6
Subbed: 80 mins (Maric)	
Shearer ⊕ ⊕ ▢	☆ 9
Goals: 24, 48 mins; Booked: 75 mins (dissent)	
sub: Marcelino	6
sub: Maric	
sub: Fumaca	
Subs not used: Harper, McClen.	

LEEDS UNITED	
Martyn	5
Mills	6
Harte ▢	7
Booked: 41 mins (foul); Subbed: 77 mins (Bowyer)	
Radebe	6
Duberry	5
Haaland ▢	7
Booked: 22 mins (foul)	
McPhail	☆ 8
Bakke ▢	7
Booked: 90 mins (foul)	
Bridges ⊕	7
Goal: 12 mins; Subbed: 80 mins (Huckerby)	
Wilcox ⊕	7
Goal: 17 mins	
Kewell ▢	7
Booked: 69 mins (unsporting behaviour)	
sub: Bowyer	
sub: Huckerby	
Subs not used: Hopkin, Robinson, Smith.	

MATCH FACTS

Shots On Target
Newcastle 7-5 Leeds

Shots Off Target
Newcastle 3 7 Leeds

Hit Woodwork
Newcastle 1-0 Leeds

Corners
Newcastle 7-6 Leeds

HOW THEY LINED UP

Given

Barton — Howey — Helder — Hughes

Gavilan — Lee — Dabizas — Domi

Shearer — Dyer

Kewell — Bridges

Wilcox — McPhail — Haaland — Bakke

Harte — Duberry — Radebe — Mills

Martyn

Newcastle staged an impressive fightback after Leeds raced into an early lead at St James' Park.

THIS WEEK...

IN THE NEWS

NEWCASTLE UNITED: Bobby Robson praises **Alan Shearer** for the captain's performances since he took over at the club. "He has been our Player Of The Season in my opinion," insists Robson... **Kieron Dyer** has settled so well on Tyneside that he claims he wants to stay with Newcastle for the next ten years... The Magpies are said to be planning a £3 million bid for Benfica midfielder **Jose Calado**... **Alessandro Pistone** plays a full game, in the reserves, for the first time since breaking his leg against Sunderland in February.

PREMIERSHIP: Man. United claim their sixth Premiership title in eight years... Arsenal reach the final of the UEFA Cup for the first time in 30 years. They face Galatasaray, conquerors of Leeds United in the semi-finals of the competition.

Newcastle United (0) 2
Coventry City (0) 0

Competition: **FA Carling Premiership**

Date: **Saturday April 29, 2000**

Attendance: **36,408**

Referee: **P Jones** (Loughborough) 7

Game 48

THE GAME: Alan Shearer marked his 150th game for United by scoring the 299th goal of his career. The captain broke the deadlock in this scrappy game against Coventry, converting from the penalty spot after a handball in the area. Alessandro Pistone returned to the first-team after a three-month absence and only one reserve game under his belt, and the left-back impressed in Newcastle's defence. But no-one questioned the Man Of The Match after seeing Robert Lee control the games from midfield. Diego Gavilan made sure of the three points with his first goal for The Magpies and it was a good end to the month for the Toon Army with only three games left.

NEWCASTLE GOALS: Shearer *(penalty 78 mins):* Shearer converted the spot-kick after Williams was adjudged to have handled in the Coventry area; **Gavilan** *(84 mins):* Scored with a powerful right-foot shot from just inside the penalty area.

MATCH RATING: ★★ **LEAGUE POSITION: 12th**

> **"I don't have to recommend Robert Lee to Kevin Keegan. Kevin knows what he can do – after all, he bought him during his time at Newcastle. Rob's one of England's most constructive players, he keeps things simple and keeps us ticking over."** BOBBY ROBSON

NEWCASTLE UNITED

Given	7
Barton	7
Pistone	7
Hughes	7
Dabizas	7
Gavilan ⊕	7
Goal: 84 mins; Subbed: 88 mins (Griffin)	
Speed	7
Lee	☆ 8
Subbed: 88 mins (McClen)	
Domi	6
Subbed: 39 mins (Ketsbaia)	
Dyer	7
Shearer ⊕	7
Goal: 78 mins	
sub: Ketsbaia	6
sub: Griffin	
sub: McClen	

Subs not used: Harper, Maric.

COVENTRY CITY

Hedman	☆ 7
Shaw	6
Williams ▢	6
Booked: 25 mins (foul)	
Breen	6
Telfer	6
McAllister ▢	6
Booked: 79 mins (dissent)	
Chippo	6
Hadji	6
Roussel	5
Subbed: 64 mins (Eustace)	
Whelan	5
Subbed: 88 mins (Betts)	
Keane	5
Subbed: 85 mins (Zuniga)	
sub: Eustace	5
sub: Zuniga	
sub: Betts	

Subs not used: Ogrizovic, Fowler.

MATCH FACTS

Shots On Target
Newcastle 5-3 Coventry

Shots Off Target
Newcastle 7-2 Coventry

Hit Woodwork
Newcastle 0-0 Coventry

Corners
Newcastle 6-2 Coventry

HOW THEY LINED UP

Given

Barton Dabizas Hughes Pistone

Gavilan Lee Speed Domi

Dyer

Shearer

Roussel Keane

Whelan McAllister Chippo Hadji

Shaw Williams Breen Telfer

Hedman

THE FINAL SCORE!

APRIL 16		
Leeds	0-4	**Arsenal**
Wimbledon	1-2	**Liverpool**
APRIL 19		
Leicester	0-1	**Tottenham**
APRIL 21		
Bradford	4-4	Derby
Everton	0-0	Liverpool
APRIL 22		
Aston Villa	2-2	Leicester
Chelsea	1-1	Middlesbrough
Sheff. Wed.	0-2	**Sunderland**
Southampton	1-3	**Man. United**
Tottenham	2-0	Wimbledon
West Ham	5-0	Coventry
APRIL 23		
Newcastle	2-2	Leeds
Watford	2-3	**Arsenal**
APRIL 24		
Derby	2-0	Southampton
Man. United	3-2	Chelsea
Sunderland	0-1	**Bradford**
APRIL 29		
Aston Villa	1-1	Sunderland
Chelsea	2-0	Liverpool
Everton	0-1	**Arsenal**
Newcastle	2-0	Coventry
Southampton	1-2	**Leicester**
Tottenham	1-1	Derby
Watford	2-3	**Man. United**
West Ham	0-1	**Middlesbrough**
APRIL 30		
Bradford	3-0	Wimbledon
Sheff. Wed.	0-3	**Leeds**

TOP OF THE PREMIERSHIP

	P	W	D	L	Pts
1. Man. United	36	26	7	3	85
2. Arsenal	34	20	6	8	66
3. Liverpool	35	19	9	7	66
12. Newcastle	35	13	8	14	47

MAY

"I'm a very proud man. When I set out at Southampton I never dreamed that I would score 300 goals. To do it at the age of 29 makes me very happy." Alan Shearer

AFTER NEWCASTLE'S WORST START TO A CAMPAIGN FOR 40 YEARS which left them in a battle for Premiership survival, The Magpies finished in a respectable 11th place. The transformation from relegation candidates to FA Cup semi-finalists was achieved by the inspirational Bobby Robson, who ended the season with a five-game unbeaten run, culminating in the thrilling 4-2 defeat of Arsenal. It gave Newcastle their 14th league win of the season and 51 points from Robson's 32 games in charge. Considering the injuries that blighted the squad throughout the season, United's final position in the Premiership and their excellent run in the FA Cup was a fine achievement.

The Magpies showed that they have a vast array of talent on their books, and with two or three more signings they'll be able to mount a more serious challenge in the 2000-2001 season. Bobby Robson made it clear that the close season would be spent strengthening the squad in a bid to challenge for silverware next season. To that end, head coach Mick Wadsworth flew to Argentina to watch midfielder Christian Bassedas playing for Velez Sarsfield. The manager knew that he had to buy wisely, though, after a financial report revealed Newcastle had spent more on transfers over five years than any other Premiership club but with no silverware to show for the expenditure.

The last month of the season saw a 2-2 draw with Middlesbrough at The Riverside in an exciting north-east derby, a goalless draw at Derby and the 4-2 thriller with The Gunners at St James' Park. Coach Steve Clarke, who had been named United's caretaker boss earlier in the season, announced his resignation, while a Newcastle old boy, Peter Beardsley, returned to the club as youth team coach. Alan Shearer flew out to Euro 2000 to play his final games for England, while a disappointed Kieron Dyer narrowly missed out on the tournament after failing to make Kevin Keegan's 22-man squad.

THE GAMES

May 2 v **Middlesbrough** (a)

May 6 v **Derby County** (a)

May 14 v **Arsenal** (h)

TRANSFERS IN

None

TRANSFERS OUT

None

MATCH facts

Matchman Of The Month

GARY SPEED
Average Rating: 8.00

Middlesbrough	(1) 2
Newcastle United	(2) 2

Competition: FA Carling Premiership

Date: Tuesday May 2, 2000

Attendance: 34,744

Game 49

Referee: M Riley (Leeds) 7

THE GAME: Honours finished even in this fast and furious north-east derby that could have gone either way. The home side were all at sea in the opening stages of the game, even after taking the lead, and United threatened to run riot. Gary Speed equalised soon after Juninho's strike and Alessandro Pistone put Newcastle ahead with his first goal for the club. The Magpies were particularly dangerous on the right wing, where Kieron Dyer and Nolberto Solano combined well, but Middlesbrough then scored a controversial equaliser when it seemed Dyer was fouled in the build-up to Festa's goal.

MIDDLESBROUGH GOALS: Juninho (5 mins): Cooper sent in a curling cross that Juninho headed past Given from eight yards out; **Festa** (78 mins): Scored with a diving header from six yards after a good cross from Stockdale.

NEWCASTLE GOALS: Speed (10 mins): Dyer cut the ball back for Speed to score with a right-foot drive that crept just inside the post from 12 yards out; **Pistone** (19 mins): Solano's corner was headed clear, but only to Shearer, who headed the ball down for Pistone to score past 'keeper Schwarzer.

MATCH RATING: ★★★ **LEAGUE POSITION:** 12th

MIDDLESBROUGH		NEWCASTLE UNITED	
Schwarzer	6	Given	6
Fleming	6	Barton	6
Vickers ▢	6	Hughes	7
Booked: 12 mins (foul)		Dabizas	6
Festa ⊕	7	Pistone ⊕	7
Goal: 78 mins		Goal: 19 mins	
Cooper	☆ 8	Solano	☆ 8
Ziege ▢	6	Subbed: 86 mins (Griffin)	
Booked: 63 mins (unsporting behaviour); Subbed: 74 mins (Stockdale)		Lee	6
Juninho ⊕	7	Speed ⊕	7
Goal: 5 mins		Goal: 10 mins	
Ince	6	Dyer	7
Summerbell		Subbed: 83 mins (McClen)	
Subbed: 14 mins (Mustoe)		Ketsbaia	6
Ricard	7	Subbed: 87 mins (Maric)	
Campbell	6	Shearer	6
Subbed: 87 mins (Kilgannon)		sub: McClen	
sub: Mustoe	7	sub: Griffin	
sub: Stockdale		sub: Maric	
sub: Kilgannon		Subs not used: Harper, Gavilan.	
Subs not used: Beresford, Maddison.			

MATCH FACTS
Shots On Target
Middlesbrough 7-4 Newcastle
Shots Off Target
Middlesbrough 7-6 Newcastle
Hit Woodwork
Middlesbrough 0-0 Newcastle
Corners
Middlesbrough 5-5 Newcastle

HOW THEY LINED UP

Schwarzer

Festa Vickers Cooper

Summerbell Ince Ziege Fleming

Juninho

Campbell Ricard

Shearer

Ketsbaia Dyer

Pistone Speed Lee Solano

Hughes Dabizas Barton

Given

Shearer and Vickers share one of their many tussles in the north-east derby.

There was plenty of pride but little quality in United's away draw at struggling Derby.

IN THE NEWS

NEWCASTLE UNITED: Bobby Robson doesn't appear for the post-match press conference after the draw at Middlesbrough, saying he was far too angry and might say something he would regret… Newspaper speculation links Bobby Robson with a £15 million joint bid for Barcelona pair **Josep Guardiola** and **Luis Enrique**… Dutch midfielder **Paul Bosvelt** is linked with a transfer to St James' Park… **Kieron Dyer** pleas with the Newcastle board not to sell winger **Nolberto Solano** following overtures from Real Madrid… The Magpies are linked with a move to sign Wimbledon's out-of-contract Scotland 'keeper **Neil Sullivan**… Bobby Robson offers UEFA Cup finalists Arsenal the chance to switch their last game of the season from Sunday to Saturday to help The Gunners in Europe… Turkish side Galatasaray are given the cold-shoulder by Newcastle as they declare an interest in making Bobby Robson their new manager.

PREMIERSHIP: Wimbledon's boss Egil Olsen is sacked by the club's Norwegian owners… Manchester United captain **Roy Keane** is voted the 2000 Footballer Of The Year.

Derby County (0) 0
Newcastle United (0) 0

Competition: **FA Carling Premiership**

Date: **Saturday May 6, 2000**

Attendance: **32,724**

Referee: **A Wiley** (Burntwood) 5

Game 50

THE GAME: Newcastle's last away match of the season was described by Bobby Robson as "Our drabbest display since September". There was little to be enthusiastic about for the Toon Army in what looked like a winding down match at the end of a long season. Derby were more interested in holding on for a draw, but this was understandable considering that Jim Smith's side were still not clear of the relegation fight in the Premiership. In keeping a clean sheet, Shay Given made an impressive save from Derby midfielder Adam Murray, while Alessandro Pistone was forced to clear soon afterwards when Georgi Kinkladze – easily the most dangerous player on the pitch – saw his fine chip rebound off the bar. This may have been a forgettable game for United, but at least they weren't regressing to the form they showed at the start of the season.

MATCH RATING: ★★★ **LEAGUE POSITION:** 12th

"The pitch deserved better." ALAN SHEARER

DERBY COUNTY

Poom	7
Laursen	6
Subbed: 90 mins (Jackson)	
Carbonari ☐	7
Booked: 68 mins (foul)	
Schnoor	7
Dorigo	7
Burley	6
Powell	0
Murray	7
Subbed: 58 mins (Bohinen)	
Kinkladze	☆ 8
Subbed: 46 mins (Sturridge)	
Christie	6
Burton	7
sub: Sturridge	7
sub: Bohinen	6
sub: Jackson	
Subs not used: Oakes, Elliott.	

NEWCASTLE UNITED

Given	7
Barton	7
Hughes	6
Dabizas	7
Pistone	
Subbed: 12 mins (Domi)	
Dyer	6
Lee ☐	7
Booked: 16 mins (foul)	
Speed	☆ 7
Solano	6
Subbed: 65 mins (Gallacher)	
Shearer	6
Ketsbaia	6
Subbed: 84 mins (Gavilan)	
sub: Domi	7
sub: Gallacher	6
sub: Gavilan	
Subs not used: Karelse, Maric.	

MATCH FACTS

Shots On Target
Derby 5-2 Newcastle

Shots Off Target
Derby 1-4 Newcastle

Hit Woodwork
Derby 1-0 Newcastle

Corners
Derby 5-2 Newcastle

HOW THEY LINED UP

```
                    Poom
   Laursen  Carbonari  Schnoor  Dorigo
      Burley  Murray  Powell  Kinkladze
            Christie   Burton

            Shearer   Ketsbaia
                  Dyer
      Speed     Lee     Solano
   Pistone  Dabizas  Hughes  Barton
                  Given
```

THE FINAL SCORE!

MAY 2		
Arsenal	2-1	West Ham
Middlesbrough	2-2	Newcastle
MAY 3		
Leeds	3-1	Watford
Liverpool	0-2	Leicester
MAY 6		
Arsenal	2-1	Chelsea
Coventry	4-1	Sheff. Wed.
Derby	0-0	Newcastle
Leicester	3-0	Bradford
Man. United	3-1	Tottenham
Middlesbrough	1-1	Watford
Sunderland	1-0	West Ham
Wimbledon	2-2	Aston Villa

TOP OF THE PREMIERSHIP

	P	W	D	L	Pts
1. Man. United	37	27	7	3	88
2. Arsenal	36	22	6	8	72
3. Leeds	36	21	4	11	67
12. Newcastle	37	13	10	14	49

The Magpies ended the season with a convincing win against Arsenal at St James' Park.

 Newcastle United (2) **4**

 Arsenal (1) **2**

Competition: **FA Carling Premiership**

Date: **Sunday May 14, 2000**

Attendance: **36,450**

Referee: **G Poll** (Tring) 7

Game 51

THE GAME: Newcastle's 51st and last competitive match of the season was a real thriller and dispelled any thoughts of early summer holidays after the previous week's lacklustre performance at Derby. Alan Shearer scored the 300th goal of his career as Newcastle tore apart a depleted Gunners side which had one eye on the UEFA Cup Final. Shearer said his 23rd minute strike was one of the best goals he'd ever scored as Bobby Robson's side romped to a 4-2 victory. Gary Speed also reached a milestone, scoring his 13th of the season – his best tally ever and a fine end to an eventful season for United.

NEWCASTLE GOALS: Speed (6 mins): Collected Shearer's overhead pass to slot the ball home with a fine first-time shot; **Shearer** (23 mins): Unleashed an explosive free-kick that tore into the net; **Speed** (59 mins): Solano's corner found Speed, unmarked, to head home; **Griffin** (63 mins): Solano carved out the chance for Griffin to shoot past Manninger from 12 yards.

ARSENAL GOALS: Kanu (7 mins): The Nigerian equalised within 45 seconds of Speed's opener, lobbing the goalkeeper after being set up by Suker; **Malz** (53 mins): Managed to hold off the attentions of Barton before shooting beyond Given.

MATCH RATING: ★★★★ **LEAGUE POSITION:** 11th

NEWCASTLE UNITED	
Given	7
Barton	7
Howey	7
Dabizas	7
Griffin ⚽	7
Goal: 63 mins	
Lee	8
Subbed: 89 mins (McClen)	
Speed ⚽⚽	☆ 9
Goals: 6, 59 mins	
Solano	7
Subbed: 85 mins (Maric)	
Dyer	7
Ketsbaia	6
Subbed: 77 mins (Gallacher)	
Shearer ⚽	8
Goal: 23 mins	
sub: Gallacher	
sub: Maric	
sub: McClen	
Subs not used: Perez, Goma.	

ARSENAL	
Manninger	6
Weston	6
Subbed: 67 mins (McGovern)	
Luzhny	6
Winterburn	6
Keown	7
Parlour	6
Subbed: 46 mins (Silvinho)	
Malz ⚽	☆ 8
Goal: 53 mins	
Vernazza	7
Cole	6
Kanu ⚽	6
Goal: 7 mins; Subbed: 71 mins (Gray)	
Suker ▢	6
Booked: 58 mins (foul)	
sub: Silvinho	6
sub: McGovern	6
sub: Gray	
Subs not used: Black, Lukic.	

MATCH FACTS

Shots On Target

Newcastle 8-7 Arsenal

Shots Off Target

Newcastle 9-6 Arsenal

Hit Woodwork

Newcastle 0-0 Arsenal

Corners

Newcastle 6-4 Arsenal

HOW THEY LINED UP

Given

Barton   Howey   Dabizas   Griffin

Solano   Lee   Speed   Dyer

Shearer   Ketsbaia

Kanu   Suker

Winterburn   Malz   Vernazza   Parlour

Cole   Weston   Keown   Luzhny

Manninger

IN THE NEWS

NEWCASTLE UNITED: Senior coach Steve Clarke, Ruud Gullit's first signing after joining in August 1998, quits the club… Peter Beardsley is offered the job of Newcastle United youth coach… Head coach Mick Wadsworth flies to Argentina to watch Velez Sarsfield's central midfield star **Christian Bassedas**… A report by Deloitte & Touche says Newcastle have spent more on transfers over the previous five years than any other Premiership club, having paid £61.5 million for new players.

PREMIERSHIP: Man. United win the Premiership for the sixth time with a record end of season run of 11 successive victories… Arsenal and Leeds United also qualify for the European Champions League but Sheffield Wednesday, Watford and Wimbledon are relegated… Sunderland striker **Kevin Phillips** finishes as the Premiership's top scorer with a total of 30 goals, while Newcastle's **Alan Shearer** is second on 23 goals… Chelsea beat Aston Villa to win the FA Cup and Arsenal lose the UEFA Cup Final to Turkish side Galatasaray.

THE FINAL SCORE!

MAY 7		
Liverpool	0-0	Southampton

MAY 8		
Leeds	1-1	Everton

MAY 9		
Arsenal	3-3	Sheff. Wed

MAY 14		
Aston Villa	0-1	**Man. United**
Bradford	1-0	Liverpool
Chelsea	4-0	Derby
Everton	0-2	**Middlesbrough**
Newcastle	4-2	Arsenal
Sheff. Wed.	4-0	Leicester
Southampton	2-0	Wimbledon
Tottenham	3-1	Sunderland
Watford	1-0	Coventry
West Ham	0-0	Leeds

TOP OF THE PREMIERSHIP

	P	W	D	L	Pts
1. Man. United	38	28	7	3	91
2. Arsenal	38	22	7	9	73
3. Leeds	38	21	6	11	69
11. Newcastle	38	14	10	14	52

1999-2000 SQUAD Games/Goals

NAME	LGE	UC	FA	WC	TOTAL
1. Shay **Given**	14/0	0/0	2/0	1/0	**17/0**
2. Warren **Barton**	34/0	5/0	6/0	1/0	**46/0**
3. Elena **Marcelino**	11/0	2/0	2/0	0/0	**15/0**
4. Didier **Domi**	27/3	4/0	4/1	1/0	**36/4**
5. Alain **Goma**	14/0	2/0	0/0	1/0	**17/0**
6. Steve **Howey**	9/0	0/0	1/0	0/0	**10/0**
7. Kieron **Dyer**	30/3	3/0	6/1	0/0	**39/4**
8. Franck **Dumas**	6/0	1/0	0/0	0/0	**7/0**
8. Diego **Gavilan**	6/1	0/0	0/0	0/0	**6/1**
9. Alan **Shearer**	37/23	6/2	6/5	1/0	**50/30**
10. Silvio **Maric**	13/0	3/2	1/0	1/0	**18/2**
11. Gary **Speed**	36/9	6/1	6/3	1/0	**49/13**
12. Andy **Griffin**	3/1	0/0	0/0	0/0	**3/1**
13. Steve **Harper**	18/0	6/0	4/0	1/0	**29/0**
14. Temuri **Ketsbaia**	21/0	3/1	4/0	0/0	**28/1**
15. Nolberto **Solano**	30/3	6/1	3/0	1/0	**40/4**
16. Laurent **Charvet**	2/0	2/0	1/0	0/0	**5/0**
17. Stephen **Glass**	7/1	3/0	1/0	1/0	**12/1**
18. Aaron **Hughes**	27/2	3/0	4/0	0/0	**34/2**
19. Jamie **McClen**	9/0	3/0	0/0	0/0	**12/0**
20. Duncan **Ferguson**	23/6	3/1	6/3	0/0	**32/10**
21. Carl **Serrant**	2/0	1/0	0/0	0/0	**3/0**
22. Gary **Caldwell**	0/0	0/0	0/0	0/0	**0/0**
23. Lionel **Perez**	0/0	0/0	0/0	0/0	**0/0**
24. Garry **Brady**	0/0	0/0	0/0	0/0	**0/0**
25. Brian **Kerr**	0/0	0/0	0/0	0/0	**0/0**
26. James **Coppinger**	0/0	0/0	0/0	0/0	**0/0**
27. David **Beharall**	2/0	0/0	0/0	0/0	**2/0**
28. Paul **Robinson**	9/0	4/1	0/0	1/0	**14/1**
29. John **Karelse**	3/0	0/0	0/0	0/0	**3/0**
30. Paul **Talbot**	0/0	0/0	0/0	0/0	**0/0**
30. Stephen **Caldwell**	0/0	0/0	0/0	0/0	**0/0**
31. Stuart **Green**	0/0	0/0	0/0	0/0	**0/0**
32. Tommy **Wright**	3/0	0/0	0/0	0/0	**3/0**
32. Kevin **Gallacher**	20/2	5/1	0/0	0/0	**25/3**
33. Des **Hamilton**	0/0	1/0	0/0	0/0	**1/0**
34. Nikos **Dabizas**	29/4	6/0	6/2	1/0	**42/6**
35. Stuart **Elliott**	0/0	0/0	0/0	0/0	**0/0**
36. Alessandro **Pistone**	15/1	2/0	3/0	1/0	**21/1**
37. Robert **Lee**	30/0	6/0	4/1	1/0	**41/1**
38. **Fumaca**	5/0	0/0	1/0	0/0	**6/0**
39. **Helder**	8/1	0/0	4/0	0/0	**12/1**

PREMIERSHIP MATCHMAN OF THE SEASON

PAOLO DI CANIO WAS NAMED THE PREMIERSHIP MATCHMAN OF the season after a sensational 1999-2000 season with West Ham. But he didn't have it all his own way, as many Newcastle stars proved in making the Premiership's top 150 players. The Magpies' top man – in 19th place with an average rating of 6.96 out of ten – was defender Nikos Dabizas. A consistent performer in Newcastle's back line, the underrated Greece international defender also contributed some vital and well-taken goals during the course of the season. Dabizas' nearest challenger, Rob Lee, was not even given a squad number by Ruud Gullit at the start of the season, so his achievement of finishing in 27th place with an average of 6.90 out of ten was particularly impressive. Newcastle's Mr Consistency, Warren Barton, finished a respectable 54th with 6.78, showing United's defence couldn't have been as bad as many critics liked to make out. Wales midfielder Gary Speed was next in 70th place with an average of 6.72, and surprisingly – despite scoring 23 goals in the Premiership last season – Alan Shearer's 6.69 average was only enough to lift the captain into 78th place. Nolberto Solano and Kieron Dyer came close behind in 82nd and 84th position respectively. In his first season in the top flight, Dyer's average of 6.65 proved his Premiership pedigree in a campaign where he made his England debut. Behind Dyer were fellow youngsters Didier Domi and Aaron Hughes, averaging 6.56 and 6.50 respectively.

1.	**PAOLO DI CANIO** *West Ham United*	29	13	7.48
2.	**Roy Keane** *Manchester United*	29	6	7.24
3.	**Paul Merson** *Aston Villa*	29	10	7.17
4.	**Harry Kewell** *Leeds United*	36	13	7.16
5.	**Thierry Henry** *Arsenal*	30	8	7.16
6.	**Neil Sullivan** *Wimbledon*	37	9	7.13
7.	**Dean Richards** *Southampton*	35	11	7.05
8.	**Tim Sherwood** *Tottenham Hotspur*	25	4	7.04
9.	**Don Hutchison** *Everton*	29	6	7.03
10.	**Ryan Giggs** *Manchester United*	30	5	7.03
11.	**Paul Ince** *Middlesbrough*	32	10	7.00
12.	**John Collins** *Everton*	34	8	7.00
13.	**Chris Makin** *Sunderland*	34	5	7.00
14.	**David Beckham** *Manchester United*	31	5	7.00
15.	**Jaap Stam** *Manchester United*	33	2	7.00
16.	**Richard Gough** *Everton*	29	2	7.00
17.	**David Ginola** *Tottenham Hotspur*	36	7	6.97
18.	**Carl Cort** *Wimbledon*	34	4	6.97
19.	**NIKOS DABIZAS** *Newcastle United*	29	4	6.96
=	**Sol Campbell** *Tottenham Hotspur*	29	4	6.96
21.	**Patrick Vieira** *Arsenal*	30	3	6.96
22.	**Darren Anderton** *Tottenham Hotspur*	22	6	6.95
23.	**Jamie Redknapp** *Liverpool*	19	4	6.94
24.	**Sami Hyypia** *Liverpool*	38	5	6.92
25.	**Matt Elliott** *Leicester City*	37	7	6.91
26.	**Muzzy Izzet** *Leicester City*	32	4	6.90
27.	**ROB LEE** *Newcastle United*	30	4	6.90
28.	**Ben Thatcher** *Wimbledon*	20	3	6.90
29.	**Gary McAllister** *Coventry City*	38	8	6.89
30.	**Niall Quinn** *Sunderland*	35	7	6.88
31.	**Stefan Schwarz** *Sunderland*	27	3	6.88
32.	**Martin Keown** *Arsenal*	27	0	6.88
33.	**Rio Ferdinand** *West Ham United*	33	3	6.87
34.	**Lucas Radebe** *Leeds United*	31	3	6.87
35.	**Thomas Sorensen** *Sunderland*	37	4	6.86
36.	**Kenny Cunningham** *Wimbledon*	37	2	6.86
37.	**Kevin Phillips** *Sunderland*	36	7	6.83

38.	Neil Lennon *Leicester City*	31	5	6.83
39.	Trevor Sinclair *West Ham United*	36	3	6.83
40.	Fredrik Ljungberg *Arsenal*	24	3	6.83
41.	Hermann Hreidarsson *Wimbledon*	24	2	6.83
42.	Christian Ziege *Middlesbrough*	29	5	6.82
43.	Mart Poom *Derby County*	28	4	6.82
44.	Lee Dixon *Arsenal*	28	1	6.82
45.	Magnus Hedman *Coventry City*	35	6	6.80
46.	Juninho *Middlesbrough*	25	6	6.80
47.	Emmanuel Petit *Arsenal*	26	3	6.80
48.	Paul Butler *Sunderland*	31	3	6.80
49.	Tony Adams *Arsenal*	21	0	6.80
50.	Robbie Earle *Wimbledon*	24	3	6.79
51.	Mark Schwarzer *Middlesbrough*	37	7	6.78
52.	David Wetherall *Bradford City*	38	4	6.78
53.	Chris Perry *Tottenham Hotspur*	37	2	6.78
54.	**WARREN BARTON** *Newcastle United*	**33**	**2**	**6.78**
55.	Gareth Southgate *Aston Villa*	31	8	6.77
56.	Gustavo Poyet *Chelsea*	31	6	6.77
57.	Marcus Gayle *Wimbledon*	36	5	6.77
58.	Paul Scholes *Manchester United*	31	4	6.77
59.	Gilles Grimandi *Arsenal*	27	0	6.77
60.	Stephen Carr *Tottenham Hotspur*	34	5	6.76
61.	Kevin Campbell *Everton*	26	1	6.76
62.	Frank Lampard *West Ham United*	34	0	6.76
63.	Dan Petrescu *Chelsea*	28	4	6.75
64.	Chris Armstrong *Tottenham Hotspur*	29	2	6.75
65.	David Seaman *Arsenal*	24	1	6.75
66.	Eirik Bakke *Leeds United*	27	4	6.74
=	Titi Camara *Liverpool*	27	4	6.74
68.	Jonathan Woodgate *Leeds United*	34	1	6.73
69.	Steve Bould *Sunderland*	19	1	6.73
70.	**GARY SPEED** *Newcastle United*	**36**	**2**	**6.72**
71.	Oyvind Leonhardsen *Tottenham Hotspur*	22	0	6.72
72.	Emile Heskey *Liverpool*	35	6	6.71
73.	Matt Clarke *Bradford City*	21	3	6.71
74.	Marc Overmars *Arsenal*	30	7	6.70
75.	Dennis Wise *Chelsea*	30	4	6.70
76.	Nordin Wooter *Watford*	20	3	6.70
77.	Mustapha Hadji *Coventry City*	33	7	6.69
78.	**ALAN SHEARER** *Newcastle United*	**36**	**4**	**6.69**
79.	Andy Cole *Manchester United*	26	4	6.69
80.	Denis Irwin *Manchester United*	25	1	6.68
81.	Paulo Wanchope *West Ham United*	34	6	6.67
82.	**NOLBERTO SOLANO** *Newcastle United*	**30**	**5**	**6.66**
83.	John Moncur *West Ham United*	21	1	6.66
84.	Brian Deane *Middlesbrough*	29	3	6.65
=	**KIERON DYER** *Newcastle United*	**29**	**3**	**6.65**
86.	Pavel Srnicek *Sheffield Wednesday*	20	1	6.65
87.	Silvinho *Arsenal*	29	0	6.65
88.	Steven Gerrard *Liverpool*	28	4	6.64
89.	Paul Jones *Southampton*	31	3	6.64
90.	Ian Walker *Tottenham Hotspur*	38	2	6.63
91.	Nigel Winterburn *Arsenal*	22	0	6.63
92.	Nick Barmby *Everton*	37	7	6.62
93.	Igor Stimac *West Ham United*	24	1	6.62
94.	Seth Johnson *Derby County*	36	5	6.61
95.	Dean Saunders *Bradford City*	31	5	6.61
96.	Ugo Ehiogu *Aston Villa*	31	2	6.61
=	Gianfranco Zola *Chelsea*	31	2	6.61
98.	Nigel Martyn *Leeds United*	38	2	6.60
99.	David Unsworth *Everton*	33	2	6.60
100.	Marcel Desailly *Chelsea*	23	2	6.60
101.	Teddy Sheringham *Manchester United*	20	2	6.60
102.	Henning Berg *Manchester United*	20	1	6.60
103.	Dwight Yorke *Manchester United*	31	4	6.58
104.	Steffen Iversen *Tottenham Hotspur*	36	3	6.58
105.	Stephen McPhail *Leeds United*	24	3	6.58
106.	Gerry Taggart *Leicester City*	31	2	6.58
107.	Richard Shaw *Coventry City*	29	2	6.58
108.	Andrew Impey *Leicester City*	28	2	6.57
109.	Kevin Pressman *Sheffield Wednesday*	19	2	6.57
110.	Ian Harte *Leeds United*	33	0	6.57
111.	Steve Guppy *Leicester City*	30	2	6.56
112.	**DIDIER DOMI** *Newcastle United*	**23**	**2**	**6.56**
113.	Marc-Vivien Foe *West Ham United*	25	1	6.56
114.	Robert Page *Watford*	36	6	6.55
115.	Patrik Berger *Liverpool*	34	6	6.55
116.	Mark Hughes *Everton*	29	3	6.55
117.	Ole Gunnar Solskjaer *Manchester United*	20	2	6.55
118.	Steve Palmer *Watford*	38	1	6.55
119.	Lee Bowyer *Leeds United*	31	4	6.54
120.	Michael Owen *Liverpool*	24	3	6.54
121.	Eric Roy *Sunderland*	22	2	6.54
=	Shaka Hislop *West Ham United*	22	2	6.54
123.	Michael Gray *Sunderland*	33	0	6.54
124.	Ray Parlour *Arsenal*	30	2	6.53
125.	Paul Williams *Coventry City*	20	2	6.53
126.	Stuart McCall *Bradford City*	34	2	6.52
127.	Stephen Clemence *Tottenham Hotspur*	19	1	6.52
128.	David Weir *Everton*	34	0	6.52
129.	Jo Tessem *Southampton*	23	0	6.52
130.	Robbie Keane *Coventry City*	31	4	6.51
131.	Robbie Savage *Leicester City*	35	3	6.51
132.	Jason Euell *Wimbledon*	37	0	6.51
=	Ed de Goey *Chelsea*	37	0	6.51
134.	Darryl Powell *Derby County*	31	2	6.51
135.	Jacob Laursen *Derby County*	36	2	6.50
136.	Matthew Oakley *Southampton*	28	1	6.50
137.	Dominic Matteo *Liverpool*	32	0	6.50
138.	**AARON HUGHES** *Newcastle United*	**24**	**0**	**6.50**
139.	Gary Neville *Manchester United*	22	0	6.50
140.	Robbie Blake *Bradford City*	25	4	6.48
141.	Dietmar Hamann *Liverpool*	27	1	6.48
142.	Nicky Butt *Manchester United*	27	1	6.48
143.	Steve Lomas *West Ham United*	25	1	6.48
144.	Horacio Carbonari *Derby County*	29	0	6.48
=	Mauricio Taricco *Tottenham Hotspur*	29	0	6.48
146.	Emerson Thome *Chelsea*	36	5	6.47
147.	Sander Westerveld *Liverpool*	36	3	6.47
148.	Alan Thompson *Aston Villa*	19	2	6.47
149.	Richard Johnson *Watford*	21	1	6.47
150.	Peter Beagrie *Bradford City*	34	0	6.47

WARREN **BARTON**

- **Position:** Defender
- **Born:** March 19, 1969 in Stoke Newington
- **Newcastle Debut:** August 19, 1995 v Coventry City
- **Total Newcastle League Apps/Goals:** 130/4
- **Transfer:** £4.5 million, June 5, 1995
- **Previous Clubs:** Leyton Orient, Leytonstone & Ilford, Maidstone United, Wimbledon
- **Club Honours:** None
- **International Honours:** Senior, England B international

Warren Barton was as reliable as ever for The Magpies during the 1999-2000 season. He spent most of the campaign in his familiar right-back role, but the versatile defender also played at centre-back and in midfield when needed. Warren would have been an ever-present last term, but he was sent-off for the first time in his career after an off-the-ball incident in the 4-1 defeat against Coventry. He apologised to his team-mates and the fans for letting them all down and was suspended for four games. Despite this rare black mark, Warren is a leader of the back line who will be looking to resolve the way the team defended from set pieces last season. This was often a weak link in the side and let The Magpies down in the Premiership because they closed down opposing teams well in open play with Warren often playing a starring role. The ex-Wimbledon man was also extremely effective with Nolberto Solano on the right wing last season, regularly joining the attack to supply dangerous crosses into the area for the aerial talents of Alan Shearer and Duncan Ferguson in the Newcastle attack.

Lge Games	Total mins	Goals	Star Ratings	Ave Rating
34	2934	0	2	6.78

Starts	Subbed off	Subbed on	Yellow	Red
33	2	1	5	1

Cup	Games/Goals	Sub on/off	Star Ratings	Yellow/Red
UEFA	5/0	0/0	1	1/0
FA	6/0	0/0	0	0/0
Worthington	1/0	0/0	0	1/0

DAVID **BEHARALL**

- **Position:** Defender
- **Born:** March 8, 1979 in Newcastle
- **Newcastle Debut:** April 17, 1999 v Everton
- **Total Newcastle League Apps/Goals:** 6/0
- **Transfer:** From Trainee, August 1, 1998
- **Previous Clubs:** None
- **Club Honours:** None
- **International Honours:** None

A product of Newcastle's School of Excellence, David Beharall made two appearances as a substitute in the Premiership last season. After coming on after 59 minutes for Alain Goma, he was unfortunate to be part of the side that squandered a 3-1 lead against Wimbledon at the start of the season. Even more daunting was his 77th minute substitution for Nolberto Solano as a ten-man Newcastle side trailed a rampant Man. United 4-1, eventually losing the game 5-1. David didn't get any other chances to show his ability last term, with other young players getting their chance to shine. Despite this, the former Magpies trainee is a highly-rated central defender who captained the Newcastle Youth side to the Northern Intermediate League title in 1998. Now a regular in the reserve team, David has been at St James' Park for eight years after joining his home town club as a 14-year-old from school. The youngster faces a battle to establish himself in the Newcastle first team with defenders like Elena Marcolino, Didier Domi, Alain Goma, Nikos Dabizas and Aaron Hughes currently ahead of him in the pecking order. His opportunities will be limited again this season, but a loan spell would offer him valuable first-team experience and the 21-year-old could yet have a bright future at St James' Park.

Lge Games	Total mins	Goals	Star Ratings	Ave Rating
2	49	0	0	5.00

Starts	Subbed off	Subbed on	Yellow	Red
0	0	2	0	0

Cup	Games/Goals	Sub on/off	Star Ratings	Yellow/Red
All Cups	0/0	0/0	0	0/0

GARRY **BRADY**

- **Position:** Midfielder
- **Born:** September 7, 1976 in Glasgow
- **Newcastle Debut:** November 23, 1998 v Everton
- **Total Newcastle League Apps/Goals:** 9/0
- **Transfer:** No fee, July 7, 1998
- **Previous Clubs:** Tottenham Hotspur, Norwich City (on loan)
- **Club Honours:** None
- **International Honours:** Scotland Under-18 international

Garry Brady was allocated a squad number by Ruud Gullit, but the right-winger failed to make an impression on the first team last season, despite nine previous appearances. Garry went on a month's loan to Norwich City in March after being formally transfer-listed by Bobby Robson a month earlier.

Lge Games	Total mins	Goals	Star Ratings	Ave Rating
0	0	0	0	0.00

Starts	Subbed off	Subbed on	Yellow	Red
0	0	0	0	0

Cup	Games/Goals	Sub on/off	Star Ratings	Yellow/Red
All Cups	0/0	0/0	0	0/0

GARY CALDWELL

- **Position:** Defender
- **Born:** April 12, 1982 in Stirling
- **Newcastle Debut:** N/A
- **Total Newcastle League Apps/Goals:** 0/0
- **Transfer:** From Trainee, August 1, 1998
- **Previous Clubs:** None
- **Club Honours:** None
- **International Honours:** None

Gary Caldwell became a professional at Newcastle in August 1998 after spending two years progressing in the youth team. The defender had an impressive run in the reserves last term, making the first-team bench on three occasions and will now be hoping to make his full debut in the 2000-2001 campaign.

Lge Games	Total mins	Goals	Star Ratings	Ave Rating
0	0	0	0	0.00

Starts	Subbed off	Subbed on	Yellow	Red
0	0	0	0	0

Cup	Games/Goals	Sub on/off	Star Ratings	Yellow/Red
All Cups	0/0	0/0	0	0/0

STEPHEN CALDWELL

- **Position:** Defender
- **Born:** September 12, 1980 in Stirling
- **Newcastle Debut:** N/A
- **Total Newcastle League Apps/Goals:** 0/0
- **Transfer:** From Trainee, August 1, 1998
- **Previous Clubs:** None
- **Club Honours:** None
- **International Honours:** Scotland Under-21 international

Stephen Caldwell, older brother of Gary, signed professional forms for Newcastle in August 1999 – two years after joining the club as a youngster from Scotland. The defender had an impressive 1999-2000 in the reserves, made the first-team bench three times and signed a new contract in March 2000.

Lge Games	Total mins	Goals	Star Ratings	Ave Rating
0	0	0	0	0.00

Starts	Subbed off	Subbed on	Yellow	Red
0	0	0	0	0

Cup	Games/Goals	Sub on/off	Star Ratings	Yellow/Red
All Cups	0/0	0/0	0	0/0

JAMES COPPINGER

- **Position:** Striker
- **Born:** January 18, 1981 in Middlesbrough
- **Newcastle Debut:** N/A
- **Total Newcastle League Apps/Goals:** 0/0
- **Transfer:** No Fee, March 25, 1998
- **Previous Clubs:** Darlington, York (on loan), Hartlepool (on loan)
- **Club Honours:** None
- **International Honours:** England Under-16 international

James Coppinger found himself in the Newcastle first team during last season's pre-season friendlies in the absence of regular strikers Duncan Ferguson and Alan Shearer. It was his first taste at the top although James has been a prolific striker in the reserve team. Last season, after becoming frustrated by his lack of opportunities, he received an offer to go on loan to Hartlepool, which he accepted. Along with fellow loan signing from Newcastle, Paul Arnison, he gained vital experience with the Third Division club. James was put on the transfer list by Newcastle in February 2000, so the young striker has more reason than most to improve his form this season.

Lge Games	Total mins	Goals	Star Ratings	Ave Rating
0	0	0	0	0.00

Starts	Subbed off	Subbed on	Yellow	Red
0	0	0	0	0

Cup	Games/Goals	Sub on/off	Star Ratings	Yellow/Red
All Cups	0/0	0/0	0	0/0

LAURENT CHARVET

- **Position:** Defender/Midfielder
- **Born:** May 8, 1973 in Beziers (France)
- **Newcastle Debut:** August 15, 1998 v Charlton Athletic
- **Total Newcastle League Apps/Goals:** 33/1
- **Transfer:** £520,000, July 16, 1998
- **Previous Clubs:** Cannes, Chelsea (on loan)
- **Club Honours:** None
- **International Honours:** None

A number of injuries restricted Laurent Charvet's appearances for Newcastle during the 1999-2000 season. This was a huge blow for the team as Charvet had been brought to Tyneside to stabilise the United defence. One of the most versatile players in the current squad, the Frenchman can play in any position across the back line, as a wing-back or as backup in midfield. Laurent made his first start of last season in the crucial UEFA Cup third round first-leg clash against Roma in Italy, where he was adjudged to have fouled Marco Delvecchio for the penalty which ultimately condemned The Magpies to defeat in the tie. If this wasn't bad enough, the defender suffered another injury in December which ruled him out until April – when he came through 90 minutes of a reserve team game against Everton unscathed. The Frenchman now faces an uphill battle to win his place back in the team, but his adaptability will give him a distinct advantage. He may be a regular on the substitutes' bench this season, but he'll need to wait for the opportunity to build on his 33 Premiership appearances for the club.

Lge Games	Total mins	Goals	Star Ratings	Ave Rating
2	108	0	0	7.00

Starts	Subbed off	Subbed on	Yellow	Red
1	0	1	0	0

Cup	Games/Goals	Sub on/off	Star Ratings	Yellow/Red
UEFA	2/0	0/0	0	0/0
FA	1/0	0/0	0	0/0
Worthington	0/0	0/0	0	0/0

NIKOS DABIZAS

- **Position:** Defender
- **Born:** August 3, 1973 in Amindeo (Greece)
- **Newcastle Debut:** March 14, 1998 v Coventry City
- **Total Newcastle League Apps/Goals:** 70/7
- **Transfer:** £1.3 million, March 13, 1998
- **Previous Clubs:** Olympiakos
- **Club Honours:** 1998 Greek Championship with Olympiakos
- **International Honours:** Senior Greece international

In January 2000 Nikos Dabizas equalled a club record that had stood for 103 years by becoming the first defender since 1897 to score in three consecutive games. His strikes against West Ham, Sheffield United and Southampton – combined with an impressive string of performances – were enough to earn him MATCH's 'Matchman Of The Month' Award for January 2000. Nikos quickly became a favourite around St James' Park after joining The Magpies in March 1998 on a four-year contract. He became the first Greek player ever to play in a FA Cup Final in 1999 but missed the first four games of last season before eventually making his first appearance of the campaign in the ill-fated defeat at home to Sunderland, after which Ruud Gullit stood down as Newcastle United's manager. Things got worse in his next game when he was sent-off for protesting to the referee that he had been pushed by Andy Cole as the striker gave Manchester United a 2-1 lead. But after his suspension he returned to the defence and was back to his best, playing comfortably in three-man and four-man defensive formations. To the delight of the United fans, Nikos signed a new four-year deal with the club at the end of last season.

Lge Games	Total mins	Goals	Star Ratings	Ave Rating
29	2568	4	4	6.96

Starts	Subbed off	Subbed on	Yellow	Red
29	1	0	6	1

Cup	Games/Goals	Sub on/off	Star Ratings	Yellow/Red
UEFA	6/0	0/0	1	0/0
FA	6/2	0/0	0	0/0
Worthington	1/0	0/0	0	0/0

DIDIER DOMI

- **Position:** Defender
- **Born:** May 2, 1978 in Sarcelles (France)
- **Newcastle Debut:** January 9, 1999 v Chelsea
- **Total Newcastle League Apps/Goals:** 41/3
- **Transfer:** £3.25 million (rising to £4 million), December 30, 1998
- **Previous Club:** Paris St Germain
- **Club Honours:** 1998 French Cup and French League Cup winner with Paris St Germain
- **International Honours:** France Under-21 international

Didier Domi certainly impressed the Newcastle supporters in his first full season for The Magpies. An attacking left-back, Didi created a host of goalscoring chances for Alan Shearer, Kevin Gallacher and Duncan Ferguson with his great crossing and superb corner-kicks. The France Under-21 international got on the scoresheet himself with goals against Wimbledon, Coventry City, Tranmere Rovers (in the FA Cup quarter-final) and Sunderland. Unfortunately, just as he was showing his best form in black and white colours, Didi missed two months of the Premiership season after damaging his ankle ligaments in November while with the France Under-21 squad. He's now fully fit though and a successful 2000-2001 with The Magpies beckons if he can stay free from injury – and if he can impress on a consistent basis in the Newcastle defence, he could find himself in the senior French national squad. Indeed, Didi is no stranger to success after winning the French League Cup and French Cup in 1998. An interesting statistic for Magpies fans is that he only picked up three bookings in 36 games last season, an envious record for Premiership defenders which combines his ball-winning ability with a sound temperament.

Lge Games	Total mins	Goals	Star Ratings	Ave Rating
27	1837	3	2	6.56

Starts	Subbed off	Subbed on	Yellow	Red
19	4	8	2	0

Cup	Games/Goals	Sub on/off	Star Ratings	Yellow/Red
UEFA	4/0	0/0	0	1/0
FA	4/1	3/0	0	0/0
Worthington	1/0	0/0	0	0/0

FRANCK DUMAS

- **Position:** Defender
- **Born:** January 9, 1968 in Bayeux (France)
- **Newcastle Debut:** August 7, 1999 v Aston Villa
- **Total Newcastle League Apps/Goals:** 6/0
- **Transfer:** £500,000, July 1, 1999
- **Previous Clubs:** Caen, Monaco
- **Club Honours:** 1997 French league winner with Monaco
- **International Honours:** None

Franck Dumas was beginning to impress boss Bobby Robson with an excellent run in the side when, in the UEFA Cup clash with Roma, the Frenchman suffered a fracture and dislocation to his right elbow, which ruled out of first-team action for six weeks. Signed by former boss Ruud Gullit, Franck looked set to settle at St James' Park but the fans were dismayed when they discovered the player was about to move back to France with Olympique Marseille. His £1.25 million transfer was made official in January – just six months after moving to Newcastle.

Lge Games	Total mins	Goals	Star Ratings	Ave Rating
6	522	0	0	6.16

Starts	Subbed off	Subbed on	Yellow	Red
6	1	0	1	0

Cup	Games/Goals	Sub on/off	Star Ratings	Yellow/Red
UEFA	1/0	0/1	0	0/0
FA	0/0	0/0	0	0/0
Worthington	0/0	0/0	0	0/0

KIERON DYER

- **Position:** Midfielder
- **Born:** December 29, 1978 in Ipswich
- **Newcastle Debut:** August 7, 1999 v Aston Villa
- **Total Newcastle League Apps/Goals:** 30/3
- **Transfer:** £6 million, July 16, 1999
- **Previous Club:** Ipswich Town
- **Club Honours:** None
- **International Honours:** Senior, England B, Under-21, Youth international

The first and only English signing by Ruud Gullit was Ipswich midfielder Kieron Dyer. Signed for £6 million in the summer of 1999, the young star was given the prized number seven shirt by Gullit at the expense of Rob Lee. Kieron offered the former Newcastle captain his shirt back when Gullit left the club, but Lee declined the offer, thanking him for his generosity. Kieron was out of action for several weeks when circulation problems in his calf required surgery, but he recovered to become an automatic choice and his first goal for Newcastle was the only thing to cheer about in the 2-1 defeat by Sunderland. Kieron scored four goals in his first season at St James' Park, but he needs to use his excellent pace and skill to improve that tally this term. His only disappointment last season was narrowly failing to make England's final Euro 2000 squad, but he will definitely star for his country in the future.

Lge Games	Total mins	Goals	Star Ratings	Ave Rating
30	2330	3	3	6.65

Starts	Subbed off	Subbed on	Yellow	Red
27	9	3	1	0

Cup	Games/Goals	Sub on/off	Star Ratings	Yellow/Red
UEFA	3/0	0/2	0	1/0
FA	6/1	1/3	1	0/0
Worthington	0/0	0/0	0	0/0

STUART ELLIOTT

- **Position:** Defender
- **Born:** August 27, 1977 in London
- **Newcastle Debut:** N/A
- **Total Newcastle League Apps/Goals:** 0/0
- **Transfer:** From Trainee, August 28, 1995
- **Previous Clubs:** Hull City (on loan), Swindon Town (on loan), Gillingham (on loan), Hartlepool United (on loan), Wrexham (on loan), Bournemouth (on loan), Stockport County (on loan)
- **Club Honours:** None
- **International Honours:** None

The only first-team appearances that Stuart Elliott made last season were for Bournemouth and Stockport County on loan. He helped United's reserves to glory in the Northumberland Senior Cup last season, scoring the fourth goal in the 4-1 win over Blue Star Seaham in the final. But despite his promise, Stuart was transfer-listed in February and joined Darlington on a free transfer before the start of the 2000-2001 season.

Lge Games	Total mins	Goals	Star Ratings	Ave Rating
0	0	0	0	0.00

Starts	Subbed off	Subbed on	Yellow	Red
0	0	0	0	0

Cup	Games/Goals	Sub on/off	Star Ratings	Yellow/Red
All Cups	0/0	0/0	0	0/0

JOSE RODRIGUES ALVES ANTUNES FUMACA

- **Position:** Midfielder
- **Born:** April 12, 1982 in Brazil
- **Newcastle Debut:** November 28, 1999 v Tottenham Hotspur
- **Total Newcastle League Apps/Goals:** 5/0
- **Transfer:** Signed on loan, September 28, 1999
- **Previous Clubs:** Catunese, Birmingham City, Colchester United (on loan), Barnsley, Crystal Palace
- **Club Honours:** None
- **International Honours:** None

Fumaca, the Brazilian-born midfielder, was signed by Bobby Robson on loan from Crystal Palace last season. The teenager was blooded in the United reserves and impressed enough for Bobby Robson to hand him his debut in the 2-1 home victory against Spurs in November. Fumaca became a regular face on the bench last season and made four further appearances as a substitute, but when his loan spell ended, the Newcastle boss decided not to offer the midfielder a permanent contract.

Lge Games	Total mins	Goals	Star Ratings	Ave Rating
5	144	0	0	6.00

Starts	Subbed off	Subbed on	Yellow	Red
1	1	4	0	0

Cup	Games/Goals	Sub on/off	Star Ratings	Yellow/Red
UEFA	0/0	0/0	0	0/0
FA	1/0	1/0	0	0/0
Worthington	0/0	0/0	0	0/0

DUNCAN FERGUSON

- **Position:** Striker
- **Born:** December 28, 1971 in Stirling
- **Newcastle Debut:** November 28, 1998 v Wimbledon
- **Total Newcastle League Apps/Goals:** 30/8
- **Transfer:** £7 million, November 1998
- **Previous Clubs:** Carse Thistle, Dundee United, Glasgow Rangers, Everton
- **Club Honours:** 1994 Scottish league and Scottish Cup winner with Glasgow Rangers, 1995 FA Cup winner with Everton
- **International Honours:** Senior, Scotland B, Under-21, Youth, Schoolboy Scotland international

Before last season, Duncan Ferguson had rarely been seen in Newcastle colours since his £7 million transfer from Everton in November 1998, but the 1999-2000 campaign heralded the return of Big Dunc. After a stop-start return to the team after two groin operations and a hamstring and calf injury, Duncan joined Alan Shearer to form one of the most lethal strikeforces in the top-flight. But after a run of 20 successive appearances he picked up a knee injury in the FA Cup semi-final against Chelsea. In that run the Ferguson-Shearer partnership netted 17 goals, including six strikes for Big Dunc. The Scotsman scored his first Premiership goal for 372 days with the winner against Aston Villa to give Newcastle their first away league win in eight games. But despite his return to form, Newcastle still had doubts about the injury-prone Scottish forward and the arrival of young striker Carl Cort from Wimbledon meant that Duncan's return to Everton on the eve of the 2000-2001 season for £3.75 million was inevitable.

Lge Games	Total mins	Goals	Star Ratings	Ave Rating
23	1509	6	0	6.35

Starts	Subbed off	Subbed on	Yellow	Red
17	8	6	1	0

Cup	Games/Goals	Sub on/off	Star Ratings	Yellow/Red
UEFA	3/1	1/1	1	0/0
FA	6/3	0/3	1	1/0
Worthington	0/0	0/0	0	0/0

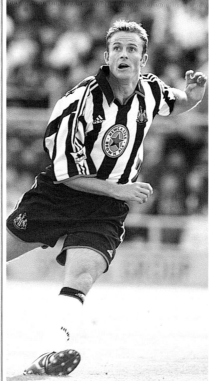

KEVIN GALLACHER

- **Position:** Striker
- **Born:** November 23, 1966 in Clydebank
- **Newcastle Debut:** October 3, 1999 v Middlesbrough
- **Total Newcastle League Apps/Goals:** 20/2
- **Transfer:** £500,000, October 1, 1999
- **Previous Clubs:** Dundee United, Coventry City, Blackburn Rovers
- **Club Honours:** None
- **International Honours:** Senior, Scotland B, Under-21, Youth Scotland international

Kevin Gallacher was Bobby Robson's first signing for United in October 1999 when he joined the club from Blackburn Rovers for £500,000. Gallacher, given an 18-month contract, was under no illusions about the reason he had been signed. He was there simply as experienced cover for Alan Shearer and Duncan Ferguson and to plug the gaps created by United's worrying injury problems at the time. He made his debut for The Magpies in the 2-1 home win over Middlesbrough but it took 13 appearances in black and white before he scored his first Newcastle goal – in the 4-1 win over Sheffield United in the FA Cup. But Kevin was a tremendous success, so when the first-choice strikers returned to fitness Robson kept him in the team, playing behind Shearer and Ferguson. Kevin was superb in Newcastle's FA Cup run, where he went further in the competition than ever before. The striker achieved another personal milestone in January 2000 by chalking up his 300th league appearance in the 5-0 thrashing of Southampton.

Lge Games	Total mins	Goals	Star Ratings	Ave Rating
20	1240	2	1	6.70

Starts	Subbed off	Subbed on	Yellow	Red
15	9	5	0	0

Cup	Games/Goals	Sub on/off	Star Ratings	Yellow/Red
UEFA	0/0	0/0	0	0/0
FA	5/1	1/3	1	0/0
Worthington	0/0	0/0	0	0/0

DIEGO ANTONIO **GAVILAN** ZARATE

- **Position:** Midfielder
- **Born:** March 1, 1980 in Asuncion (Paraguay)
- **Newcastle Debut:** February 5, 2000 v Sunderland
- **Total Newcastle League Apps/Goals:** 6/1
- **Transfer:** £1 million, January 28, 2000
- **Previous Club:** Cerro Porteno
- **Club Honours:** None
- **International Honours:** Senior, U-20, U-17 Paraguay international

Diego Gavilan became the first Paraguayan ever to grace the Premiership after Bobby Robson signed the midfielder from Cerro Porteno for a cut-price £1 million at the turn of the year. The Paraguay club had wanted twice as much money for the international, but Gavilan still signed in January 2000 before making a brief debut as an 88th minute substitute in the 2-2 draw at Sunderland a week later. Unfortunately, his World Cup qualifying commitments restricted his first-team opportunities last season but he made his first start in late April against Leeds and scored his first goal in the 2-0 win over Coventry.

Lge Games	Total mins	Goals	Star Ratings	Ave Rating
6	213	1	0	6.00

Starts	Subbed off	Subbed on	Yellow	Red
2	2	4	0	0

Cup	Games/Goals	Sub on/off	Star Ratings	Yellow/Red
All Cups	0/0	0/0	0	0/0

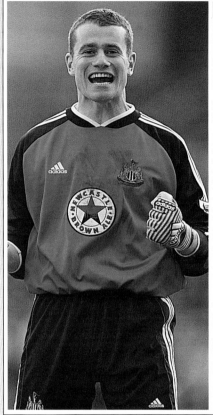

SHAY **GIVEN**

- **Position:** Goalkeeper
- **Born:** April 20, 2976 in Donegal
- **Newcastle Debut:** August 9, 1997 v Sheffield Wednesday
- **Total Newcastle League Apps/Goals:** 69/0
- **Transfer:** £1.5 million, July 14, 1997
- **Previous Clubs:** Celtic, Blackburn Rovers, Swindon Town (on loan), Sunderland (on loan)
- **Club Honours:** 1996 Division One winner with Sunderland
- **International Honours:** Senior, Under-21, Youth Republic Of Ireland international

Republic of Ireland goalkeeper Shay Given was allocated the number one shirt by Newcastle boss Ruud Gullit and clearly started last season as The Magpies' first choice. However, a finger injury sustained in pre-season ruled him out for the start of 1999-2000 and he wasn't even considered for the first team until October 12 when he was named as a substitute for the Worthington Cup clash at First Division Birmingham. The dismissal of Steve Harper in that 2-0 defeat gave Shay his first start of the season against Coventry City in the very next game, but while his display in goal contributed to a 4-1 defeat he made amends in his next appearance as Newcastle gained only their second clean sheet of the season in a 2-0 win over Derby. The Irishman then lost his place in the side, which also coincided with Newcastle's unbeaten run, so he didn't even make the bench for five successive games and had to act as understudy to Steve Harper. But Shay returned to the side on February 20 for the FA Cup quarter-final against Tranmere, and went on to play in all but one of the remaining 12 games.

Lge Games	Total mins	Goals	Star Ratings	Ave Rating
14	1260	0	1	6.35

Starts	Subbed off	Subbed on	Yellow	Red
14	0	0	0	0

Cup	Games/Goals	Sub on/off	Star Ratings	Yellow/Red
UEFA	0/0	0/0	0	0/0
FA	2/0	0/0	0	0/0
Worthington	1/0	1/0	0	0/0

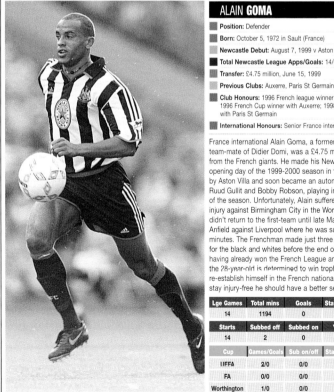

ALAIN **GOMA**

- **Position:** Defender
- **Born:** October 5, 1972 in Sault (France)
- **Newcastle Debut:** August 7, 1999 v Aston Villa
- **Total Newcastle League Apps/Goals:** 14/0
- **Transfer:** £4.75 million, June 15, 1999
- **Previous Clubs:** Auxerre, Paris St Germain
- **Club Honours:** 1996 French league winner with Auxerre; 1994, 1996 French Cup winner with Auxerre; 1998 French Cup winner with Paris St Germain
- **International Honours:** Senior France international

France international Alain Goma, a former Paris St Germain team-mate of Didier Domi, was a £4.75 million summer signing from the French giants. He made his Newcastle debut on the opening day of the 1999-2000 season in the 1-0 home defeat by Aston Villa and soon became an automatic choice under Ruud Gullit and Bobby Robson, playing in the first 13 matches of the season. Unfortunately, Alain suffered a knee ligament injury against Birmingham City in the Worthington Cup and he didn't return to the first-team until late March for the game at Anfield against Liverpool where he was substituted after 57 minutes. The Frenchman made just three more appearances for the black and whites before the end of the campaign, but having already won the French League and the French Cup, the 28-year-old is determined to win trophies with United and re-establish himself in the French national side. And if he can stay injury-free he should have a better season in 2000-2001.

Lge Games	Total mins	Goals	Star Ratings	Ave Rating
14	1194	0	1	6.57

Starts	Subbed off	Subbed on	Yellow	Red
14	0	0	5	0

Cup	Games/Goals	Sub on/off	Star Ratings	Yellow/Red
UEFA	2/0	0/0	0	0/0
FA	0/0	0/0	0	0/0
Worthington	1/0	0/0	0	0/0

STEPHEN **GLASS**

- **Position:** Midfielder
- **Born:** May 23, 1976 in Dundee
- **Newcastle Debut:** August 30, 1998 v Liverpool
- **Total Newcastle League Apps/Goals:** 29/3
- **Transfer:** £650,000, July 1, 1998
- **Previous Club:** Aberdeen
- **Club Honours:** 1995 Scottish League Cup winner with Aberdeen
- **International Honours:** Senior, Under-21 Scotland international

After recovering from a seven-month lay-off with a knee injury, Stephen Glass only made two starts for Newcastle in the last campaign. The direct winger put in a written transfer request in February 2000, but had a change of heart in the summer and told Bobby Robson that he wanted to stay and fight for his place. Stephen was in fantastic form before his injury and the Toon Army will be delighted if he can get back to his best.

Lge Games	Total mins	Goals	Star Ratings	Ave Rating
7	183	1	0	6.50

Starts	Subbed off	Subbed on	Yellow	Red
1	0	6	0	0

Cup	Games/Goals	Sub on/off	Star Ratings	Yellow/Red
UEFA	3/0	0/3	0	0/0
FA	1/0	1/0	0	0/0
Worthington	1/0	0/0	0	0/0

STUART GREEN

- **Position:** Midfielder
- **Born:** June 15, 1981 in Whitehaven
- **Newcastle Debut:** N/A
- **Total Newcastle League Apps/Goals:** 0/0
- **Transfer:** From Trainee, August 1, 1999
- **Previous Clubs:** None
- **Club Honours:** None
- **International Honours:** None

Teenage midfielder Stuart Green came closest to making his long-awaited first-team debut in Ruud Gullit's final game in charge of Newcastle. He found himself among the substitutes with Alan Shearer, Duncan Ferguson, Steve Harper and Aaron Hughes, but it was the only time he appeared on the bench all season. However, with some fine performances in the reserve team and after scoring an impressive five goals in 20 games from midfield for the Under-19s, Stuart was offered a four-year contract, showing just how highly they rate the youngster at St James' Park. The forthcoming season could be the one in which he finally makes his first-team debut with the club.

Lge Games	Total mins	Goals	Star Ratings	Ave Rating
0	0	0	0	0.00

Starts	Subbed off	Subbed on	Yellow	Red
0	0	0	0	0

Cup	Games/Goals	Sub on/off	Star Ratings	Yellow/Red
All Cups	0/0	0/0	0	0/0

ANDY GRIFFIN

- **Position:** Defender
- **Born:** March 7, 1979 in Wigan
- **Newcastle Debut:** February 7, 1998 v West Ham United
- **Total Newcastle League Apps/Goals:** 21/1
- **Transfer:** £1.5 million, January 30, 1998
- **Previous Club:** Stoke City
- **Club Honours:** None
- **International Honours:** England Under-21, Youth international

Andy Griffin was restricted to two late substitute appearances and an end-of-season run-out against Arsenal that amounted to a mere 98 minutes of playing time in 1999-2000. The young defender, who signed a four-year contract when he joined The Magpies in January 1998, had suffered a serious back injury – diagnosed as a stress fracture of his lower spine – during the summer. It was a long and hard road to recovery, and it was eight months before Andy could return to training, playing in the reserves before declaring himself fit in April. The defender made his first start in the last game of the season but better things are to come for the England Under-21 international.

Lge Games	Total mins	Goals	Star Ratings	Ave Rating
3	98	1	0	7.00

Starts	Subbed off	Subbed on	Yellow	Red
1	0	2	0	0

Cup	Games/Goals	Sub on/off	Star Ratings	Yellow/Red
All Cups	0/0	0/0	0	0/0

DES HAMILTON

- **Position:** Defender/Midfielder
- **Born:** August 15, 1976 in Bradford
- **Newcastle Debut:** September 27, 1997 v Chelsea
- **Total Newcastle League Apps/Goals:** 12/0
- **Transfer:** £1.5 million, March 27, 1997
- **Previous Clubs:** Bradford City, Sheffield United (on loan), Huddersfield Town (on loan), Norwich City (on loan)
- **Club Honours:** None
- **International Honours:** England Under-21 international

Des Hamilton had been at the club for three years after being signed from Bradford City in 1997 by Kenny Dalglish, but had struggled to establish himself in the first team. Before making a substitute appearance in place of Nolberto Solano in the UEFA Cup clash with CSKA Sofia last season, he had not played in the United first team since March 1998. Those six minutes were to be his only contribution to the senior side in 1999-2000. Des was transfer-listed in February and spent the last two months of last season on loan at Norwich City.

Lge Games	Total mins	Goals	Star Ratings	Ave Rating
0	0	0	0	0.00

Starts	Subbed off	Subbed on	Yellow	Red
0	0	0	0	0

Cup	Games/Goals	Sub on/off	Star Ratings	Yellow/Red
UEFA	1/0	1/0	0	0/0
FA	0/0	0/0	0	0/0
Worthington	0/0	0/0	0	0/0

STEVE HARPER

- **Position:** Goalkeeper
- **Born:** March 14, 1975 in Easington
- **Newcastle Debut:** November 28, 1998 v Wimbledon
- **Total Newcastle League Apps/Goals:** 26/0
- **Transfer:** No Fee, July 5, 1993
- **Previous Clubs:** Seaham Red Star, Bradford (on loan), Stockport County (on loan), Hartlepool (on loan), Huddersfield Town (on loan)
- **Club Honours:** None
- **International Honours:** None

Although Ruud Gullit handed Shay Given the No.1 shirt at the start of the 1999-2000 season, it was Steve Harper who spent much of the campaign as Newcastle's first-choice goalkeeper. Steve got his opportunity to impress between the posts when injury forced Given to sit out. He played the first two games of the season, against Aston Villa and Spurs, but was relegated to the bench for the next game. Steve returned for the UEFA Cup clash with CSKA Sofia and from that point onwards the commanding 'keeper only featured in a losing Magpies side on two occasions. His best performance was during the 1-0 win at Aston Villa in which he pulled off one of the saves of the season to deny Benito Carbone. The healthy competition for the No.1 spot at Newcastle can only be good for the club.

Lge Games	Total mins	Goals	Star Ratings	Ave Rating
18	1620	0	2	6.77

Starts	Subbed off	Subbed on	Yellow	Red
18	0	0	0	0

Cup	Games/Goals	Sub on/off	Star Ratings	Yellow/Red
UEFA	6/0	0/0	0	1/0
FA	4/0	0/0	0	0/0
Worthington	1/0	0/0	0	0/1

HELDER MARINO RODRIGUES CRISTOVAO

- **Position:** Defender
- **Born:** March 25, 1971 in Luanda (Angola)
- **Newcastle Debut:** November 12, 1999 v Tottenham Hotspur
- **Total Newcastle League Apps/Goals:** 8/1
- **Transfer:** Signed on loan, November 19, 1999
- **Previous Clubs:** Estoril, Benfica, Deportivo La Coruna
- **Club Honours:** 1994 Portuguese league winner with Benfica; 1993, 1996 Portuguese Cup winner with Benfica
- **International Honours:** Senior Portugal international

Angola-born Helder was signed on loan from Spanish club Deportivo La Coruna last season as backup for defenders like Steve Howey who was struggling with injury for most of the campaign. Helder made an impressive debut in the win over Tottenham in November and claimed his first goal for United at Sunderland on their way to a 2-2 draw. The powerful and experienced defender was beginning to build an impressive partnership with Nikos Dabizas until injury struck after three games. This kept him out until February and after making only five more league starts he returned to Deportivo La Coruna.

Lge Games	Total mins	Goals	Star Ratings	Ave Rating
8	672	1	1	7.13

Starts	Subbed off	Subbed on	Yellow	Red
8	2	0	1	0

Cup	Games/Goals	Sub on/off	Star Ratings	Yellow/Red
UEFA	0/0	0/0	0	0/0
FA	4/0	0/3	0	2/0
Worthington	0/0	0/0	0	0/0

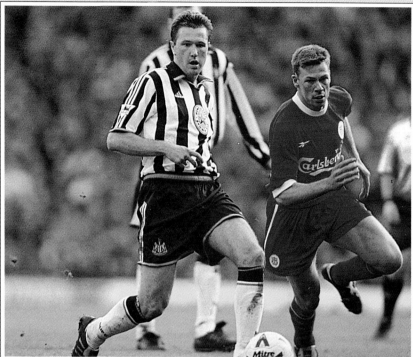

STEVE HOWEY

- **Position:** Defender
- **Born:** October 26, 1971 in Sunderland
- **Newcastle Debut:** May 13, 1989 v Manchester United
- **Total Newcastle League Apps/Goals:** 191/6
- **Transfer:** From Trainee, December 11, 1989
- **Previous Clubs:** None
- **Club Honours:** 1993 Division One Champions with Newcastle
- **International Honours:** Senior England international

The return of Steve Howey was a welcome sight last season after the former England defender's career had been blighted by injury. A problem with his calf ruled him out for most of the 1996-97 season and then a series of minor injuries hindered Steve's contribution to United's cause in the 1997-98 season. In 1998-99 he ruptured an Achilles tendon during the FA Cup semi-final clash with Tottenham at Old Trafford, which ruled him out for almost a year. But he was back playing for the reserves in January 2000 and returned to the first team as a substitute in February during the 2-0 win away to Sheffield Wednesday. Steve made his first start a week later in the 1-0 defeat by Chelsea and finished the season with seven starts, but he was sold to Man. City in the summer for £3 million as Bobby Robson looked to cut down the size of his squad.

Lge Games	Total mins	Goals	Star Ratings	Ave Rating
9	694	0	1	6.00

Starts	Subbed off	Subbed on	Yellow	Red
7	0	2	1	0

Cup	Games/Goals	Sub on/off	Star Ratings	Yellow/Red
UEFA	0/0	0/0	0	0/0
FA	1/0	0/0	0	0/0
Worthington	0/0	0/0	0	0/0

AARON HUGHES

- **Position:** Defender
- **Born:** November 8, 1977 in Belfast
- **Newcastle Debut:** November 26, 1997 v Barcelona
- **Total Newcastle League Apps/Goals:** 45/2
- **Transfer:** From Trainee, March 11, 1997
- **Previous Clubs:** None
- **Club Honours:** None
- **International Honours:** Senior, Under-21, Youth Northern Ireland international

Aaron Hughes spent much of last season in and out of the first team, covering for almost the entire Newcastle defence when he was needed. His adaptability was a huge asset for Bobby Robson and he was eventually rewarded with a regular place at left-back from February until the end of the season. At one stage he played in three different positions in three successive games – at left back, centre-back and right-back. Aaron got off the mark for Newcastle with the first goal in the 8-0 thrashing of Sheffield Wednesday. The Northern Ireland defender is now a valuable member of the squad and can look forward to an even better season in 2000-2001.

Lge Games	Total mins	Goals	Star Ratings	Ave Rating
27	1995	2		6.50

Starts	Subbed off	Subbed on	Yellow	Red
22	3	5	0	0

Cup	Games/Goals	Sub on/off	Star Ratings	Yellow/Red
UEFA	3/0	1/0	1	0/0
FA	4/0	1/1	0	0/0
Worthington	0/0	0/0	0	0/0

JOHN KARELSE

- **Position:** Goalkeeper
- **Born:** 1970 in Kapelle (Holland)
- **Newcastle Debut:** August 15, 1999 v Southampton
- **Total Newcastle League Apps/Goals:** 3/0
- **Transfer:** £750,000, August 13, 1999
- **Previous Clubs:** Wemeldigen, NAC Breda
- **Club Honours:** None
- **International Honours:** None

Dutch goalkeeper John Karelse was Ruud Gullit's last buy before leaving St James' Park in August 1999. The £750,000 signing was bought to ease the injury crisis affecting United's 'keepers, but his debut was one he would rather forget. Two days after completing his transfer he conceded four goals in Newcastle's 4-2 defeat at Southampton. In the next game he was beaten on three occasions by the Wimbledon forward line at home as The Magpies twice squandered a two goal lead. John sustained a knee injury in training soon after and was replaced by the on loan Tommy Wright, but the Dutchman's first-team opportunities were limited under Bobby Robson. In January, John asked for a loan move so he could get first-team football and was later formally transfer-listed by the club.

Lge Games	Total mins	Goals	Star Ratings	Ave Rating
3	270	0	0	6.00

Starts	Subbed off	Subbed on	Yellow	Red
3	0	0	0	0

Cup	Games/Goals	Sub on/off	Star Ratings	Yellow/Red
All Cups	0/0	0/0	0	0/0

BRIAN KERR

- **Position:** Midfielder
- **Born:** October 12, 1981 in Motherwell
- **Newcastle Debut:** N/A
- **Total Newcastle League Apps/Goals:** 0/0
- **Transfer:** From Trainee, July 1, 1999
- **Previous Clubs:** None
- **Club Honours:** None
- **International Honours:** Scotland Under-18, Under-17, Under-16, Under-15 international

Brian Kerr joined Newcastle as a schoolboy after he had been spotted playing for Glasgow Rangers. He signed professional forms before the start of last season and was close to making his debut for Newcastle in 1999-2000 when Kieron Dyer went down after a challenge at Wimbledon. He didn't make it onto the pitch, but remains in the first-team squad for 2000-2001.

Lge Games	Total mins	Goals	Star Ratings	Ave Rating
0	0	0	0	0.00

Starts	Subbed off	Subbed on	Yellow	Red
0	0	0	0	0

Cup	Games/Goals	Sub on/off	Star Ratings	Yellow/Red
All Cups	0/0	0/0	0	0/0

TEMURI **KETSBAIA**

- **Position:** Striker
- **Born:** March 18, 1968 in Gale (Georgia)
- **Newcastle Debut:** August 9, 1997 v Sheffield Wednesday
- **Total Newcastle League Apps/Goals:** 78/7
- **Transfer:** No Fee, July 1997
- **Previous Clubs:** Dinamo Sukhumi, Dinamo Tblisi, Anorthosis Famagusta, AEK Athens
- **Club Honours:** 1997, 1998 Greek Cup winner with AEK Athens
- **International Honours:** Senior Georgia international

Popular Georgia international Temuri Ketsbaia was the cover for Alan Shearer, Duncan Ferguson and Kevin Gallacher last season. He made some telling contributions to the side when he was called upon, but sitting on the subs bench frustrated the talented striker. Temuri expressed his disappointment to Bobby Robson in the summer and he made a £900,000 move to Wolves with the best wishes of the Toon Army behind him.

Lge Games	Total mins	Goals	Star Ratings	Ave Rating
21	1173	0	0	6.35

Starts	Subbed off	Subbed on	Yellow	Red
11	7	10	0	0

Cup	Games/Goals	Sub on/off	Star Ratings	Yellow/Red
UEFA	3/1	1/2	0	0/0
FA	4/0	4/0	0	0/0
Worthington	0/0	0/0	0	0/0

ROBERT **LEE**

- **Position:** Midfielder
- **Born:** February 1, 1966 in London
- **Newcastle Debut:** September 23, 1992 v Middlesbrough
- **Total Newcastle League Apps/Goals:** 265/43
- **Transfer:** £700,000, September 22, 1992
- **Previous Clubs:** Pegasus, Sovereign Hornchurch, Charlton Athletic
- **Club Honours:** 1993 Division One Champions with Newcastle
- **International Honours:** Senior, England, B, Under-21 England international

Former club captain and England midfielder Robert Lee was out in the cold under Ruud Gullit. Under the Dutch manager's reign he wasn't even allocated a squad number at the start of the 1999-2000 season – he was placed on the transfer list and not even considered for selection. However, following Gullit's departure, Newcastle's caretaker boss Steve Clarke handed Rob the number 37 shirt and immediately included him in the team to face Manchester United at Old Trafford. After Bobby Robson's arrival, the ex-England manager was so impressed with Rob's contribution he argued that the former Charlton man should return to the England team, calling him the 'best midfielder in the country'. Robson couldn't believe that such an influential figure could have been considered surplus to requirements, so once he realised Rob was on the transfer list he took him off immediately, saying he wouldn't even consider selling him. A gifted, hard-working player who can play in either a holding role or as an attacking midfielder, his only goal of the season was against Chelsea in the FA Cup semi-final.

Lge Games	Total mins	Goals	Star Ratings	Ave Rating
30	2567	0	4	6.90

Starts	Subbed off	Subbed on	Yellow	Red
30	9	0	5	0

Cup	Games/Goals	Sub on/off	Star Ratings	Yellow/Red
UEFA	6/0	0/2	1	1/0
FA	4/1	0/0	0	1/0
Worthington	1/0	0/1	0	0/0

ELENA SIERRA **MARCELINO**

- **Position:** Defender
- **Born:** September 26, 1971 in Gijon (Spain)
- **Newcastle Debut:** August 7, 1999 v Aston Villa
- **Total Newcastle League Apps/Goals:** 11/0
- **Transfer:** £5 million, June 24, 1999
- **Previous Clubs:** Sporting Gijon, Real Mallorca
- **Club Honours:** None
- **International Honours:** Senior Spain international

Central defender Marcelino was another to be struck by injury in his debut season for United. A £5 million signing from Real Mallorca, he has looked promising at the back when he has played, but after making his debut on the opening day of the season he suffered a groin strain and further injuries kept him out of action for two months. This season he'll be looking for a good run in the side to repay the faith the club has in him.

Lge Games	Total mins	Goals	Star Ratings	Ave Rating
11	881	0	0	6.27

Starts	Subbed off	Subbed on	Yellow	Red
10	1	1	2	0

Cup	Games/Goals	Sub on/off	Star Ratings	Yellow/Red
UEFA	2/0	0/0	0	0/0
FA	2/0	1/0	0	0/0
Worthington	0/0	0/0	0	0/0

SILVIO **MARIC**

- **Position:** Midfielder
- **Born:** March 20, 1975 in Zagreb (Croatia)
- **Newcastle Debut:** March 7, 1999 v Everton
- **Total Newcastle League Apps/Goals:** 14/0
- **Transfer:** £3.5 million, February 5, 1999
- **Previous Clubs:** Croatia Zagreb, Segesta Sisak (on loan)
- **Club Honours:** 1996, 1997, 1998, 1999 Croatian league winner with Croatia Zagreb; 1996, 1997, 1998 Croatian Cup winner with Croatia Zagreb
- **International Honours:** Senior Croatia international

Croatia international Silvio Maric was on the transfer list for most of last season at Newcastle after admitting that he was unhappy at St James' Park. The midfielder announced his intention to quit Tyneside as early as August, just five months after joining the club. A series of disciplinary problems did not endear him to the coaching staff at Newcastle – he reported late for United's UEFA Cup trip to CSKA Sofia and was fined by manager Bobby Robson. A move back to Croatia Zagreb looked on the cards for a cut-price £2 million but the Croatian club could not afford the fee. His lack of appearances for the first-team threatened Maric's work permit, and to compound problems he failed to turn up for the end-of-season tour of the Caribbean. He was mostly left on the bench last season, and was even substituted after coming on for Carl Serrant against Southampton. Significantly, he only finished one game in 1999-2000 – in the Worthington Cup at Birmingham – and moved to Porto for £2 million before the new season started.

Lge Games	Total mins	Goals	Star Ratings	Ave Rating
13	427	0	0	5.66

Starts	Subbed off	Subbed on	Yellow	Red
3	3	10	0	0

Cup	Games/Goals	Sub on/off	Star Ratings	Yellow/Red
UEFA	3/2	0/3	0	0/0
FA	1/0	1/0	0	0/0
Worthington	1/0	0/0	0	0/0

JAMIE McCLEN

- **Position:** Midfielder
- **Born:** May 13, 1979 in Newcastle
- **Newcastle Debut:** April 5, 1999 v Tottenham
- **Total Newcastle League Apps/Goals:** 10/0
- **Transfer:** From Trainee, August 1, 1997
- **Previous Clubs:** None
- **Club Honours:** None
- **International Honours:** None

Jamie McClen has been with his favourite club since the age of ten and graduated to the first team for his Newcastle debut against Tottenham in April 1999. Last season, the energetic midfielder made three starts against Wimbledon, Sunderland and Leeds, plus six appearances from the substitutes bench. Another product of Newcastle's School of Excellence, it looks like Jamie has an exciting future at St James' Park.

Lge Games	Total mins	Goals	Star Ratings	Ave Rating
9	309	0	1	6.50

Starts	Subbed off	Subbed on	Yellow	Red
3	1	6	2	0

Cup	Games/Goals	Sub on/off	Star Ratings	Yellow/Red
UEFA	3/0	3/0	0	0/0
FA	0/0	0/0	0	0/0
Worthington	0/0	0/0	0	0/0

LIONEL PEREZ

- **Position:** Goalkeeper
- **Born:** April 26, 1967 in Bagnols Coze (France)
- **Newcastle Debut:** N/A
- **Total Newcastle League Apps/Goals:** 0/0
- **Transfer:** No Fee, June 30, 1998
- **Previous Clubs:** Nimes, Bordeaux, Laval, Sunderland, Scunthorpe United (on loan), Cambridge United (on loan)
- **Club Honours:** None
- **International Honours:** Senior France international

French goalkeeper Lionel Perez was signed from arch-rivals Sunderland on a free transfer in June 1998, but failed to make a single first-team appearance for Newcastle. In order to play some competitive first-team football, Lionel moved on loan to Scunthorpe United and Cambridge United, but then rejected another loan approach by West Brom. Under Bobby Robson, the experienced 'keeper proved to be surplus to requirements at St James' Park and was put on the transfer-list. He signed for Cambridge United on a free transfer in July 2000.

Lge Games	Total mins	Goals	Star Ratings	Ave Rating
0	0	0	0	0.00

Starts	Subbed off	Subbed on	Yellow	Red
0	0	0	0	0

Cup	Games/Goals	Sub on/off	Star Ratings	Yellow/Red
All Cups	0/0	0/0	0	0/0

ALESSANDRO PISTONE

- **Position:** Defender
- **Born:** July 27, 1975 in Milan (Italy)
- **Newcastle Debut:** August 9, 1997 v Sheffield Wednesday
- **Total Newcastle League Apps/Goals:** 46/1
- **Transfer:** £4.3 million, July 31, 1997
- **Previous Clubs:** Vicenza, Solbiatese, Crevalcora, Inter Milan, Venezia (on loan)
- **Club Honours:** None
- **International Honours:** Italy Under-21 international

The departure of Ruud Gullit from Tyneside was welcomed by Alessandro Pistone after Gullit had made it clear to the Italian left-back that he was not in his plans for the future. A former captain of the Italy Under-21 team, Alessandro did not figure in the starting line-up for 14 months but he was finally given an opportunity by Bobby Robson in the victory over Derby in November. However, his impressive run in the side came to an abrupt end after a 37th minute collision with Sunderland's Nicky Summerbee, which broke his leg and ruled him out for three months. The Toon Army was delighted to see him return to first-team action before the end of the campaign, playing in two of the last three Premiership games, but at the end of the season Alessandro moved to Everton in a £3 million deal.

Lge Games	Total mins	Goals	Star Ratings	Ave Rating
15	1216	1	0	6.06

Starts	Subbed off	Subbed on	Yellow	Red
15	2	0	1	0

Cup	Games/Goals	Sub on/off	Star Ratings	Yellow/Red
UEFA	2/0	0/0	0	0/0
FA	3/0	0/1	0	0/0
Worthington	1/0	1/0	0	1/0

PAUL ROBINSON

- **Position:** Striker
- **Born:** November 20, 1979 in Sunderland
- **Newcastle Debut:** August 21, 1999 v Wimbledon
- **Total Newcastle League Apps/Goals:** 11/0
- **Transfer:** £250,000, March 27, 1998
- **Previous Club:** Darlington
- **Club Honours:** None
- **International Honours:** None

With international strikers like Alan Shearer, Duncan Ferguson and Kevin Gallacher in front of him, Paul Robinson found his chances limited at Newcastle. In the first half of the season he acted as regular cover on the bench, making 13 substitute appearances and only two starts – in the games against Wimbledon and Sunderland. Paul helped the reserve team to glory in the Northumberland Senior Cup – scoring twice in the 4-1 defeat of Blue Star Seaham in the final – but he became frustrated at his lack of first-team opportunities and agreed a £1.5 million move to Wimbledon during the close season.

Lge Games	Total mins	Goals	Star Ratings	Ave Rating
9	262	0	1	6.50

Starts	Subbed off	Subbed on	Yellow	Red
2	1	7	0	0

Cup	Games/Goals	Sub on/off	Star Ratings	Yellow/Red
UEFA	4/1	4/0	0	0/0
FA	0/0	0/0	0	0/0
Worthington	1/0	1/0	0	0/0

CARL SERRANT

- **Position:** Defender
- **Born:** September 12, 1975 in Bradford
- **Newcastle Debut:** August 30, 1998 v Liverpool
- **Total Newcastle League Apps/Goals:** 6/0
- **Transfer:** £500,000, July 7, 1998
- **Previous Club:** Oldham Athletic, Bury (on loan)
- **Club Honours:** None
- **International Honours:** England B, England Under-21, Youth international

An injury after 13 minutes of his second appearance of the campaign effectively ended Carl Serrant's season. The former Oldham defender only made one more appearance from the bench for Newcastle and was due to go on loan to Sheffield United before surgery to rectify a cartilage problem ended the move. He was transfer-listed by Bobby Robson towards the end of last season and has competition from Didier Domi at left-back but remains part of the first-team squad at United.

Lge Games	Total mins	Goals	Star Ratings	Ave Rating
2	87	0	0	5.00

Starts	Subbed off	Subbed on	Yellow	Red
2	2	0	0	0

Cup	Games/Goals	Sub on/off	Star Ratings	Yellow/Red
UEFA	1/0	1/0	0	0/0
FA	0/0	0/0	0	0/0
Worthington	0/0	0/0	0	0/0

ALAN SHEARER

■ **Position:** Striker
■ **Born:** August 13, 1970 in Newcastle upon Tyne
■ **Newcastle Debut:** August 17, 1996 v Everton
■ **Total Newcastle League Apps/Goals:** 115/64
■ **Transfer:** £15 million, July 30, 1996
■ **Previous Clubs:** Southampton, Blackburn Rovers
■ **Club Honours:** 1995 Premier League Champions with Blackburn Rovers
■ **International Honours:** Senior, England B, England Under-21 international

Alan Shearer had another eventful season in the spotlight during the 1999-2000 season. The club's record £15 million signing was sent-off for the first time in his career on the first day of the campaign and was relegated to the subs' bench for the infamous derby encounter with Sunderland. The Magpies skipper scored just one goal in his first seven appearances of the campaign and admitted he wasn't firing on all cylinders with the team experiencing a bad run of form. But the arrival of Bobby Robson transformed The Magpies and Shearer was soon back to his brilliant best as he scored five goals in the 8-0 drubbing of Sheffield Wednesday. A series of milestones followed for Big Al, including his 100th league appearance for the club against Wimbledon, his 80th goal for Newcastle, his 300th career goal and his best goalscoring tally for United by netting 29 goals. In February, the England captain announced that he would retire from international football after Euro 2000 to devote all of his energies to his home-town club, which was fantastic news for the Toon Army and a warning to every other team in the Premiership for the 2000-2001 season.

Lge Games	Total mins	Goals	Star Ratings	Ave Rating
37	3259	23	4	6.69

Starts	Subbed off	Subbed on	Yellow	Red
36	0	1	3	1

Cup	Games/Goals	Sub on/off	Star Ratings	Yellow/Red
UEFA	6/2	0/1	1	2/0
FA	6/5	0/0	2	2/0
Worthington	1/0	0/1	0	0/0

NOLBERTO SOLANO

■ **Position:** Midfielder
■ **Born:** December 12, 1974 in Lima (Peru)
■ **Newcastle Debut:** August 22, 1998 v Chelsea
■ **Total Newcastle League Apps/Goals:** 59/9
■ **Transfer:** £2.5 million, July 12, 1998
■ **Previous Clubs:** Alianza Lima, Sporting Crystal, Boca Juniors
■ **Club Honours:** None
■ **International Honours:** Senior Peru international

Nolberto Solano is now established as one of the Toon Army's favourites at St James' Park and with good reason. The Peru international is one of the most gifted players in the team and created many of Newcastle's goals last season, providing perfectly flighted corners from either flank as well as pinpoint crosses and exquisite free-kicks. Nol has scored some superb goals during his spell with The Magpies, but he'll be looking to improve his tally of three Premiership goals in the 2000-2001 campaign. Nol would have been an ever-present last season but his skills were needed for his country, which he captained, to play in Peru's Gold Cup and 2002 World Cup qualifying campaigns. He got into trouble after playing for his country while carrying an injury, but the subsequent rumours about a move away from St James' Park proved unfounded. Nobby says he wants to stay with Newcastle, even though he will be required to play for Peru in World Cup qualifiers next season, which will rule him out of the United team for several weeks.

Lge Games	Total mins	Goals	Star Ratings	Ave Rating
30	2489	3	5	6.66

Starts	Subbed off	Subbed on	Yellow	Red
29	15	1	6	0

Cup	Games/Goals	Sub on/off	Star Ratings	Yellow/Red
UEFA	6/1	0/2	0	0/0
FA	3/0	0/0	0	0/0
Worthington	1/0	0/1	0	0/0

GARY **SPEED**

- **Position:** Midfielder
- **Born:** September 8, 1969 in Mancot
- **Newcastle Debut:** February 7, 1998 v West Ham
- **Total Newcastle League Apps/Goals:** 87/14
- **Transfer:** £5.5 million, February 6, 1998
- **Previous Clubs:** Leeds United, Everton
- **Club Honours:** 1992 League Champions with Leeds United; 1990 Division Two Champions with Leeds United
- **International Honours:** Senior Wales, Under-21, Youth international

Gary Speed is one of the most influential figures at Newcastle with his vast experience and undoubted class. Arguably one of the club's best players last season, the talented midfielder was a virtual ever-present during 1999-2000, missing only two Premiership games. He was particularly outstanding during Newcastle's 6-1 thrashing of Tottenham in the FA Cup third round, scoring the first goal and inspiring Bobby Robson's side to a memorable win. The Wales international was also a regular goalscorer for The Magpies last season, achieving a personal record of 13 league and cup goals – many of them from corners and set-pieces with his trademark, unstoppable headers. Gary gets into some superb goalscoring positions by sprinting from deep to meet crosses. After making his name on the left wing with Leeds, he has rejuvenated his career by moving into the centre with United, regularly breaking down opposition attacks and supplying defence-splitting passes for his team-mates. Gary is one of the most reliable and valued members of the squad and will be priceless next season if The Magpies are going to challenge for honours.

Lge Games	Total mins	Goals	Star Ratings	Ave Rating
36	3240	9	2	6.72

Starts	Subbed off	Subbed on	Yellow	Red
36	0	0	6	0

Cup	Games/Goals	Sub on/off	Star Ratings	Yellow/Red
UEFA	6/1	0/0	0	1/0
FA	6/3	0/0	2	1/0
Worthington	1/0	0/0	1	0/0

PAUL **TALBOT**

- **Position:** Defender
- **Born:** August 11, 1979 in Gateshead
- **Newcastle Debut:** N/A
- **Total Newcastle League Apps/Goals:** 0/0
- **Transfer:** From Trainee, November 1, 1993
- **Previous Clubs:** York City (on loan), Norwich City (on loan)
- **Club Honours:** None
- **International Honours:** None

Gateshead-born Paul Talbot was given the number 30 shirt by Ruud Gullit and was hoping to make his Newcastle debut last season. Unfortunately, the defender didn't make the first-team and went on loan to York City and then Norwich City. Paul was transfer-listed in February 2000 and has not been given a squad number for the 2000-2001 campaign.

Lge Games	Total mins	Goals	Star Ratings	Ave Rating
0	0	0	0	0.00

Starts	Subbed off	Subbed on	Yellow	Red
0	0	0	0	0

Cup	Games/Goals	Sub on/off	Star Ratings	Yellow/Red
All Cups	0/0	0/0	0	0/0

TOMMY **WRIGHT**

- **Position:** Goalkeeper
- **Born:** August 29, 1963 in Belfast
- **Newcastle Debut:** January 14, 1989 v Aston Villa
- **Total Newcastle League Apps/Goals:** 85/0
- **Transfer:** Signed on loan, August 24,1999
- **Previous Clubs:** Linfield, Newcastle United, Hull City (loan), Nottingham Forest, Reading (loan), Manchester City (loan), Manchester City.
- **Club Honours:** 1993 Division One Champions with Newcastle
- **International Honours:** Senior, Under-23 Northern Ireland international

Tommy Wright played for Newcastle between 1988 and 1993 and returned to St James' Park on loan from Manchester City in August 1999 to solve the goalkeeping crisis that ruled out first-choice stoppers Shay Given and Steve Harper. Incredibly, Tommy played for three different Newcastle managers while he was on loan with The Magpies, but they were all keen to retain his services, recognising the experience he would bring to the side as cover. He played in Ruud Gullit's last game and was included in the side selected by caretaker boss Steve Clarke for the 5-1 defeat by Manchester United. He then featured in Bobby Robson's first match in charge, a 1-0 defeat against Chelsea. Tommy's previous spell had seen him play for former managers Willie McFaul, Jim Smith, Ossie Ardiles and Kevin Keegan. He was even part of the set-up at Newcastle when The Magpies won promotion to the Premiership in 1993 under Keegan and has been a fine servant to the club, not just last season, but from when he first joined United 13 years ago.

Lge Games	Total mins	Goals	Star Ratings	Ave Rating
3	270	0	1	7.00

Starts	Subbed off	Subbed on	Yellow	Red
3	0	0	0	0

Cup	Games/Goals	Sub on/off	Star Ratings	Yellow/Red
All Cups	0/0	0/0	0	0/0

TRANSFER ROUND-UP

In their quest for a European place at the end of the season and a good run in the domestic cup competitions, the Newcastle squad has been strengthened by the arrival of England Under-21 striker Carl Cort, a player that Bobby Robson knows can perform at the highest level. Duncan Ferguson's return to Everton, combined with the departures of Silvio Maric, Temuri Ketsbaia and Paul Robinson, makes Cort's £7 million transfer from Wimbledon a key signing for The Magpies.

The Argentinian pair of Christian Bassedas and Daniel Cordone are less famous names, but Robson has been chasing the players for some time and the experienced manager clearly has an eye for talented footballers having coached some of the biggest names in the business.

After taking time to assess his charges, the management at Newcastle decided to trim the squad to a more manageable number by placing 13 players on the transfer list in February 2000. There were several surprises, with first-team squad members like Silvio Maric, Stephen Glass and Carl Serrant all being told that they could leave the club at the end of the season. While Maric has already departed, the other players on the list can still prove that they are worthy of a place in the Newcastle side.

If Bobby Robson's squad can remain mostly injury-free, The Magpies could make a serious impact this season. After making their worst start in the league for 40 years last season, the 2000-2001 campaign could be the one that the passionate Toon Army have been waiting for – the passionate United fans certainly deserve it.

CARL **CORT**

- ▪ **Position:** Striker
- ▪ **Born:** November 1, 1977 in Southwark
- ▪ **Newcastle Debut:** August 20, 2000 v Manchester United
- ▪ **Transfer:** £7 million, July 5, 2000.
- ▪ **Previous Clubs:** Wimbledon, Lincoln City (on loan)
- ▪ **Club Honours:** None
- ▪ **International Honours:** England Under-21 international

Carl Cort is a product of Wimbledon's youth scheme who has developed into one of the best young strikers in the country. Quick, strong and powerful in the air, Carl has been a vital member of the England Under-21 squad in recent years and will be looking to gain full international honours during his time at Newcastle. Carl managed 15 goals as Wimbledon were relegated last season, so the £7 million signing should enjoy playing alongside a host of established internationals in an improving Newcastle side. He'll also relish playing up front with Magpies legend Alan Shearer, which could help Carl to realise his own international ambitions with England.

CARLOS DANIEL **CORDONE**

- ▪ **Position:** Midfielder/Striker
- ▪ **Born:** November 6, 1974 in Buenos Aires (Argentina)
- ▪ **Newcastle Debut:** August 20, 2000 v Manchester United
- ▪ **Transfer:** £500,000 (loan fee), June 28, 2000
- ▪ **Previous Clubs:** Racing Club
- ▪ **Club Honours:** None
- ▪ **International Honours:** None

CHRISTIAN **BASSEDAS**

- ▪ **Position:** Midfielder
- ▪ **Born:** February 16, 1973 in Buenos Aires (Argentina)
- ▪ **Newcastle Debut:** N/A
- ▪ **Transfer:** £3.5 million, June 2000
- ▪ **Previous Clubs:** Velez Sarsfield
- ▪ **Club Honours:** 1993, 1995, 1996, 1998 Argentina league Champions with Velez Sarsfield; 1996 Americas Cup winner with Velez Sarsfield; 1994 Intercontinental Cup winner with Velez Sarsfield; 1997 Recopa winner with Velez Sarsfield; 1995 Pan American Games winner with Argentina Under-23s
- ▪ **International Honours:** Senior, Under-23 Argentina international

Newcastle spent most of the 1999-2000 season trying to sign Argentinian midfield ace Christian Bassedas, but the transfer fee proved a major stumbling block. The two clubs eventually reached a compromise, though, agreeing on a five-year deal for £3.5 million. Christian boasts a host of top honours from Argentina and South America and holds a dual nationality – Argentinian and Italian – passport, which means he can avoid work permit problems that non-EC players often experience when they come over to play in England. Christian featured in Argentina's 1998 World Cup qualifiers, played in the Argentina Under-23 side that won the 1995 Pan American Games and featured in the Olympic team at Atlanta '96.

Having arrived at St James' Park on a one-year loan deal for £500,000, Daniel Cordone has the option to add an extra two years to his contract if the move works out for both club and player. The versatile front man – who is equally comfortable as a lone striker, playing up front with another forward, or playing just behind the front two – will certainly give United options this season. One of Daniel's reasons for moving to Newcastle was to prove what he can do in one of the best leagues in the world as he stakes his claim for international recognition with Argentina. Bobby Robson plans to use Daniel in midfield, but he should score plenty of goals if he lives up to his reputation.

THE SQUAD

1. Shay **Given**
2. Warren **Barton**
3. Elena **Marcelino**
4. Didier **Domi**
5. Alain **Goma**
6.
7. Robert **Lee**
8. Kieron **Dyer**
9. Alan **Shearer**
10. Christian **Bassedas**
11. Gary **Speed**
12. Andy **Griffin**
13. Steve **Harper**
14.
15. Nolberto **Solano**
16. Carl **Cort**
17. Daniel **Cordone**
18. Aaron **Hughes**
19. Stephen **Glass**
20.
21. Diego **Gavilan**
22. Jamie **McClen**
23.
24. Garry **Brady**
25. Brian **Kerr**
26. James **Coppinger**
27. David **Beharall**
28.
29. John **Karelse**
30. Stephen **Caldwell**
31. Stuart **Green**
32. Kevin **Gallacher**
33. Des **Hamilton**
34. Nikos **Dabizas**
35.
36. Gary **Caldwell**
37. Laurent **Charvet**
38.
39. David **McMahon**
40. Carl **Serrant**

Carl Cort will be hoping to form a potent strikeforce with United captain Alan Shearer.

NEWCASTLE UNITED FIXTURES

Date	Opponent	H/A	Date	Opponent	H/A
Aug. 20	Manchester United	A	Dec. 26	Leeds United	H
Aug. 23	Derby County	H	Dec. 30	Manchester United	H
Aug. 26	Tottenham Hotspur	H	Jan. 1	Tottenham Hotspur	A
Sept. 6	Coventry City	A	Jan. 13	Coventry City	H
Sept. 9	Chelsea	H	Jan. 20	Leeds United	A
Sept. 16	Southampton	A	Jan. 31	Chelsea	A
Sept. 23	Charlton Athletic	H	Feb. 3	Southampton	H
Sept. 30	Manchester City	A	Feb. 10	Charlton Athletic	A
Oct. 16	Middlesbrough	A	Feb. 24	Manchester City	H
Oct. 21	Everton	H	Mar. 3	Everton	A
Oct. 28	West Ham United	A	Mar. 17	Middlesbrough	H
Nov. 4	Ipswich Town	H	Mar. 31	Bradford City	A
Nov. 11	Leicester City	A	Apr. 7	Arsenal	H
Nov. 18	Sunderland	H	Apr. 14	Ipswich Town	A
Nov. 25	Liverpool	H	Apr. 16	West Ham United	H
Dec. 2	Aston Villa	A	Apr. 21	Sunderland	A
Dec. 9	Arsenal	A	Apr. 28	Leicester City	H
Dec. 16	Bradford City	H	May 5	Liverpool	A
Dec. 23	Derby County	A	May 19	Aston Villa	H